Tradition and Innovation in Psychoanalytic Education

Clark Conference on Psychoanalytic Training for Psychologists

Tradition and Innovation in Psychoanalytic Education

Clark Conference on Psychoanalytic Training for Psychologists

Edited by

MURRAY MEISELS
Eastern Michigan University

ESTER R. SHAPIRO
University of Massachusetts, Boston

LEA LAWRENCE ERLBAUM ASSOCIATES, PUBLISHERS
1990 Hillsdale, New Jersey   Hove and London

Lawrence Erlbaum Associates, Inc., Publishers
365 Broadway
Hillsdale, New Jersey 07642

Library of Congress Cataloging-in-Publication Data

Clark Conference on Psychoanalytic Training for Psychologists (1986 :
   Clark University)
      Tradition and innovation in psychoanalytic education / Clark
   Conference on Psychoanalytic Training for Psychologists ; edited by
   Murray Meisels, Ester R. Shapiro.
         p.   cm.
      Conference held Oct. 24–27, 1986 at Clark University, Worcester,
   Mass.
      Dedicated to the memory of Helen Block Lewis.
      Includes bibliographical references.
      ISBN 0–8058–0386–6   ISBN 0–8058–0791–8 (pbk.)
      1. Psychoanalysis—Study and teaching—Congresses.   2. Lewis,
   Helen Block—Congresses.   I. Meisels, Murray.   II. Shapiro, Ester
   R.   III. Lewis, Helen Block.   IV. Title.
      [DNLM: 1. Psychoanalysis—education—congresses.   WM 18 C592t
   1986]
   RC502.C53   1986
   616.89'17'076—dc20
   DNLM/DLC
   for Library of Congress   89–23453
                                                                  CIP

Printed in the United States of America
10 9 8 7 6 5 4 3 2 1

Contents

Dedication

This book is a record of the October 1986 Clark Conference on psychoanalytic education, sponsored by the Division of Psychoanalysis of the American Psychological Association. The book is dedicated to Helen Block Lewis, in gratitude for her many contributions to the Division and to the Clark Conference. Helen Block Lewis was a courageous woman, not given to illusions, and willing to confront self-serving ideas. Championing the necessity for re-examination and further development of all ideas in psychoanalysis, she strongly engaged and helped actualize those who worked with her. It is with sadness and loss that we write that Helen Block Lewis died several months after the Clark Conference. She is still missed, still mourned, and still a part of us.

Proceeds from this book will go to the Helen Block Lewis Memorial Fund, established by the Division to provide an annual award for the best article in *Psychoanalytic Psychology,* the Division's journal, of which Helen Block Lewis was founding editor.

Murray Meisels
Ester R. Shapiro

Clark Conference Participants (1986)

Bottom row, left to right: Carol Michaels, Zenia Fliegel, Murray Meisels, Helen Block Lewis, Stanton Marlan, Anne-Marie Sandler, Ester Shapiro, Anna Antonovsky, and Rochelle Kainer;

Second row, left to right: Norma Simon, not identified, Charles Spezzano, Sabert Basescu, Gerald Stechler, Marvin Hyman, and Ava Siegler;

Third row, left to right: Stanley Gochman, Bernard Kalinkowitz, George Silberschatz, Jonathan Slavin, Paul Wachtel, Magda Denes, Murray Bilmes, Jan Drucker, Robert Lane and Bertram Karon;

Top row, left to right: Herbert Schlesinger, Stephen Appelbaum, George Goldman, Susannah Gourevitch, John Gedo, Milton Horowitz, James Barron, and Robert Aguado.

Contributors

Nathan Adler, Ph.D., Professor, California School of Professional Psychology, Berkeley-Alameda, and faculty of their Center for Integrative Psychoanalytic Studies.

Anna M. Antonovsky, Ph.D., Fellow, training and supervising analyst, William Alanson White, and Clinical Associate Professor of Psychology in Psychiatry, Cornell University Medical College, and is in private practice in New York City.

Stephen A. Appelbaum, Ph.D., Faculty, Karl Menninger School of Psychiatry and Mental Health Sciences in Topeka, at the Colorado Society for Psychology and Psychoanalysis in Denver, and is in private practice, Prairie Village, Kansas.

Sabert Basescu, Ph.D., Clinical Professor, New York University Postdoctoral Program in Psychoanalysis and Director, Westchester Center for the Study of Psychoanalysis.

Murray Bilmes, Ph.D., Professor of Psychology, California School of Professional Psychology, Berkely/Alameda, and Associate Clinical Professor, Department of Psychiatry, Stanford University.

John Gedo, M.D., training and supervising analyst, Chicago Institute for Psychoanalysis, Clinical Professor of Psychiatry, University of Illinois (Chicago), and is in private practice in Chicago.

Susannah Gourevitch, Ph.D., teaches object relations theory at the Advanced Psychotherapy Program of the Washington School of Psychiatry and is in private practice in Washington, DC.

Milton J. Horowitz, Ph.D., is a training and supervising analyst, Los Angeles Institute for Psychoanalytic Studies and is in private practice in Los Angeles.

Marvin Hyman, Ph.D., teacher, Michigan Society for Psychoanalytic Psychology, is in private practice in West Bloomfield, Michigan.

Rochelle G. K. Kainer, Ph.D., teaching and supervising faculty at the Washington School of Psychiatry, and faculty of the Washington Society of Psychoanalytic Psychology, and is in private practice in Washington, DC.

Helen Block Lewis, Ph.D., is described in the book.

Murray Meisels, Ph.D., teacher, Michigan Society for Psychoanalytic Psychology, and Professor, Department of Psychology, Eastern Michigan University, and is in private practice in Ann Arbor, Michigan.

Dale Mendell, Ph.D., faculty and supervisor, Postgraduate Center for Mental Health; faculty and senior supervisor, National Institute for the Psychotherapies; and is in private practice, New York City.

Jean Baker Miller, M.D., Clinical Professor of Psychiatry, School of Medicine, Boston University and former Secretary and Trustee, American Academy of Psychoanalysis.

Fred Pine, Ph.D., training and supervising analyst, New York University Postdoctoral Program in Psychotherapy and Psychoanalysis and at the New York Freudian Society, and Professor, Department of Psychiatry, Albert Einstein College of Medicine.

Anne-Marie Sandler is training and supervising analyst and lecturer at the British Psychoanalytic Society and is former President of the European Psycho-Analytic Federation.

Herbert J. Schlesinger, Ph.D., is Alfred J. Marrow Professor of Psychology at the New School for Social Research, and training and supervising analyst, Columbia Center for Psychoanalytic Training and research.

Ester Shapiro, Ph.D., is active in the Massachusetts Association for Psychoanalytic Psychology, Secretary of the Board, Massachusetts Institute for Psychoanalysis, and is Assistant Professor, University of Massachusetts, Boston.

Ava L. Siegler, Ph.D., is Dean of Training, Psychoanalytic Institute, Postgraduate Center for Mental Health, is Associate Adjunct Professor at New York University's graduate program in clinical psychology, and is in private practice in New York City.

George Silberschatz, Ph.D., is with the Mount Zion Psychotherapy Research Group at Mount Zion Hospital, is assistant clinical professor, Department of Psychiatry, University of California Medical Center, and is in private practice in San Francisco.

Jonathan H. Slavin, Ph.D., Director of the Counseling Center, Tufts University, has been president of both the Massachusetts Association for Psychoanalytic Psychology and the Massachusetts Institute for Psychoanalysis.

Charles Spezzano, Ph.D., has been president of the Colorado Society for Psychology and Psychoanalysis, and is in private practice in Denver.

Gerald Stechler, Ph.D., is Professor of Psychiatry, Boston University Medical School, and Vice President, Community Care Systems Inc., Boston, MA.

Paul L. Wachtel, Ph.D., is Distinguished Professor of Psychology at the City College and the Graduate Center of the City University of New York.

Lenore Walker, Ph.D., is at the Professional School of Psychology, University of Denver, and at Walker and Associates, in Denver.

1 Introduction: The Colorful Background of the Clark Conference

Murray Meisels

BACKGROUND

Reuben Fine launched the Division of Psychoanalysis in 1978: Signatures were collected at the 1978 annual meeting of the American Psychological Association (APA), whose Council approved the petition at the 1979 annual meeting. It was one of those developments that led some to wondering why it took so long for one of the earliest psychologies to organize itself in APA. Indeed, 10 years before, at another APA annual meeting, several psychologist-psychoanalysts did call a meeting to organize a Division, but I've heard that there was anxiety that psychologists would start forming training Institutes if there were a psychoanalytic division—apparently, the idea of psychologists training themselves was not regarded as desirable—and the result of that 1968 convening was a compromise formation called Psychologists Interested in the Study of Psychoanalysis (PISP), a research group. The 1968 "anxiety" that psychologists would form training Institutes if there was a psychoanalytic Division was a real one, because this is precisely what happened once the Division of Psychoanalysis was established a decade later.

Once formed, the main political antagonism that emerged within the Division represented an adumbration of the 1968 anxiety, since on one pole there was a group that identified with the standards of the International Psychoanalytic Association (IPA) and the American Psychoanalytic Association (the American), while the other pole was comprised first of a group that considered it premature to define psychoanalytic praxis and, later, of the emerging local chapters.

Some of the original political antagonism originated in New York City, since approximately 55% of the Division membership came from either more tradition-

1

al or less traditional New York area Institutes, which apparently had never interacted although they now had representatives sitting at Divisional Board meetings. The traditional group organized itself first. Essentially it comprised the entire membership of the early Qualifications Committee and then formed itself as the Division's first section, the Section of Psychologist-Psychoanalyst Practitioners (Section I). Section I required that psychoanalysis consist of at least three sessions per week, and that therapy of any less frequency be considered psychoanalytic psychotherapy. While this was not as high as the four- or five-weekly frequencies advocated by the IPA and the American, it was enough to antagonize the less traditional groups. The less traditional group organized itself more slowly, as did the local chapters: The Section of Local Chapters (Section IV) was formed in 1985, and the Psychologist-Psychoanalyst Forum (Section V) in 1986.

The interval after the emergence of Section I and before the emergence of Sections IV and V was a colorful period, filled as it was with intense political and emotional strife, parochialism, and some painful, even horrid, Board meetings. The political strife was between Section I and (eventual) Section V, the parochialism was the persistent and remarkable obliviousness of many New Yorkers to psychologist's needs in the rest of the United States, and Division board meetings erupted into periodic political infighting as now one issue, now another, was perceived as the latest battleground on which the issue of standards was being fought. Some of the battlegrounds entailed meaningful content, such as battles over the composition of the ABPP committee or about whether the Division should sponsor this Clark Conference, but other of the battles were quite distant from the issues, such as the battle over who is the proper Section I representative, or whether section membership should be included in a membership directory. At this point, I should like to sketch the three positions.

The Section I Position

Although the Division was founded as an interest group and remains open to any APA member, within months of its founding efforts were under way to attempt to credential psychologist-psychoanalysts. Within a year, Meisels and Hyman (1980) wrote a proposal to that effect, a symposium on the subject was held at the APA annual meeting in Montreal, and the Qualifications Committee was appointed. By 1982 the Division board had approved the recommendations of the Qualifications Committee, so that *the thrice-weekly standard is the Division's definition of qualification.* Section I then used the Division's standards as a membership requirement: This requirement, that only psychologists who met the Division's standards for qualification in psychoanalysis could join Section I, led to the widespread perception—widespread even in the leadership of Section I—that Section I was engaging in unofficial credentialing. However, Section I had acted strictly within APA and Division rules.

The Section I position, broadly, was: The field of psychoanalysis has defined standards of practice which entail a high frequency of contact; to play a role in the international psychoanalytic community it is necessary for the Division to maintain these standards: and that, practically speaking, the thrice-weekly standard was itself a compromise, so that any effort to reduce frequency requirements further—or to impose a concept such as "equivalency"—must be fought with alacrity and determination. These were fiercely held convictions. These convictions, interestingly, did not have an ideological cast: Section I admitted psychologists of all theoretical stripes, and also admitted psychologists who were not trained in Institutes, colleagues who had engaged in "bootlegged" or, better, self-directed, training. It was the frequency/intensity dimension that Section I fiercely defended, not a particular theory.

The Section V Position

It was apparently the Division's official establishment of Section I that galvanized the (future) Section V people into organization and action. Hitherto, they had played a minor role, and the major Division initiatives had derived from Section I (these were the agreement on standards for qualification, the establishment of the Division's first section, and the possibility of ABPP credentialing). Now, however, New Yorkers whose Institutes accepted some twice-weekly treatments became concerned since they perceived that even if Section I were not engaging in official credentialing (since it gave no credential but was, by APA rules, a membership organization), it was certainly doing unofficial credentialing (since so many in the Division so viewed it). Many New Yorkers were concerned that graduates of their Institutes would not be admitted to Section I, and they were joined by some non-New Yorkers who also demanded grandparenting or equivalency of training. This, Section I was unwilling to do. It must be borne in mind that this was 2 or 3 years before the Division reached the organizational resolution of establishing another section for these less traditional psychologist-psychoanalysts, and that, at the time, there was widespread agreement—or a wish—that the Division should have a standard of psychoanalytic qualification that is acceptable to all.

In any event, in 1982–1986, the result was internecine warfare. The future Section V people were demanding a hearing, or calling for the decertification of Section I, and Section I felt under severe attack, and devoted enormous energy to the struggle. The Division board itself was obsessed with this conflict, which was the fundamental agenda item of several board meetings; and the issue was indeed the focus of conflict at board meetings, and derivatives of the conflict attached themselves to numerous tangential issues, and the two ideologies would have at each other again and again. There was much unhappiness. Some, including this writer, had fears that the Division might split.

The Local Chapters

This intense emotional issue of standards, which had so preoccupied the Division board and the Section I board for years, was almost irrelevant to non-New Yorkers. As a Michiganian who championed local chapter formation, I vividly recall many meetings of the Division board and the Section I board at which I broached the topic of encouraging local chapter development, only to find that the reactions ranged from indifference to minor interest, and that the issue quickly turned back again to the issue of standards. The New York parochialism which focused such intense emotion on the issue of standards led to the benign neglect of the rest of the country.

The central, focal emotional issue for psychologists outside of greater New York City was the lack of training opportunities because of the successful exclusionary policy of the American. Except for the many Institutes in New York City and the one in Los Angeles, psychoanalytically minded psychologists in the remainder of the United States were virtually unable to train in psychoanalysis unless the local Institute of the American gave them permission (in which case they had to undergo the odious waiver procedure). It has long seemed to me that the central success of U. S. psychiatrist-psychoanalysts was in establishing a national organization, the American, and that the central difficulty for psychologists was the lack of a central organization. Once Division 39 came into existance, once psychologists had their national organization, they immediately began to form local societies, exactly as had been "feared" in 1968.

THE SHIFT FROM "STANDARDS" TO LOCAL CHAPTERS

Before 1979 the American was the major national psychoanalytic organization, with a network of local units throughout the country, and psychologists had neither a national organization nor a network: There were areas of the country where psychoanalytically minded psychologists had literally never seen a psychologist who was a psychoanalyst. Once the Division was launched, a network of local chapters began to emerge. By 1981, a Committee on Local Chapters was established, chaired by an innovative Chicagoan, Oliver J. B. Kerner. He and I worked together to propose that the Division establish a national program to train psychologists in the hinterlands (Meisels & Kerner, 1982)—a proposal which never did materialize—and we also recommend that the Division establish a Foundation for Psychoanalytic Education and Research. The Foundation did materialize, but to date has garnered money only with great difficulty, and not in amounts large enough to impact on local training programs.

By late 1984, the Division's major agenda had shifted from standards to local training issues. There were two developments here. First, by 1984, Bryant

Welch, Nathan Stockhamer, and Ernest Lawrence had organized a group to sue the American for restraint of trade, and a lawsuit was filed on March 1, 1985. The purpose of the suit was to force local Institutes of the American to admit psychologists, and the specific intent was to help psychologists throughout the United States. The lawsuit, with its expenses and purposes—and its focus on non-New Yorkers—would become a primary Division agenda item for many years.

The second development in 1984 was that Helen Block Lewis assumed the presidency of the Division. Lewis, a stalwart of the less traditional viewpoint, had long appreciated and strongly supported the importance of local chapter development. Upon assuming the presidency she appointed me chair of the newly created National Program Committee—in line with the idea of developing a national program—and she and I called for a Nationwide Conference on Psychoanalytic Training, which was held in New York City on Dec. 1–2, 1984. What a wonderful conference that was! There were representatives from Boston, Washington, Los Angeles, San Francisco, Chicago, Cleveland, Michigan, Philadelphia, Phoenix, Miami, Tampa, New Haven, and Denver, and all delegates were fascinated to hear about the other local chapters, about other groups in various phases of development, all of which had heretofore been isolated groups but which now had representation at this meeting of the Division of Psychoanalysis.

Immediately, the participants issued a call for further conferences and further dialogue about matters such as organizational development and training issues. It seemed reasonable to hold a series of meetings, and indeed to hold a major conference on psychoanalytic training, an idea that suited the local chapters who were experimenting with new educational forms, and also suited the (future) Section V group, who wanted dialogue with Section I. However, conferences require funding, and this would likely not be forthcoming from the Division, given the political situation. Accordingly, Helen Block Lewis set out to gain grant funding, and in short order the Exxon Foundation granted $25,000 to be used first for preconference and then for a major conference on psychoanalytic training. The preconference, which was the second convening of local chapters, was partially supported by the Exxon foundation and met in Ann Arbor, Michigan, on June 21–23, 1985. The major training conference, of course, is this Clark Conference, which was in great part supported by the Exxon grant.

In 1985, representatives of local chapters realized the necessity of a political power base within the Division in order to press for their goals, and petitions to form a Section of Local Chapters were circulated. The Division board approved the Section of Local Chapters (Section IV) in October, 1985.

I wish at this point to describe the quirky, convoluted politics of the 1984–1986 phase of the Division's development. In 1984, Section I was still dominant and the future Section V was still unclear, and these antagonists now took opposite sides in reference to the emerging local chapters, with the future Section

V people strongly supporting local chapters and the Section I people in opposition—not in opposition to local chapters, just in opposition to the developments that were unfolding. Perhaps the most peculiar aspect of this political scene is that the local groups, so far as standards was concerned, were strongly identified with the values of Section I. Hence, they could easily have become the allies of Section I. Indeed, in 1983, had Section I been so inclined (which it decidedly was not!), it could have organized the local chapter movement, rather than the Division doing so a year later.

The reason that local chapters were most clearly identified with Section I values seems clear enough. Psychologists in places such as Michigan, Chicago, Denver, Dallas, Washington, and Boston were essentially aware of only one model of psychoanalysis, that of the local Institute of the American. Often these psychologists hung around the fringes of the local medical society, and were analyzed, supervised (psychotherapy, of course), and taught by members of the American. In Michigan, for example, a 1981 survey of the fledgling Michigan Society for Psychoanalytic Psychology found not one interpersonalist among the respondents, indicating that the interpersonal approach had not quite made it to the Midwest. Thus, the theoretical focus of most non-New Yorkers was mostly what I label mainstream American Freudian, so that these psychologists were natural allies of Section I, so far as standards were concerned.

On the other hand, the founders of local chapters (see, in this Volume, the articles of Gourevitch, Hyman, Kainer, Meisels, Shapiro, Slavin, and Spezzano) were strong-willed individualists: They had defied the local authority of the American, had courageously launched new organizations, and were well aware that any training activities in their areas would require nontraditional, creative educational forms. It was *this* that Section I apparently opposed. At the time, Section I people largely controlled the Division's Education and Training Committee, and they seemed to have the idea that the Education and Training Committee should set standards and requirements for local training groups. Already, at the December, 1984, Nationwide Conference—the first conference—conflict between the local chapters and the Educational and Training Committee had emerged, for local leaders were outraged at the idea that, having finally achieved local autonomy for psychologists, they would be asked to surrender that autonomy to a new central authority, even to the central authority of their own Division.

In the event, Section I leaders were generally opposed to the events that were unfolding. They were either opposed to, or were fighting rearguard actions against, such developments as the National Program Committee; the December, 1984, New York conference; the June, 1985, Ann Arbor conference; even to the formation of the Section of Local Chapters; and to this Clark Conference. Section I, which in its first years had launched the initiatives that had provided the Division's agenda, had misread the major currents that were developing, and had lost the initiative.

AFTERMATH

In retrospect, it might be said that the Division is constituted of diverse constituencies, much like the APA itself, and that the history of the Division is characterized by the emergence of these constituencies (the other two major groups that were not controversial were the Section on Childhood and Adolescence, and the Section on Women and Psychoanalysis). The intense, emotional, colorful conflict of the 1982–1986 period may be understood as a playing out of some of the major antipathies in the field of psychoanalysis, prior to the time that the Division developed the organizational solution of establishing new sections to accommodate emerging constituencies. Since then, since 1986, conflict has largely subsided. In the end, there was more eros than thanatos, and all constituencies seemed to agree that, to paraphrase, "If we don't hang together, we may hang separately."

DISCUSSION

I shall now discuss this historical material from the point of view of two common fantasies. First I shall present the fantasies and then indicate how I think they impacted on the history of the Division.

Fantasy No. 1: There is a Higher Justice

One of the persistent themes in the history of humankind, and in the Division, is a complaint about being mistreated and misunderstood, accompanied by an appeal that some higher authority might rectify the situation. For example, I have heard a number of psychiatrist-psychoanalysts bemoan their mistreatment by federal and state legislatures, for they feel that they have been injured, have been dealt a grave injustice, and they await the age when justice will prevail and the legislatures will declare that psychoanalysis—indeed, psychotherapy—is the province of medicine.

So, too, have I heard numbers of Freudians who are aggrieved because so many non-Freudians label themselves psychoanalysts. Why don't they call themselves something else instead, they ask. These individuals await the day of justice, when their rivals will see the light, and leave the term "psychoanalysis" to its proper Freudian home.

And psychologists and social workers—and others—who have so long felt betrayed and abused by the American Psychoanalytic Association (the American) and the International Psychoanalytic Association (the International), who have felt the sting of discrimination, have longed for the day that the American, and the International, would realize that they have committed horrible injustices, would rue the errors of their ways, and would finally admit psychologists and social workers (and others) as peers.

In point of fact, it appears unlikely that legislatures will decide that talk is the province of medicine; or that Kleinians would forsake the designation of psychoanalyst; or that the American or International would voluntarily change their policies. In raw reality, there is evidence of just how unlikely it was or is that the American or International would ever "see the light," would ever "recognize the errors of their ways," would ever make reparation for their discriminatory actions. That evidence comes from the 1985 lawsuit that psychologists filed against the American and International, particularly from depositions of leaders of the American. I have read five of six of these depositions, and what emerged is that the psychiatrist-psychoanalysts who comprise the leadership of the American are very much identified with the field of psychiatry; that many have little contact with the social sciences; and that their attention was focused on the internal workings of their organization, and on psychiatry and medicine. One of the very striking features of these depositions was the callousness of these leaders toward the plight of psychologists. Psychologists have experienced years of frustration, years of disappointment and dashed hopes, and entire psychoanalytic careers have gone undeveloped, and have been mourned. Yet the attitude towards this among leaders of the American—even leaders who favor training for psychologists—was bland indifference. No one expressed regret, or compassion, or seemed to feel a need to make repair. So much for the fantasy that "they" would realize an error.

In terms of the history of the Division of Psychoanalysis, the fantasy that there is a higher justice seemed to inform every development. Section I certainly felt entitled to define psychoanalysis in its traditional form, and considered that all who disagreed should "see the light," realize that they were not doing psychoanalysis, and redefine their activities. The future Section V people were looking to Section I for justice, hoping that Section I would be reasonable and hold an objective discourse about psychoanalytic process, more or less as nonpsychiatrists had hoped the American would listen and understand. And, the response of Section I to the Section V people was very similar to the response of the American to psychologists and social workers: Namely, indifference. And, the local chapters felt unjustly treated by a Division that barely supported or approved of their actions, a Division that was preoccupied with other issues.

There appears to be a psychoanalytic conclusion to be drawn from these observations. I am reminded here that Erich Fromm once wrote that the search for justice is universal because we all experienced injustices as children. Children are relatively helpless, and it is striking to me that one of the characteristics of the fantasy of a higher justice entails a theme of helplessness: There is a complainer who is unable to do for oneself, so someone else must "realize" something. In the history of the Division, the frustration of the search for justice led to the eventual recognition that a higher justice would never materialize—the American would never admit psychologists, so psychologists must form their own organization, their own practitioner section, or launch a lawsuit; and those in Section V realized that Section I would never listen, and thus set up their own section; and local chapters recognized the need for a power base within the Division, so another section was born. In sum, the plea for a higher justice is a statement of helplessness, and the proper reply is empowerment. It is the empowerment of psychologists through their national and local organizations that has mitigated their sense of injustice.

Fantasy No. 2: The Perfectly Analyzed Analyst

This is the term used by Glover (1955), and is the reflection, in psycho-analysis, of the human search for perfection. The perfectly analyzed analyst, then, is someone who does everything just right, someone who has resolved all of his or her transferences, who has no countertransferences, and who is seem-ingly not affected by past realities or even by present realities. This analyst is able to use analytic technique correctly, and the transferences become focused, and are resolved properly, by interpretation. It is hard to know just who such an analyst might be, and there is much analytic mythology here. Certainly I've heard it said that a young analyst could not be such an analyst, for young analysts lack seasoning and experience. Certainly, I've heard it said, someone who has been thrice divorced, or drives a sports car, or is a Jungian, could not be such an analyst. Graduation from an Institute is certainly no guarantee, as anyone who knows Institute graduates can readily attest. So the number of *analysts, real analysts,* by which is meant perfectly analyzed analysts, becomes fewer and fewer. This raises another problem, because there is no guarantee that an adjudged "perfectly analyzed analyst"—say, a married 55-year-old training analyst, a graduate of a first-rate Institute who also has an excellent reputation—will not start living with a former patient in another year, or change theoretical orientation.

The Roman Catholic Church, of course, has solved its version of the perfectly analyzed analyst by not decreeing perfection—sainthood—until 100 years after the person dies. That way, the person cannot change, and all who knew what that person was really like are dead.

In my contribution to the Clark Conference, I have documented a variation on the theme. To anticipate, the training analysis is widely viewed as a failure, and the cause is widely attributed to the fact that the analyst reports on the progress of the candidate's analysis as part of the institute's educational reviews. However, most Institutes do not report, and surveys of Institute graduates show great satisfaction with the training analysis! In my judgment, the reason that the training analysis is viewed as a failure is because many candidates—perhaps two in three—go on to further treatments, which presumably, would not occur if a "perfect" analysis had been conducted. I conclude arguing that the bad reputa-tion of the training analysis, and of reporting, are distractions from the far more penetrating issue of why multiple analyses are so commonplace among psychoanalysts. For some, it may be preferable to be distracted by the reporting function than to surrender the fantasy of the perfect analyst.

In reference to Division 39, it seems that the fantasy of the perfectly analyzed analyst was most intensely manifested in Section I. Indeed, I well recall an address by a Section I leader which argued that one learns the analyzing function by internalizing the analyzing functions of one's analyst, which meant, for that writer, that one's analyst's capacities prescribe the limits of one's own capacities, a variation on the lineage myth. Note that such an argument means that virtually no one thinks for themselves, that no one learns from experience. In my opinion, the fantasy of the perfectly analyzed analyst held such sway over the Section I leadership that it had difficulty coping with the changing agenda of the Division, much as the same fantasy, in the American, caused it grave difficulties in coping with the changing composition of mental health professionals in the United States.

REFERENCES

Glover, E. (1955). *The technique of psychoanalysis.* New York: International Universities Press.

Meisels, M., & Hyman, M. (1980). A proposal for accrediting psychoanalyst psychologists. *Psychologist-Psychoanalyst, 1,* 3–9.

Meisels, M., & Kerner, O. J. B. (1982). A proposal for a national program of psychoanalytic education. *Psychologist-Psychoanalyst, 3*(Fall), 7–8.

2

Helen Block Lewis, In Memoriam: Her Vision of the Clark Conference on Psychoanalytic Training for Psychologists

Ester R. Shapiro

In Murray Meisels's introduction, he suggests that in order to develop their own psychoanalytic training programs, psychologists need the support of their own national organization, the Division of Psychoanalysis. How can the Division serve this supportive function, without becoming a new, rigidified organization which imposes its own vision of training on developing programs? How will psychologists, with the new opportunities for developing their own training offered by the formation of the Division and by the development of local chapters, approach questions of psychoanalytic training? Will we psychologists rely on the educational model developed by the medical psychoanalysts, or will we create our own models? Can we learn from the past, and still leave room for new ideas, without rigidly imposing this past on the present and the future? Can we support the development of local chapters with our own view of the educational needs in our particular communities?

Helen Block Lewis saw the importance of these questions in the development of psychoanalytic training programs, both within the Division, and more broadly on behalf of the development of psychoanalysis as a science and as a therapy. During her presidential year, she facilitated the development of local chapters, and encouraged discussions of the variety of evolving training programs in different communities. Most importantly, she enabled all of us working with local chapters to look within ourselves for our own authority as we explored alternative educational models. She felt that the best way to facilitate this creative development of educational alternatives was to hold a series of conferences which offered an opportunity for dialogue and collaboration.

Dr. Lewis's vision for the Clark Conference was at the same time ambitiously intellectual and immensely practical. She felt that psychoanalysis had failed to

11

change, as a science and as a therapy, because of its isolation from different points of view. She believed that if the Division brought together the broadest group of psychoanalytic theorists and educators, and facilitated their mutually respectful dialogue on issues of psychoanalytic theory and training, it would provide an opportunity for creative intellectual exchange and discovery. It would also offer the local chapters a broader view of psychoanalytic educational alternatives, especially in communities where the medical Institutes were the only point of reference.

Dr. Lewis died on January 18, 1987, at the age of 72, a few months after the conference was held. With her death, psychoanalytic psychology lost one of its most clear and innovative voices. Lewis felt ill at the time of the conference, but participated fully in the conference by drawing deeply from her remaining resources for the energy and vitality which was characteristic of her throughout her life. Lewis left us the significant legacy of her unique perspective as a psychoanalyst-psychologist, devoted clinician and teacher, innovative researcher and writer. The Clark Conference was a special opportunity for her to weave the threads of her vision together in one time and place.

Lewis's contributions to psychoanalysis have been highly significant, and are most visibly documented in her five important books, and many published articles and chapters, on cognitive style, on the importance of shame and guilt in relationships, on gender differences, and on a rethinking of Freud in the light of modern psychology (Lewis, 1971, 1976, 1981, 1983, 1988; Witkin et al., 1954). Lewis was a psychoanalyst-researcher in the fullest sense of both words: her clinical work, research, and theoretical formulations were coherently devoted to the goal of making psychoanalysis as effective as possible in relieving human suffering. In Lewis, intellectual rigor combined with humanitarian aims to create an urgency of commitment to the current and future welfare of patients. She was remarkably and unsentimentally capable of listening to new ideas and letting the data change her mind, whether the new information came from research, from her understanding of her patients, or from dialogue with colleagues.

Lewis also made a formative contribution to the Division of Psychoanalysis of the American Psychological Association, as an active member, president in 1984, and founding editor of the Division's journal, *Psychoanalytic Psychology*. She created the journal as a forum for the particular perspective of psychologists, whom she felt approached psychoanalysis with the healthy skepticism toward ideas which had emerged from their background of academic scholarship. Lewis was devoted to psychoanalytic process in the best sense of the word, sufficiently so that she believed psychoanalysis could best flourish in a climate where psychoanalytic ideas were argued and examined open-mindedly, through challenging discussion and through systematic research.

Helen Block Lewis's commitment to future generations was a strong motivating force in her final years, especially in her devotion to issues of psychoanalytic training. She felt that at a time when psychologists were developing their own psychoanalytic training programs and identities as psychoanalysts, psycho-analytic psychologists had the exciting opportunity to assess the nature of the psychoanalytic enterprise in new ways. She believed that psychology, with its unique tradition of academic scholarship and research, offered a much needed perspective for the continuing development of psychoanalysis as a scientific and clinical discipline.

Lewis was especially committed to exploring and understanding the costs and benefits of institutional training programs, compared with programs of independent study. Lewis, like many psychologists of her era, had arrived at her psychoanalytic training through "bootlegged" or independent study. Looking back on her self-initiated training, she believed that the opportunity to create a program which best fit her own educational needs, borrowing from a wide range of teachers and supervisors available to her in New York, was for her an ideal situation. Lewis freely pursued intellectual and humanitarian psychoanalytic goals, without defending a particular pedagogical method or a particular institution. As psychologists became more involved in traditional psychoanalytic education, she wanted to be sure that the field didn't lose sight of the distinct advantages of independent study out of a wish to be considered legitimate members of the American psychoanalytic community.

In addition, Lewis's intensive study of the superego emotions of shame and guilt made her acutely sensitive to the emotional difficulties inherent in relationships where one person nurtures the development of another. Fundamental to her theory of normal and symptomatic personality development were two propositions: Attachment in close relationships is the essential driving force in life, and undischarged or strangulated affect is the basis from which self-constricting defenses and symptom formation can best be understood (Shapiro, 1988). Lewis observed that a state of shame inevitably accompanies any close relationship with inequality of status. She found that in interpersonal situations where a dependent person felt rejected or criticized and could not make direct reparation, an intrapsychic process was initiated as a means of self-regulation. Humiliated rage at the relational injury was followed by shame and guilt at the unwarranted hatred of the beloved, often followed by attempts to punish the self as a reparation toward the internalized, idealized image of the other, or else by attempts to devalue the other and bring them down from their position of power.

Because of her detailed study of the intrapsychic consequences of these interpersonal sequences, Lewis was especially concerned about the unconscious exploitation of authority by parents, clinicians, or teachers, and the emotional consequences for children, patients, and students of their unacknowledged humiliations in dependent relationships. She believed it was vitally important to bring in new information from child development, feminist theory, and family systems theory, not only to expand psychoanalytic theory as it might be taught in a curriculum, but also to enhance our understanding of the interplay between attachment processes, internalization of authority, and self-regulation within relationships in the training process itself. Because of her own close attention to these relational processes, Lewis knew how to listen to her patients, students, and colleagues in a way that conveyed the respectful appreciation for the experience of the other which most enabled self-understanding.

In Lewis's writing on the development of the Clark Conference, she emphasized that psychoanalytic training had evolved with limited responsiveness to changes in the science of psychology and in the clinical needs of the communities requiring psychological services. This dual goal, to review psychoanalytic training in the light of scientific advances, and to move toward the goal of becoming more responsive to patient needs, provided her guiding orientation to the organization of the program. Lewis agreed with the accumulated wisdom of the field, that the training model combining coursework, supervision, and a personal analysis continued to be the most effective means of training future psychoanalysts.

However, the questions Lewis asked of the traditional, tripartite training model were so fundamentally challenging that they required the most open-minded reassessment of the most basic theoretical and technical assumptions in psychoanalysis. She proposed, in a preliminary draft for the conference program, that the tripartite model needed to respond to the following three areas of difference:

1. *Differing theoretical viewpoints on therapeutic efficiency*, and on psychoanalysis versus psychotherapy, both within psychoanalysis and outside it. Within psychoanalysis, the different theoretical and technical contributions of Freudian, interpersonal, or Jungian theories; psychoanalytic approaches to group, family, and systems theory, humanistic psychoanalysis, and crisis intervention needed to be considered. Outside of psychoanalysis, behavioral, cognitive-behavioral, and drug therapy approaches and their place in therapeutic efficacy needed to be included for their aid to therapeutic efficacy as well.

2. *Differing needs of different populations.* Differences in the treatment of children, adolescents, adults, and the aging; gender issues; the treatment of neurotic patients, personality disorders, or psychotic patients.

3. *Differing goals of psychoanalysis*: The goal of personal growth, compared with the goal of relief of suffering. How is psychoanalytic treatment different for psychoanalytic "candidates" in training, compared with other patients?

The Clark Conference was conceived as a collaborative working conference, encouraging dialogue among a diverse faculty and participants who represented the broadest range of psychoanalytic points of view. Lewis's own creative energy, excitement about new ideas, and readiness to learn from new experiences inspired all of us who worked with her in planning the conference to design an environment where a creative exchange could freely take place. In collaboration with Murray Meisels, cochair of the conference planning committee, and the other committee members, Lewis provided the leadership for an ambitious and challenging program which promised dialogue of such diversity that no one who participated fully in the conference could leave with all of their previous assumptions unchallenged.

The following two chapters best represent Helen Block Lewis's views on psychoanalytic training. These were written and presented in 1985, during Lewis's year as president of Division 39. Although they were not presented at the Clark Conference, these chapters provide a clear statement of the guiding principles which oriented the conference and therefore this book of proceedings. Lewis's presidential address at the Division's 1985 spring meeting, "Some Thoughts About Becoming a Psychoanalyst: Anno 1985," was meant to shake up traditional ideas on psychoanalytic training, and to open up discussion of new pathways for the future. Lewis argued that from the time of Freud, psychoanalysis had confounded its research and training aims with its treatment aims. She believed that it was vital for the future of psychoanalysis to separate institutional goals from the treatment goal of relieving human suffering as efficiently and effectively as humanly possible. Her life work as a psychologist, which is resonantly voiced in this chapter, was based on her unique combination of a wide-ranging, vigorous capacity for intellectual exploration, and a respectful, compassionate understanding of the nature of people's lives.

In her final presidential address, "Psychoanalysis as Therapy Today," Lewis begins by acknowledging her surprise at the depth of passion aroused by her call for a reconsideration of the methods and goals in psychoanalytic training. She proposed that in order to grow in the future, psychoanalysis needed to become responsive to new research and theoretical formulations rather than to close ranks in response to criticism. In the past, new theoretical formulations and technical innovations were banished from the field of psychoanalysis into the separate and less valued area of psychodynamic psychotherapy. Lewis asserts in this chapter that this development occurred, in part, because psychoanalysis became separated from its treatment goal of symptom relief and instead became devoted to achieving character restructuring. As outcome studies increasingly show that supportive psychotherapies are at least as effective as psychoanalysis, the field of psychoanalysis has become more preoccupied with achieving an analysis, and failures are chalked up to the "unanalyzability" or character defects of the analysand. Perhaps for this reason, psychoanalysis has become an increasingly lengthy, expensive process, now used most often by other mental health professionals rather than the general community as the treatment of choice.

In sum, the Clark Conference was profoundly shaped by Helen Block Lewis, by her intellectual and humanitarian missions. She felt that psychoanalytic theory and clinical practice could be expanded, on behalf of both the field of psychoanalysis and the community of people psychoanalysis can help, by a mutually respectful dialogue among theorists and practitioners with diverse points of view. The subtitle of the conference, "Tradition and Innovation in Psychoanalytic Training," was meant to reflect the respectful balance between the teachings offered by experience of the past and the creativity required for the future. The purpose of the collaborative working conference was to express points of view, develop a discourse, explore different models of training, and encourage a research perspective.

The conference itself was an extremely intensive experience, in both its high level of scholarship and its interpersonal atmosphere of respectful collegial exchange. It was densely packed with programmed talks and unprogrammed interpersonal engagement as the participants offered, heard, and integrated new ideas about training. The conference was attended by 180 persons, 40 of whom were invited faculty. Participants came from all over the country, and had a diverse range of backgrounds in psychoanalysis, which contributed richly to all our discussions, in both the large conference and the small groups. The eminent faculty was a valuable resource, but the program itself was so full we had too little time for the lively responses which the talks were meant to generate. The coffee breaks and lunches which punctuated the meetings had a constant hum of animated conversation, which showed just how enthusiastically participants were responding to the issues presented in the formal talks. The small-group workshops, which met four times during the conference, provided an additional opportunity for discussion.

In the end, all of us who participated in planning the conference felt satisfied that the "holding environment" for the conference had successfully provided a setting where participants transcended their customary divisions and learned from each other in mutually enhancing ways. The conference had high intellectual and interpersonal goals, and the measure of its success is the lively dialogue on training which it catalyzed, and which continues in the development of creative psychoanalytic training programs within the local chapters of Division 39. Hopefully, in the translation from conference to the printed pages of this book, we will continue to expand the important dialogue on these issues of psychoanalytic training beyond the conference participants.

Helen was so fully, intensely productive and engaged with life in her last years, and at the time of the Clark Conference, that most of us who worked closely with her were unprepared for her sudden death. Yet looking back on my work with her in supervision, now that my memories are the place where I find her, I remembered Helen's comments on my therapy with a cancer patient, in which she told me her thinking about living one's life in the face of death. In talking with her about my therapeutic work with a young woman who had undergone surgery for breast cancer and who was waiting for her 5-year verdict on its recurrence, I wondered whether I colluded with the patient and avoided talking about her illness out of my own grief on her behalf. Helen told me that this patient was living with the shadow of Moloch, the angel of death, and I was helping her to bear this painful reality. The patient could not go on with her life while giving herself over to death, and as her therapist I had to help her keep her mind on life over death. The dilemma of the therapy, as Helen saw it, was that we couldn't urge her to face death when we didn't know if death was imminent, but neither could we look away from death if she was to live her life fully. Helen chose to live and work fully, to the last months of her life, in the face of death. Her presence and active participation at the Clark Conference was one of her final gifts.

Helen Block Lewis gave us the conceptual and personal leadership for the Clark Conference, as does any good teacher, to support the creative development of a future in which she herself would not directly participate. In intergenerational dialogue, she was extraordinarily capable of drawing on what she had learned in the past, engaging fully in the present, and holding a vision for the future, in a way that enhanced past, present, and future. Her work was infused with her generous and creative spirit, and she has left us the powerful legacy of that spirit to enrich our futures.

REFERENCES

Lewis, H. B. (1971). *Shame and guilt in neurosis.* New York: International Universities Press.

Lewis, H. B. (1976). *Psychic war in men and women.* New York: New York University Press. Reprinted as *Sex and the superego.* Hillsdale, NJ: Analytic Press, 1988.

Lewis, H. B. (1981). *Freud and modern psychology* (Vol. 1). *The emotional basis of mental illness.* New York: Plenum.

Lewis, H. B. (1983). *Freud and modern psychology* (Vol. 2). *The emotional basis of human behavior.* New York: Plenum.

Shapiro, E. R. (1988). *Shame, guilt, and family development: The interpersonal superego.* Paper presented at a symposium in honor of Helen Block Lewis, Division 39 spring meeting, San Francisco.

Witkin, H., Lewis, H., Hertzman, M., Machover, K., Meissner, P., & Wapner, S. (1954). *Personality through perception.* New York: Harper.

3 Some Thoughts on Becoming a Psychoanalyst: Anno 1985

Helen Block Lewis

Let me say first how honored and delighted I am to be delivering a presidential address at Division 39's first spring meeting and its first meeting in my still-beloved New York, the city that can boast of having the largest number of training institutions for psychologists who want to become psychoanalysts—probably the largest concentration in the world. I have chosen to discuss some questions about how to train in psychoanalysis in the light of the accumulation of almost a hundred years of knowledge since our field came into existence. It is also a very appropriate time to think about how training should be conducted since our Division has lauched its exciting three-part program: arranging with ABPP for developing a procedure for certification in psychoanalysis; supporting a class-action lawsuit just launched by four clinical psychologists against the American Psychoanalytic Association, in order to end many years of discrimination against psychologists in psychoanalytic training; and beginning to develop its own nationwide training programs. While this is a number of years down the road, it is not too early to start talking about how we should do this and we will need many meetings and conferences at which the informed opinion of our membership and of the field's experts should be solicited.

Let me say at once that I am raising questions to which I do not have the answers. I do not have any specific program or curriculum to propose, except for two points that I want to exclude from argument before I proceed because they are not at issue in my thinking. The first of these is that our training Institutes of the future must incorporate training in clinical and experimental research into curricula in a much more systematic way than now occurs; this includes responsibility to do research on the effectiveness of their own training programs. Had such a research base been built into the training institutions that have evolved,

19

both medical and nonmedical, our field would be much less given to acrimonious disputes and to the development of schisms about what constitutes "true doctrine" or "real psychoanalysis" than it is now. The second point on which I think there should be no disagreement is the necessity for would-be psychoanalysts to be analyzed themselves. I permit myself this article of faith because of the empirical evidence that therapists' warmth and empathy are key factors that have been isolated as contributing to a good therapeutic outcome. Without an analysis of their own to strengthen them against their patients' unconscious hostility, analysts can hardly hope to maintain these essential affective positions.

I am aware that I may be raising painful identity questions at a time when our profession is under attack from the increasing dehumanization of our society. Our professional identity is also suffering at the moment from the growing evidence that psychoanalysis as a therapeutic instrument is not quite so potent as it was once thought to be—in the early 1940s, for example, when I first entered training. While external threats tend to unite us, evidence of our possible deficiencies as therapists tends to divide us because talking about deficiencies may seem like a threat to our professional identity. Because it has not had a good research arm, our profession has a history of responding to new ideas by worrying about the supposed watering down of psychoanalysis and a resulting "lowering of standards," and by reading critics out of the fold. This is a defensive maneuver that is familiar to all of us. The critic has nothing worthwhile to say, therefore he or she cannot shame us for our mistakes; he or she should rather be shamed for not upholding standards or being provocative, or rebellious, or some such label. Although the necessary process of thinking through our own training program may be painful, I have little doubt that if we keep our eye on what is good for patients, and refer our different prescriptions for training to the arbitration of research (where it exists) we will be able to use our own analytic expertise to help us with our growing pains.

Riccardo Steiner's admirable account, just published in the *International Review of Psychoanalysis*, of the so-called controversial discussions between Anna Freud and Melanie Klein is a part of our history from which we can learn some lessons. The liveliest debate was about the admissibility of Klein's notion of "unconscious phantasy," which Anna Freud's group believed would demolish what they had come to regard as the secure foundation of psychoanalysis. (This is the same threat that Anna Freud saw in Masson's publication of *all* of Freud's letters to Fliess on the subject of the seduction theory.) As Steiner points out, psychoanalysis in Britain at the time had no research base. Some of the Viennese "wished to defend Freud's writings to the very letter including his theory of primary narcissism which Klein had abandoned because they believed that to accept Klein's ideas would be to open the door to a perversion of psychoanalysis and the loss of professional identify as psychoanalysts" (p. 58). Ironically, it was one of the Melanie Klein's analysands, John Bowlby, who, while putting aside her theoretical formulations about a death instinct, carried out empirical investigations about infants' phantasmic and affective life. And, in fact, Klein's notions of infants' early depressive and paranoid positions in relation to the caretaker and her concept of reparation comes closer to capturing the ongoing social character of infant experience than the classical concept of infant narcissism. Steiner's account of the controversial discussions makes no reference to the role of Bowlby's empirical work in ending the Freud-Klein controversy. Nor does he make reference to the long years during which direct observation of children in a nonanalytic setting was considered a suspect activity which had no relevance to psychoanalysis. The moral of this story, then, is twofold: (1) We must beware of the response to questions which threatens us with shame and guilt by association with those who would pervert or demolish psychoanalysis; and (2) We must remember to refer our questions to solution by research, both clinical and experimental.

Before coming back to questions of training, let me very briefly summarize for you my own 40 years of experience as a psychologist-psychoanalyst so that I may better convey to you where I am coming from and why. In this way you can assess the professional and personal background out of which my strong interest in training has evolved. I will not detail to you the sad, and often funny story of my own anonymous teachers. The class-action lawsuit filed by my four younger colleagues should go far to remedy that kind of bottleneck to training. I need, rather, to describe very briefly my odyssey from a classical training in which Edith Jacobson and Marcel Heiman were my anonymous teachers and Margaret Mahler was among my open ones. (None of the above is responsible in any way for my errors.)

I have traveled from my classical training into a somewhat different mode of listening with benign neutrality to the patients' stream of consciousness and free associations. While my technique relies completely on this very classical aspect of listening, what is new is my *focus* on the sequelae from patients' evoked states of shame and guilt as these appear in the stream of communications. I have found that this focus comprehends both the childhood traumata and sufferings that slant the transference and the "resistances" which dog the patient–therapist relationship and inhibit the patients' flow of communications. The sequence from shame into humiliated fury and simultaneously into guilt is elucidated. The patient thus comes to see the many ways in which an unanalyzed tangle of shame and guilt leads by the well-described (but still not clearly understood) route of primary-process transformation into symptoms. I do not imagine that I understand this process so that I cannot call it a causal sequence, but it clearly is an experiential one. My present-day best guess is that the causal factors pushing the sequence of emotional states lie in the motivational system—the need to restore or maintain the threatened affectional bonds that are basic to human nature.

I was led into my focus on the affective-cognitive states of shame and guilt by the small but surprising number of failures in patients whose analysis we both thought had been successful. This unhappy experience of mine in the 1950s and

1960s seems to have coincided roughly in time with the negative experiences described by Kohut and Kernberg, which led them to postulate a separate category of patients, namely, borderlines. My hypothesis about my failures did not involve a new category of patients, however, but rather the neglect of shame in the analysis.

A second set of experiences which ultimately helped me to crystallize my focus on shame and guilt came from my work with H. A. Witkin on the cognitive style that we came to call field dependence. This work of ours during the 1940s and 1950s was part of the New Look in perception and cognition which resulted from the spread of psychoanalytic concepts. An early finding, one of many linking field dependence/independence to differing forms of pathology was of a connection between field dependence and depression, and of a corresponding connection between field independence and paranoia. Robust evidence now confirms connection between field dependence and depression and good evidence has also accumulated for the link between field independence and paranoia. Playing with the relationship between cognitive style and the then-prevalent concept of an archaic or merciless superego as the villain in symptom formation led me to speculate that field-dependent patients should be more prone to shame and field-dependent patients more prone to guilt as their prevailing a superego style. (Both kinds of patients would be overflowing with both miseries.) Witkin, Edmund Weil, and I were able to put this speculation into a set of hypotheses which we then put to experimental test, and our hypotheses were well confirmed by our results. This experience increased my confidence in the wisdom of studying shame and guilt as well as yielding 180 transcripts of psychotherapy sessions for study. There was also an extra, unpredicted bonus: My focus on these states and their sequelae considerably increased my therapeutic efficiency. While I have no outcome studies to support this claim, my experience has been that patients feel better sooner and come back less often when treated with this focus. The students I have taught over the past 15 years or so have also reported good results with this focus.

In any case, my experience taught me that, over and above my own deficiencies as a therapist, there was something missing in the excellent training that I received. It taught me, rather painfully at first, that these omissions were not cause for shame or guilt on anybody's part. Rather they should be the spur to discovering as best we can what it is that we do not know. And this process absolutely requires that mistakes, such as the neglect of shame, be acknowledged in our work without weaseling. Acceptance of mistakes is facilitated if training institutes do indeed have a functioning research arm.

My odyssey has now taken me to identifying the areas of information that were not available in Freud's time: the social and cognitively organized nature of infant behavior; the overriding importance of the infant–caretaker dyad; the discovery of REMS; the growing evidence of the universal human emotions, including the positive ones; the evidence of the cultural nature of human nature and the burgeoning of information about sex differences, arising in part from feminist critiques of scholarship. Each new area of information has an impact on practice and many of them have already been well identified in many existing Institutes. But psychoanalytic knowledge will proceed more rapidly if we also recognize the necessity for building bridges between us and academia and if we pay special attention to our own tendency to be parochial—to operate as if all knowledge relevant to psychoanalysis were contained in existing psychoanalytic journals. Our research-based APA journals can also be very useful.

Thus I come back to my first fundamental of a training program: its built-in research arm. The history of the psychoanalytic movement in relation to research deserves a moment's reflection. Psychoanalysis actually began with a confound between listening to free associations as a way into a person's emotional life, for a therapeutic purpose, and listening with the purpose of research into the origin of the trouble. The implications of this fact of our history have never been fully articulated. That the use of an extended long-term program of free association as a research tool might actually conflict with its use as a therapeutic instrument has never really been faced, although this idea has been in the wings of the movement surely as early as the 1920s if not earlier. For example, I recently learned from reviewing Paul Roazen's biography of Helene Deutsch that as early as 1926, she had abandoned the "phantom" of the "Freudian method which I now recognize I must regard as an area of research and not a therapeutic method." She goes on in the same letter to her husband, Felix Deutsch, to specify what she calls a "swindle," namely that "certain people (the professor himself) in full awareness—do not openly disavow the therapeutic—whereas others, on the one hand out of identification and on the other hand out of narcisistic need to have some special ability, unconsciously elevate psychoanalysis to be their battle cry, to be the one and only path to blessedness." According to her biographer, Helene Deutsch never made these views public. What is so important here is that a problem was known but not addressed, apparently out of regard for the feelings of the Founder.

The confound between psychoanalysis as a research tool and psychoanalysis as a therapeutic instrument also had as one of its ill effects, a confound between finding the cause of genesis of an illness or symptoms and finding the means of cure. The two tasks are by no means identical. Freud was aware of this on occasion as when he wrote that the technique of free association was meant to locate the causal chain into illness, but that, theoretically, any intervention that broke the chain, even a chemical one, would be welcome to psychoanalysis. This was written long before there was any notion of the existence of mood-altering drugs. But it does remind us, as an aside that our training programs must address the problem of establishing collegial relationships between people who can prescribe useful drugs and ourselves; it also seems to me wise to suggest, as some Institutes do, that candidates make themselves personally conversant with the rudiments of psychopharmacology.

The careful distinction between genesis and cure was ultimately lost in the more or less unquestioned assumption that psychoanalysis can be both a research and a therapeutic instrument without loss to either undertaking. As Gill has suggested, a focus on reconstructing a patient's history does have some costs to be evaluated along with benefits. Moreover, we have become aware of the dangers of retrospective falsification as we try to reconstruct our patients' pasts with our methods of free association. This is one reason why some of our colleagues now speak of distinguishing between narrative and historical truth. Training Institutes that have a research arm can help us to keep our research and therapeutic aims from further confound.

Still another kind of confound has arisen in the course of our history: the confound between the needs of candidates and the needs of ordinary patients. There is little doubt that by now, a large proportion of analysands are people who wish to become or are mental health professionals themselves. Estimates put the proportion as at least 50%, if not more. This fact alone may inadvertently create a climate in which the intensive and thorough treatment needed by candidates becomes the unconscious standard by which therapy for ordinary mortals is evaluated. There is good evidence, moreover, that the more senior the analyst, the more likely it is that his or her practice will be devoted to treating candidates. Our senior professionals are thus dealing with relatively more put-together patients, while their junior colleagues are struggling with more severe symptoms in sicker patients. Perhaps because of some halo effect, the junior professionals regard the second enterprise as lower-order; instead of themselves as simply junior. When, in addition, the senior professionals are not only senior, but elevated to the institutionalized status as training analysts, the tendency becomes even stronger to think of workers in the field, doing the everyday tasks in the community, as somehow inferior. If this were only snobbishness, it could be addressed and overcome. But the institution of training analyst does tend, as many have indicated before this, to make us less open to new experiences arising out of our work.

Ordinary mortals, moreover, come for relief of depression, hysteria, phobia, and obsessional neurosis. The tendency that has developed for psychoanalytic technique to be in the "one size fits all" mode, based, in part, on the model of the reasonably well-put-together candidate, may hinder our fuller understanding of differing conditions. We know, for example, that situation phobics, formerly called agoraphobics, are likely to be more field-dependent people than people with specific phobias, who tend to be field-independent. These results were predicted on analytic grounds. As another example, there is some evidence that suggests that behavior methods for depression and phobia are at least as success-ful in offering symptom relief as a course of psychoanalysis. Now psycho-analysis surely has the potential of offering more than symptom relief. But this claim should not be used to derogate symptom relief which is what some people may be quite willing to settle for. Should we not now offer our candidates a careful overview of established, competing therapies, in the manner of Appelbaum and Wachtel? Both of these writers have shown us how much there is to learn from encounters with the larger therapeutic world. In addition, there are many treatment modalities, such as group and family therapy, in which psychoanalytic approaches play a very significant role. There are many analysts who practice group and family therapy. Do they cease being psychoanalysts when they do?

And so we come to the thorny question of the relationship between psychoanalysis and psychoanalytic psychotherapy. As you can see, I have come to think that both deserve the embrace of psychoanalysis as equal sisters. And before you respond that I am lowering standards, let me remind you that most research on the effectiveness of the psychoanalytic approach has combined psychoanalysis and psychotherapy in its reckoning. Let me remind you also, that when people think of psychoanalysts today, they do not make any hierarchy of differing schools. All of us are "followers" of Freud: Adler, Jung, Horney, Sullivan, Fromm, Existential Psychoanalysis, Object-relations, Ego psychology, all have been somewhat homogenized, because every group has taught us something. We are now fortunately more united in being psychoanalysts than we are divided in our theoretical views. This is how some training Institutes operate now, although when our professional began, the "real psychoanalysis" was being protected from criticism by one split after the other.

One of my much respected colleagues and friends wrote me after my first President's Column that he did not understand what I mean by the term, "brief psychoanalysis." I had used this descriptor to refer to David Malan's work, which Malan regards as distillation of the best in psychoanalysis, just as I do my work. Malan, however, always used the term brief dynamic psychotherapy to characterize his work. I was in error, of course, in using a term for Malan's work that Malan does not use. But I do not know what I mean by brief psychoanalysis. It means what Freud did with the Rat-Man—unraveled his symptoms in 9 months. It is true that they worked 6 days a week. But was it a successful psychoanalysis for this reason or for some more intrinsic reason?

The problem of the relationship between psychoanalysis and psychotherapy is clearly still timely. Gill's recent brilliant piece in the *International Review* to which I have already referred, is only the latest in a series that has occupied him since 1954. Gill distinguishes between external and internal criteria of psychoanalysis. By external criteria he means frequency of sessions, use of the chair versus the couch, length of treatment, relative health of the patient and relative experience of the therapist. By intrinsic criteria he means the analysis of the transference which he has come to reconceptualize as an interpersonal transaction. He has spelled out for us some of the implications of taking seriously a "two-person view" of the transference. Since I am persuaded of the importance of the two moral, social emotions, shame and guilt, in the transference I readily see his point. Within this altered framework, he suggests that the intrinsic feature psychoanalysis as he redefines it should be employed as much as possible "even if the patient comes less frequently than usual, uses the chair rather than the couch, is not necessarily committed to a treatment of relatively long duration, is sicker than usually considered analysable, and even if the therapist is relatively inexperienced" (p. 163). Gill ends his paper by asking what to call the process he is describing and suggests the answer: that we not worry about the name right now. My suggestion is that we face it, and call the enterprise psychoanalysis, even if it does not have the familiar external criteria.

When we look at the evidence on the relationship between psychoanalysis and psychotherapy from empirical research, we find, as Fisher and Greenberg tell us, that the trend since Freud's time has been to blur the distinction between the two. The most famous of the studies on the outcome of psychoanalysis was the Menninger Project, which was conducted by psychoanalytically trained researchers, and a concluding report of which was written by our own Stephen Appelbaum in his book. Although the study was not designed to compare psychoanalysis and psychotherapy, the naturalistic setting involved assigning people with greater degrees of ego strength to psychoanalysis and people with lesser strengths to psychotherapy. There was, however, no significant difference between the patient groups in their overall improvement. If anything, therapists judged less skilled did better when the treatment mode was psychoanalysis than in psychotherapy, a finding that can be interpreted as indicating either that psychotherapy requires more skill than psychoanalysis or that the relative leisure of the psychoanalytic enterprise allows the mistakes of less skillful therapists to dissipate, or both. A principal finding was that those patients who were better endowed to begin with profited more from both psychoanalysis or psychoanalytic therapy that those who were sicker to start. In any case, no clear-cut evidence of the therapeutic superiority of psychoanalysis emerged from the long and arduous Menninger Project. In fact, "structural changes" occurred in the course of so-called supportive psychotherapy. (This reminds us as an aside that the term "supportive" may be becoming a bit passé, now that so many of us are talking about the importance of the support of the "self–other" and the necessity for the support that inheres in "mirroring.")

What I am proposing is that we think through the implications of this knowledge in planning how we train psychologists to be psychoanalysts. I go back now to my second fundamental of training an analyst, his or her personal analysis. For this we need a continuing stream of analysts who focus on the questions and techniques involved in training candidates, keeping clearly in mind the special goals of this enterprise. Candidates, in turn, need the experience of analyzing selected, suitable patients, much like themselves in degree of health, but only with different analytic goals, than the candidates. So far, this is pretty much *all* we do right now. What I am suggesting is that we need to do more. We need to train candidates directly for their awesome task of helping the rest of the suffering community, with fewer hours at their disposal and with very flexible psychoanalytic interventions, a la Malan, for example. Since many candidates will have come to us with a great deal of experience on the front line, we need moreover, to help them (and ourselves) to integrate their rich and varied experiences into the fabric of psychoanalytic thinking. In my view, this is an equally psychoanalytic enterprise which should occupy a healthy proportion of our institute curricula. Let me emphasize that this proposal *raises* standards, since it adds a whole curriculum unit to what we traditionally now do. Would it not make sense, for example, to regard a certain number of hours spent in supervised dynamic psychotherapy with sicker patients as at least equivalent in value of one supervised analytic case conducted with a better integrated patient? Should our Institutes not focus more on the intrinsic rather than the extrinsic criteria of psychoanalysis?

I am aware that there are pressing guild problems that motivate us to set up our own new Institutes as like as possible to the old so that "they" will not derogate us. I am aware that there are many well-functioning Institutes for psychologists in the more populated areas of our country. These have been operating successfully for years and may regard the development of new training programs with a certain degree of understandable caution. In any case, I look forward to our joint work toward an ideal—that the coveted title of psychoanalyst be applied to analyzed persons with a doctoral degree in psychology or its equivalent, who learn by many and widely varying means, including acknowledging mistakes, how to render the most effective and efficient "talking cures" to the suffering people they serve.

4

Psychoanalysis as Therapy Today[1]

Helen Block Lewis

A presidential address is, of course, also a farewell address by the retiring president. I want, first, to express my gratitude to the membership for enabling me to have a gratifying (on balance) as well as a most informative experience. Among the pieces of incidental intelligence that I collected in the course of my presidency, for example, is that there are over 26,000 private charitable foundations in this country, many thousands of which offer support for educational and mental health programs! As you undoubtedly know, one of them, the Exxon Education Foundation, is funding our Division's forthcoming Conference on Psychoanalytic Training to be held at Clark University in October, 1986. Another kind of enlightenment during my presidency came from encountering some of the passionate feelings that surround the idea of reviewing the training procedures for becoming a psychoanalyst. As some of you who participated in the balloting that elected me may remember, I ran on a platform in which I said that, whoever was elected, I was sure that person would encourage a thorough review of our training procedures. I have discovered in the course of my presidency, however, that not all our members are as enthusiastic about this idea as are some others. I had really not anticipated the depth of passions that can be aroused when one of us suggests that training for psychoanalysis needs some re-thinking. As I consider why this is, I realize that psychoanalysis as a therapy today is under considerable attack for its profoundly humanistic values. The psychoanalyst's role as what Freud called the "curer of souls" is not congenial to many segments of psychology and to many tough-minded segments of the larger community.

[1] Presidential address to Division 39, APA, at the 93rd annual convention of the American Psychological Association, Los Angeles. Copyright ©1985 Helen Block Lewis. All rights reserved.

29

The natural response to such criticism is to tighten ranks and to defend our humanistic premises and practices. And when one of us from within the movement calls attention to some of our deficiencies as therapists which seem to derive from some of our standard training procedures—that person is sure to be regarded as misguided, if not some kind of threat to psychoanalysis itself.

What surprised me, as I have said, was the depth of the passions aroused. On reflection, I think this has happened because so many of us have gone through a rigorous training process ourselves. Some of us are inclined to equate their own rigorous training with the best that there is in training today. Alas, this is not necessarily so. It may be the best that there was, but the signs now point to some need for change. Anyway, the messenger who brings this kind of news should not be surprised if she evokes protest responses.

On balance, reviewing my presidential year, I am glad to be able to say that I have at least fulfilled my promise to our membership. As president, and with the able help of Murray Meisels and many active members of the local chapters committee, including George Goldman and Robert Lane, I have been able to secure for the Division a grant of $25,000 from the Exxon Education Foundation in support of a series of conferences on developing our own national training program. And I am happy to announce also that Clark University has invited our Division to hold its nationwide conference on training psychologists to become psychoanalysts. As the president of Clark University wrote in his invitation to us, Clark, which did so much to disseminate Freud's views, will also be helping in the development of psychoanalysis some 75 years later. Our Clark University Conference is scheduled for October 24–27, 1986, and I hereby invite our membership with ideas about training to be in touch with Murray Meisels or me.

What, then, are the issues that need conferences to discuss? As I see our problems in broad outline, they derive from the paradox that I developed in my *Freud and Modern Psychology*, especially in Volume 1. On the one hand, Freud's fundamental discoveries about the emotional basis of mental illness and the emotional basis of human behavior are still having a growing influence on the development of psychology and psychiatry. For example, the newly formed International Society for Research on Emotions, an interdisciplinary group, which held its first meeting at Harvard this June, has as charter members Silvan Tomkins, John Bowlby, Margaret Mahler, Hartvig Dahl, and myself. Freud's remarkably accurate descriptions of "primary-process" transformations under the press of emotional conflict engendered by shame and guilt and his descriptions of the defenses we all employ to protect the self's relationship to significant others have been accepted not only into the apperceptive mass of the behaviorists, but into the 20th-century *Zeitgeist*. Freud's metapsychology, however, is still undergoing fundamental, necessary revisions. Psychoanalysis as a therapy today is caught in the paradox that we possess a powerful, descriptive insight into emotional distress that is still embedded in an inadequate theoretical framework. Each suggested revision of the theoretical framework, beginning with Adler's and including Horney's, Fromm's, Thompson's, Sullivan's, Hartmann's and including more recent theoretical revisions, Bowlby's, Kohut's, Kernberg's, Schafer's, Spence's, Gill's and my own has caught some facet of the complex emotional forces that drive us all to stay connected with significant others. But our therapeutic techniques, although they are as powerful as they are because they zero in on the complexities of emotional distress, have had to struggle against the confinement of a formal, rigid, therapeutic system that still reflects Freud's metapsychology—that is, his individualistic drive theory. Our therapeutic paradigm also still reflects only Freud's original few prescriptions for technique. And, again, paradoxically, this is so even though Freud refused to specify his prescriptions for technique, describing psychoanalysis as like a chess game— open-minded with respect to the moves that may be made, provided they hit the emotional nodes. Our techniques for training candidates to become psychoanalysts tend to perpetuate a rigidified version of Freud's prescriptions for technique. And the situation is bound to continue because the medical establishment has been notoriously deficient when it comes to building appropriate arrangements for research into the question of their therapeutic efficiency.

Let me quickly make clear what I mean by this. I do not mean encouraging candidates and graduates to do research in general. We all do this. I mean building in to the structure and curriculum of our training Institutes—the ones we psychologists will run—an ongoing process of collecting, analyzing, and interpreting data about how well our therapeutic techniques are working to help our patients. I mean making such checks regularly and often. And I mean including some information directly from the patients themselves as well as from the analysts. If we do not review our therapeutic efficiency and its relationship to training processes regularly, using research as the arbiter of our differences, psychoanalysis will have a harder time than it needs to in fulfilling its inherent promise as a powerful therapeutic instrument. It is for this reason that I am devoting my farewell address as president of Division 39 to a brief discussion of our therapeutic deficiencies, as well as the relationship between these issues and psychoanalytic training.

Let's look first at outcome studies of the therapeutic efficiency of psychoanalysis. The most famous of outcome studies is the Menninger project, conducted by psychoanalytically trained investigators, which yielded relatively unsatisfactory outcome results. The concluding report of this long and arduous study was written by our own Stephen Appelbaum, in his book, *The Anatomy of Change*. The basic data on which this study relied were dynamically based psychological tests made before, after and 2 years after termination of psychoanalysis or psychotherapy. And these test data were better at predicting outcome than the psychiatrist-psychoanalyst's judgments.

Although the study was not designed to compare psychoanalysis with psychotherapy, its naturalistic setting involved assigning people with lesser ego strength to psychotherapy. There was, however, no significant difference between the patient groups in their overall improvement. If anything, therapists judged less skilled did better when the treatment made was psychoanalysis than when it was psychotherapy. This is a finding that can be interpreted as indicating either that psychotherapy requires more skill than psychoanalysis, or that the relative leisure of the psychoanalytic enterprise allows the mistakes of less skillful therapists to dissipate, or both. A principal finding was that those patients who were better endowed to begin with profited more from psychoanalysis *or* psychotherapy than those who were sicker to start. In any case, no clear-cut evidence of the therapeutic superiority of psychoanalysis emerged from the Menninger Project. In fact, "structural changes" occurred in the course of so-called "supportive" psychotherapy. This reminds us that the term supportive may be becoming a bit déclassé, now that so many of us are talking about the importance of necessary support from the self–other in psychoanalysis.

The most recent outcome study, which has just been published in the *International Review of Psychoanalysis*, shows results which echo the weak findings of the Menninger Project. Data come from the work of the Columbia Psychoanalytic Center in New York, a medically directed facility, over the period from 1945–1971. Data collection began in 1959, and was supported by a background population of more than 9,000 cases. This research has the great methodological advantage of being a prospective study. It is, however, deeply flawed, in my opinion, by having no data whatsoever from patients' experience. Its data base consists entirely of judgments from analysts and candidates about the outcome of psychotherapy and psychoanalysis. (As usual, patients judged higher in ego strength were assigned to psychoanalysis and those with lesser strength to psychotherapy.) These judgments, although all from one side of the story, were made in many categories, all of them thoughtful reflections of psychoanalytic "clinical wisdom." They included 34 categories of judgments about the patients' characteristics, for example, ego strength, social relations, work gratification, and 15 judgments about the analysts (candidates as well as senior analysts) such as therapeutic ability, freedom from difficulty, and experience in psychoanalysis. The authors tell us that these judgments were highly reliable. They make no statement, however, as to the validity of these judgments, as might have been possible if there had been attempt to validate them against some outside criterion, or some independently administered tests.

Measures of therapeutic benefit were also derived from this data bank, using three perspectives: circumstances of termination (therapy ended by mutual consent, vs. prematurely ended), direct clinical judgments of improvement, and change scores. As already indicated, no measures of therapeutic benefit were obtained from patients themselves.

The results are reported in terms both of "therapeutic benefit" and in terms of whether the patient "achieved an analytic process" (p. 131), and was therefore " 'analyzable' by the particular analyst given the conditions which prevailed at the time" (p. 131). "Analyzability," moreover, refers not to a prospective assessment of whether the patient could "achieve an analysis," but to a retrospective judgment whether or not the patient did do so. These two methods of assessing benefits were used because, as the authors tell us, "therapeutic benefit is not synonymous with the process of analysis" (p. 131). This is a rather bland statement of a difference that might seriously reflect the limitations of psychoanalysis as a therapy. It represents a long-standing tradition in psychoanalysis of placing the achievement of an analysis as an even higher-order aim than therapeutic benefit. Eissler argued for this position in some detail more than 20 years ago. It is a distinction that leaves us wide open to the suspicion that we value therapeutic benefit less than the analytic process itself, a position that may find us chasing our tails. If we cannot achieve therapeutic benefit, at least we have achieved an analytic process. Or if we cannot achieve therapeutic benefit, it was because the patient was not analyzable—the patient couldn't achieve it. As psychoanalysts we ought to be able to recognize easily how the mechanisms of projection and rationalization can hide behind the concept of "achieving an analytic process."

All these caveats would be moot, however, if the prospective study had been able to predict either therapeutic benefit or analyzability. But this was very definitely not the case. Clinical predictions made by the admissions service chiefs, all senior analysts, showed no relationship between the chief's expectations and either measures of therapeutic benefit or analyzability. Five different clinic chiefs were included and although their assessments were made on the basis of accepted clinical wisdom, their "expectations were largely not met." When the picture is viewed from the perspective of the relationship between the raw data of clinical assessments, and final clinical outcomes, the story is the same. No consistent pattern of relationships occurs. Even when there is a modest correlation, as in the case of prospectively assessed ego strength, this measure correlates with outcome for psychotherapy but *not* for psychoanalysis. This, despite the fact that patients with *lower* ego strength were originally assigned to psychotherapy. Measures of analyst characteristics, such as clinical ability and experience in psychoanalysis, also showed no correlation with outcome.

The authors do their best to make the best of these findings, but their attempt at explanation does not seem cogent. They write that the "prudent conclusion from these findings is not that therapeutic benefit or analyzability are *per se* unpredictable, but that once a case has been carefully selected as suitable for an analysis, its eventual fate remains relatively indeterminate" (p. 135). I find the difference between unpredictable and indeterminate hard to understand. As for the factor of careful selection, one would surely expect good prediction where there is careful selection, and poor prediction to be even more likely with difficult and unsuitable cases who are almost by definition relatively unpredictable.

The study also reports retrospective judgments in which all groups of patients achieved therapeutic benefits and in which psychoanalysis comes off better than psychotherapy. Treatment length, however, was the only independent factor consistently related to final outcome in analytic cases. Of course, if you ask the treating analyst to make retrospective judgments about outcome (and do not ask the patient), you are likely to get the result that the patients who stayed longer did better in their analysts' eyes. Analyzability, however, was only modestly associated with therapeutic benefit. The authors do not present the actual correlations here, telling us only that they ranged from .3 to .4, with no report of statistical significance of these figures. Moreover, only 40% of the patients who remained in analysis for a long time were characterized as having been analyzed at termination. Clearly, the medical analysts treating these patients knew less about what they were doing than they thought they did. In short, this picture of the outcome of psychoanalysis as a therapy is not one that has us cheering, even when we use "achieving an analytic process" as our criterion, not just therapeutic benefit.

The authors remind us, finally, that the generalizability of even these findings is limited by the fact that the analysts in the study were all from the same (medical) Institute. They point out that working definitions of psychoanalysis, of the meaning of analyzability, of therapeutic benefit, all exist within various conceptual frameworks—and they tell us this limitation is of particular moment in the "contemporary climate of proliferating psychoanalytic paradigms" (p. 137).

It is this last comment by the authors of this outcome study that gives me some reason for optimism. At the same time that I confront this unconvincing evidence of the effectiveness of medically run psychoanalysis, I am reminded that since its inception psychoanalysis has had many faces. The trouble is rather that we have not yet learned how to integrate into our techniques the vast clinical knowledge that is behind "proliferating paradigms." This is in part because the medical establishment has been so lax about research, relying more on citations from authority, and in part because established psychoanalysis has had a rigid attitude toward new findings.

Michael Rustin's piece on the social organization of secrets, just published in the *International Review of Psychoanalysis*, gives us a lucid description of the sociology of our movement. It helps us also to see the enormous social consequences of the course we choose to pursue. In Great Britain, for example, the Tavistock Clinic, staffed by psychoanalytically trained and oriented people has a community orientation, and is funded by the National Health Service. The British Psychoanalytic Association, in contrast, is mainly oriented toward private practice. Similar differences can be described in our country as well. Rustin points out that the British Psychoanalytic Association fosters an approach which

> Principally seeks to conserve and maintain the essence of psychoanalytic insight in the safe-keeping of those proved fit to be trusted with it. . . . while the other (Tavistock) seeks a more active diffusion of this form of insight into as many

settings as will receive it. The concern of the former approach is with maintaining standards and the purity of the analytic essence, even if this means renouncing any substantial attempt to convert a wider circle to psychoanalytic approaches. (p. 151)

Rustin is careful not to confound differences in approach with vested economic interests and I heartily agree with him in this respect. But I do not think that we are in a position at this point in our history to "conserve" psychoanalytic essence. The outcome study in the same issue of the journal that published Rustin's paper is not encouraging along these lines. I am suggesting that the maintenance of essence is premature and that we need rather to go with both approaches, seeking to integrate new information into old essences. New information ought not to have to run the risk of being called a "parameter" of established technique, as if we had a research-based notion on what psychoanalytic procedure is surely effective. Of course, if we did have an established method of proven therapeutic effectiveness, an attitude of caution toward new ideas would make more sense. What does happen is that we behave as if we do have a strong foundation of information about therapeutic benefit when we do not.

Good therapeutic ideas, of course, have a way of becoming quietly integrated into the mainstream of psychology and into the mainstream of humanistic therapies. We can begin with Alexander's suggestion for role playing how an analyst perceives the patient's transference, which was treated contemptuously by Ernest Jones but has found its way not only into Gestalt therapy, but into the offices of many psychoanalytically oriented therapists as well. They ought not to be afraid that they might not be entitled to be called psychoanalysts if they use such techniques. We remember Gill, Brenman's and Kubie's work with hypnosis and know that there are many psychoanalysts, like our own Erika Fromm, who find this useful. We can cite the "corrective emotional experience" and the importance of the "therapeutic alliance," and now the importance of "mirroring" by the self–other. It will be noted that all these ideas stress the importance of emotional bonding and speak to the existence of the attachment emotions, a concept the evidence for which was not available in Freud's time.

When it comes to ideas like Malan's focus on the core conflict as a way of shortening psychoanalytic treatment, or my focus on the sequences from unanalyzed superego emotions of shame and guilt into symptom formation—these ideas have to run the risk of being considered only dynamic psychotherapy. As Malan has said, he regards his focus as a tribute to psychoanalysis, not an attack on it. I share this attitude about my own focus.

Lester Luborsky has just published a jewel of a manual describing expressive-supportive dynamic psychotherapy, which I am reviewing for *Psychologist-Psychoanalyst*. He tells us, of course, that the parent of his manual is psychoanalysis. What I have in mind as a goal is the day when psychoanalysis will publish a companion manual for research. I am sure there will be great overlap between the two manuals. My best guess is that the manual for psychoanalysis would be written for the training of therapists and other relatively put-together people who wish to further their personal growth—to achieve a solid "analytic process." But most important of all, psychoanalytic methods, like the ones Luborsky describes, and which are derived from the exigencies of shortening treatment, ought not to have to forfeit the title of psychoanalysis. They are methods of brief psychoanalysis. I am sure that it was not because Freud saw the Rat Man six times a week, but because he was following something intrinsic in psychoanalysis that he was able to cure the Rat Man in 9 months. We all lost something when Freud ran up against the Wolf Man's affect of indifference—the "Russian tactics" which helped the Wolf Man to bypass shame. The lengthened treatment of obsessionals that has since been assumed to be par for the course is not intrinsically psychoanalytic.

The best way I have found of understanding the dilemma that confronts present-day psychoanalysis as a therapy is to look at our history. Hopefully if we remember, we will not need to repeat so much of our past. Once upon a time, psychoanalysis began as the psychoanalysis of hysteria. In a brilliant insight, its originator came to discover that similar phenomena of emotional conflict were also underneath phobias, and then—even more miraculously—underneath such a different appearance from hysteria as obsessional neurosis. Also in a very different appearance were the same forces underlying our nightly dreams. And then such different illnesses as depression and paranoia could be brought under one roof. No wonder the early psychoanalysts, impressed as they should have been by the fundamentals of emotional conflict, stopped thinking so much in terms of differing symptoms—although clearly the differences among symptoms (especially the striking sex differences in susceptibility) were and are of paramount importance in understanding the whole story. So psychoanalysts stopped thinking so much in terms of psychoanalysis of specific illnesses and symptoms and started thinking more in terms of analyzing more generally fundamental emotional conflicts. Specific symptoms became less important. In fact, psychoanalysis, following the thinking of its Founder, developed a shibboleth that symptom relief was bound to be unstable. This notion seems to have originated with Freud's one and only published attempt to cure symptoms of hysteria by suggestion *without* emotional catharsis. In any case, there is no evidence that I know for this belief—if anything, symptom relief improves the general character picture. Somehow, also, as I have already indicated, symptom relief became a lesser goal. This is an attitude that serves our defenses if we cannot produce change. Patients who come to psychoanalysis for symptom relief may be understandably more grateful for it than for character reorganization. In any case, psychoanalysis as a therapy followed the Founder not only in derogating symptom relief but in downgrading therapeutic benefit in what I regard as a compensatory movement honoring "achieving an analysis." Once symptom relief and therapeutic benefit are both downgraded, it should not be cause for wonder if our therapeutic skills become blunted. Instead of a specifically oriented psychoanalysis, we have a "one size fits all" (the large size) model and those who do not benefit from this approach must have been unanalyzable to begin with.

Another unfortunate remnant of our history is the confound which began it—the confound between listening to free associations for a therapeutic purpose and listening for the purpose of research into the origin of the trouble. The implications of this fact of our history have never been clearly articulated. That the use of an extended long-term program of free associations might actually conflict with its use as a therapeutic instrument has never really been faced, although this idea has been in the wings of the psychoanalytic movement since the 1920s, as I learned from the recent biography of Helene Deutsch. As Gill has suggested, however, a focus on reconstructing patients' history does have some costs to be evaluated along with benefits. We have, moreover, become aware of the dangers of retrospective falsification as we try to reconstruct our patients' pasts with our methods of free association. This is one reason why Spence speaks of narrative versus historical truth. On the other side, we are beginning to relearn the extent to which our patients' free associations do not reflect only fantasies but the brutal realities of seduction, abuse, and betrayal.

The confound between psychoanalysis as a research tool and psychoanalysis as a therapeutic instrument also has had as one of its ill effects, a confound between finding the cause or genesis of an illness or symptoms and finding the means of cure. The two tasks are by no means identical. Freud was well aware of this on occasion as when he wrote that the technique of free association was meant to locate the causal chain into illness, but that theoretically any intervention that broke the chain, even a chemical one, would be welcome to psychoanalysis. (This was written long before the discovery of mood-altering drugs.) The careful distinction between genesis and cure, however, was ultimately lost in the more or less unquestioned assumption that psychoanalysis can be both a research tool and a therapeutic instrument without loss to either undertaking.

Still another confound that has arisen in the course of our history is that between the needs of ordinary patients and the needs of candidates. One of my colleagues, replying to this suggestion, reminded me that a training analysis is actually no different from an ordinary one. This is, of course, true insofar as the technique of free association and interpretation of the transference are concerned. But the goals of an analytic candidate and an ordinary sufferer are very different, indeed. One wants relief of suffering, the other wants to become a healer. There is no good reason that I can see for confusing the two sets of perfectly reasonable goals. Also, we need to remember that in the case of candidates, we try to clone ourselves a bit. For other patients, we need to have their goals clearly in mind.

There is little doubt that by now, a large proportion of analysands are people who wish to become or are already mental health professionals as well. Estimates put the proportion as at least 50%, if not more. This fact alone may inadvertently create a climate in which the intensive and thorough, long-term treatment needed by candidates in order to withstand the rigors of practice becomes the unconscious standard by which therapy for ordinary mortals is evaluated. There is good evidence, moreover, that the more senior the analyst, the more likely it is that his or her practice will be devoted to treating candidates. Our senior professionals are thus dealing with relatively put-together candidates, while their juniors are practicing dynamic psychotherapy with sicker patients and fewer resources of time and money. Perhaps because of some halo effect, the junior professionals are regarded as doing something lower-order. This, in turn, tends to divert attention from the tremendous resources that psychoanalysis has at its disposal. Psychoanalysis can foster an integration of the insights gained from treating groups, families, posttraumatic stress victims, victims of child and sexual abuse, incest victims, anorexia-bulimia, drug abusers, to say nothing of the experience of those, like Bert Karon and Gary VandenBos, who treat schizophrenics with dynamic psychotherapy as the "treatment of choice." What I am saying is that we ought to foster the attitude that we have much to learn from the workers in the field, as well as teaching them the parental wisdom of psychoanalysis.

And so we come to the thorny question of the relationship between psycho-analysis and psychotherapy. As you can see, I have come to think that both deserve the embrace of psychoanalysis as equal sisters. Gill's brilliant piece in the recent *International Review of Psychoanalysis* distinguishes between intrinsic and extrinsic criteria of psychoanalysis. He was pushed to this position by realizing that the transference needed to be reconceptualized as a "two-person" phenomenon. By external criteria, he means the frequency of sessions, use of the chair versus the couch, length of treatment, relative health of the patient and relative experience of the therapist. By intrinsic criteria, he means the analysis of the transference. Psychoanalysis as thus redefined should be employed as much as possible even if the patient "comes less frequently than usual, uses the chair rather than the couch, is not necessarily committed to a treatment of relatively long duration, is sicker than is usually considered analyzable, and even if the therapist is relatively inexperienced." Gill ends his paper by asking the question what to call this enterprise and suggests that we not worry about this question now. I suggest that we face it, and call the enterprise psychoanalysis even if it does not meet the familiar external criteria. As I suggested earlier, by this set of internal criteria Luborsky's beautiful manual might become the pattern for a manual of the technique of psychoanalysis as well. And when the day comes, as I am sure it will, that we have differing manuals for the major symptoms with which suffering people come to us—then we can offer a psychoanalysis of depression, of hysteria, of phobia, of paranoia, all with evidence of proven efficacy. (A manual for "interpersonal" treatment of depression is already in use in the nationwide collaborative NIMH study of the effectiveness of differing treatments of depression.) As Anna Freud put it, in 1954:

> If all the skill, knowledge and pioneering effort which was spent in widening the scope of application of psychoanalysis (she meant into general psychotherapy) had

been employed instead on intensifying and improving our technique in the original field (by which she meant hysteria, phobia and compulsive disorders) I cannot help but feel that, by now, we would find the treatment of the common neuroses child's play, instead of struggling with their technical problems as we have continued to do.

We did broaden our scope, and we can now integrate what we have learned into an understanding of what is intrinsic in psychoanalysis, and what is extrinsic.

These are some of the issues, then, which we can profitably discuss at our forthcoming Conference on Training. We psychologists are at an important crossroad at which we can make the choice, implicit in our having formed a Division of Psychoanalysis, to carve out our own training programs. We really have come of age. This does not mean that we should not make use of all available resources, including the best of the medical establishment. But we need to rely, as well, on the tremendous potential of psychoanalytically oriented workers in the field. These resources exist not only in populated cities but in many areas of our vast country.

And so I have turned over the gavel to my able successor, Nat Stockhamer, with the cheerful conviction that a process of review has been started that is bound to take hold. On balance, I am very glad that I came out of my ivory tower to participate in the work of the Division. I need now to turn back to my own postponed work—trying to make clear to my colleagues how unanalyzed and therefore undischarged states of shame and guilt operate to form symptoms, and how a technique of focus on these states facilitates recovery. In this enterprise I am sure I shall profit from the insights that came with the privilege of being Division president.

5 Introduction: Keynote Address

Ester R. Shapiro

Anne-Marie Sandler was invited as keynote speaker for the conference, because of her study of diverse psychoanalytic training programs in Europe (Sandler, 1982). With her respectful review of different models of training, Mrs. Sandler introduced a broadly cross-cultural perspective on psychoanalytic education. In contrast to the United States, where most psychoanalytic training has been conducted under the uniform guidelines of the medical American Psychoanalytic Association, the European community has more fully preserved the diversity and interdisciplinary quality of psychoanalysis.

In her 1982 review, Mrs. Sandler quoted Max Eitingon's 1925 call for systematic training requirements to emphasize that in the early development of psychoanalysis, it was vital to preserve the unique identity of psychoanalysis, and to protect it from premature fusion with other fields of thought and methods of investigation and technique. With this goal in mind, Eitingon and others in the early psychoanalytic movement felt it imperative to guide the development of the next generation of analysts, since the future of psychoanalysis would now be in their hands. Mrs. Sandler pointed out that current concerns on behalf of the future of psychoanalysis involve very different issues:

> More than half a century after Nunberg's and Eitingon's recommendations there is still the same concern for the quality of psychoanalytic training and for the future of psychoanalysis. But the situation is rather different now. Well-organized training programmes exist and training analysts have become central figures in most Institutes and Societies, exerting a great deal of influence and control over the workings of their institution. The danger now is towards a tendency to unhealthy conservatism which may result in rigidity, in a kind of ossification and a lack of openness to adaptive change. It is vitally important, therefore, to explore, from

time to time, whether our training Institutes and Societies really are "maintaining and developing that which Freud has created." Are there ways in which improvements can be made? Have we reached a point where we have to begin to think of radical revisions in our training methods? (1982, p. 386)

Mrs. Sandler concluded her survey by recommending attention to the structure of institutions as they impacted on training and in this way on the future development of psychoanalysis.

Mrs. Sandler's survey of the training analysis in Europe was part of a special issue of the *International Review of Psychoanalysis*. In that issue, Sandler (1982) reviewed Europe, Cabernite (1982) reviewed Latin America, Orgel (1982) reviewed North America, and Weinshel (1982) wrote a summary paper. Cabernite (1982) stated that because the personal analysis not only imparts theoretical and technical training but also involves personality change, candidates unconsciously internalize aspects of the person of the analyst, relationships among faculty, and power relationships within the institution. He argued that these mental activities will inevitably be reflected in the structure of training institutions. Orgel (1982) cautioned that with the emphasis on the training analysis as the major component of psychoanalytic training, and with the secondary position of seminars and supervision, psychoanalysis is losing its intellectual and scientific foundation. These writers pointed to serious concerns about the confusion of institutional or educational goals with therapeutic goals in the training analysis system most frequently used throughout the world.

In a final summary, Weinshel (1982) reviewed the realistic problems in the training analysis system. However, he concluded by quoting Freud in "Analysis Terminable and Interminable" that analysis may have joined the two other impossible professions, government and education. Because analysts know more about analysis than about education and politics, Weinshel recommended that analysts explore the intrapsychic conflicts reflected in the candidate's response to these institutional problems, rather than initiate more ambitious goals of institutional change. Weinshel's conclusion is a curious non sequitur, because it appears to condone ignorance of education and politics. It is perhaps germane to remember Aristotle's aphorism that politics is the fundamental science. Weinshel's conclusion is another instance in which the traditional leadership in psychoanalysis chooses to analyze the reaction to political and social problems, rather than to address the need for social change.

In her conference paper, Mrs. Sandler described two training models available in Europe: the traditional, faculty-centered Institute which has distinct requirements for graduation, and a selection procedure for admission; and an "open," student-centered model which involves a self-directed program of study. Mrs. Sandler found that while the traditional Institute, including her own British psychoanalytic Institute, provided a sense of community within which candidates could define their identities, such a model emphasized compliance with external authority, and was vulnerable to creating mediocre analysts who emphasized the meeting of requirements. With the open model, she found, candidates tended to take a longer course of study, were more creative but also more cynical or anarchistic about psychoanalytic theory and practice. She concluded that there is no one ideal model for psychoanalytic training, and proposed that the merits of both models and their potential integration need to be debated and explored openly.

REFERENCES

Cabernite, L. (1982). The selection and function of the training analyst in analytic training institutes in Latin America. *International Review of Psychoanalysis, 9*(38), 398–417.

Orgel, S. (1982). The selection and function of the training analyst in North American Institutes. *International Review of Psychoanalysis, 9*(38), 386–398.

Sandler, A. (1982). The selection and function of the training analyst in Europe. *International Review of Psychoanalysis, 9*(38), 357–385.

Weinshel, E. (1982). The functions of the training analysis and the selection of the training analyst. *International Review of Psychoanalysis, 9*(38), 435–446.

6 Comments on Varieties of Psychoanalytic Training in Europe

Anne-Marie Sandler

When I received the most welcome invitation to give this address I was provided with a title for my talk, viz. "Psychoanalytic Training Including Open and Lockstep Models." Lockstep is a very unfamiliar word to me, and one which, I must confess, does not fall comfortably on my European ears. When I first wrote on this topic I referred to "open" and "closed" methods of training, and although these terms are not all that satisfactory I shall ask you to bear with me in my use of them. I also have to ask your indulgence for the reality that my knowledge of methods of psychoanalytic training relates almost exclusively to training in Europe, and that my acquaintance with training methods in the U.S.A. and Latin America is limited. Let me say, however, that psychoanalytic geography is rather bizarre, in that Europe—at least as far as the International Psychoanalytical Association (IPA) is concerned—includes Australia, India, Israel, and Japan; and I suspect that there is a battle going on between Europe and the United States for possession of Korea!

Perhaps one of the reasons for my receiving an invitation to speak was the fact that I am currently the president of the European Psychoanalytical Federation (until spring 1987) and some years ago published a survey of psychoanalytic training in Europe. On that continent the variation between different training methods is certainly far greater than it is in the United States at present. From the point of view of the IPA there is only one psychoanalytical Association in the U.S.A.—the American Psychoanalytic Association—which exerts overall control over the methods and standards of its training Institutes. So the IPA relates at present to its one component organization in the United States: the American Association. However, in Europe it relates directly to almost a score of different and differing component bodies. At the inception of the European Federation,

45

some two decades ago, it was only the clear understanding that the Federation would have no power whatsoever to interfere in the internal affairs of the Societies that allowed it to come into being. There was to be no control by the Federation over the methods and standards of training. This was to be left entirely to the IPA. That such an arrangement was arrived at was entirely understandable because of the anxiety felt by many European Societies (perhaps mostly by the French) in relation to the possibility that changes in training methods might be imposed from above. Each Society had made a major effort over many years to develop what were in its view the best methods of training that could be devised within the constraints of practicability, the Society's traditions, and the local culture. So, in regard to its structure and function, the European Federation was and is markedly different from the American Psycho-analytic Association.

You will have noticed that I have spoken of a Federation of Societies, whereas, in the U.S. there seems to be a clear division between training Institutes and local Societies.

This division is not all so clear-cut in Europe, where it is the Societies which undertake training as well as being professional associations of psychoanalysts. So, in England, for example, the British Psychoanalytical Society provides analytic training, and although there is an Institute of Psychoanalysis, this is an administrative body for legal purposes, not connected with training at all. Some societies do have training Institutes which belong to them and which they control. In Germany, for instance, there are some 12 different training Institutes in different parts of the country. All are responsible to the German Psychoanaly-tic Association. The same is true in Italy, where there is a training Institute in Milan and two in Rome; but there is only one Italian Society. In Spain the Spanish Society (based in Barcelona) and the Madrid Society are separate component organizations of the IPA and have no formal link with each other except through the IPA and the European Federation. Similarly, in France we have the French Association and the Paris Society (the latter being the only Society in Europe which has an administratively divorced training Institute). I should add that the size of European Societies varies substantially. We have small Societies of perhaps 30 to 40 members and others with 10 times that number. Further, the ratio of analysts to candidates is not the same for all Societies. In some countries there has been in the postwar years an increasing demand for psychoanalytic training, and as a result the ratio of candidates to members is high. But, as I will try to show later, the definition of a psychoanaly-tic candidate can differ significantly from one Society to another.

Before coming to the differences between the various training methods in Europe I should like to remind you of something of the history of the whole notion of psychoanalytic training. It was not until 1918, quite some time after the psychoanalytic movement had come into existence, that the notion introduced by Dr. Hermann Nunberg that all analysts should, in order to do their work, have undergone a personal analysis. This was called an "instructional" analysis, and was probably very different from what we would know as a training analysis. At first it was thought that such a requirement would be an impossible one to meet, but within a years it became unthinkable that people would not undergo a training analysis. In 1925, at the Ninth Congress of the IPA in Bad Homburg, Dr. Max Eitingon, who was at that time working in Berlin, made another controversial recommendation, that is, that regular supervision of analyses should be introduced as part of analytic training. He believed that it was only by taking full responsibility for the training of prospective analysts that the future of the psychoanalytic movement could be guaranteed. So he suggested that Institutes specially concerned with training should be established in each country. Let me quote Eitingon:

> It is the duty of our Association to be ceaselessly diligent in maintaining and developing that which Freud has created, to guide it from a premature fusion and so-called synthesis with other fields of thought and different methods of investigation and work, and ever to give clear definition to that which is specifically our own. Now the fate of our work is in the hands of our successors, and it is to them more and more that we must turn our attention. We must endeavor to meet this our most pressing need by making suitable provision.

We may well ask ourselves how the psychoanalytic movement in Europe responded to this plea over the ensuing 60 years. What stands out is the seriousness with which psychoanalytic Societies have tackled the problem of the transmission of psychoanalytic knowledge and skills to succeeding generations of analysts. However, in this there has always been a central conflict. On the one hand there has been a tendency to maintain things as they were, particularly if the training methods had been functioning satisfactorily in the past. On the other hand, there has been a pressure to modify the training system as new knowledge and experience was gained and as new ideas and tendencies developed. So Societies have had to respond both to the pressures towards conservatism and towards change. Change was often seen as threatening because the attractiveness of new ideas could (and often did) conceal resistances to the necessarily slow and painstaking acquisition of psychoanalytic skills. As a consequence it is understandable that there has been a considerable reluctance to change, a reluctance which in many Societies has unfortunately led to rigidity and excessive authoritarianism. However, it is clear that in Europe training Institutes have developed in a number of different ways—the extreme differences being exemplified by the "open" and "closed" systems which I shall describe later in this chapter. I should emphasize, however, that all psychoanalytic trainings (at least those recognized by the IPA) insist upon a personal analysis (by IPA standards a minimum of four times a week), the treatment of analytic cases (also to be seen four times a week) under supervision, and systematic education—usually through lectures and seminars—in psychoanalytic theory and technique. The *differences* in training methods arise from a number of factors. One of these is the tendency for the training in any one country to reflect the general structure of higher education in that country; there are great differences in this regard between, for example, England and France. Another factor is the influence of the individuals who founded the local Societies, and of their followers. Where Societies have split into two, the split is usually accompanied by the emergence of differences in the method of training or in the content of what is taught, or both. Of the many other influences bringing about differences between Societies I would mention only the language barriers in Europe which foster separate development, and the effect of World War II in either destroying or damaging Institutes so that they had to be rebuilt after the war ended. In contrast, the American Psychoanalytic Association, which achieved a period of rapid growth after the war, could exert a standardizing and unifying influence over its own training Institutes. This standardization in the U.S.A. was all the greater in that psychoanalysis within the American Association was more or less completely restricted to physicians who were psychiatrically trained. The situation is completely different in Europe, as Societies admit nonmedical candidates to full training, and although in most Societies these candidates tend to be psychologists, there are a good number of members of other professions given full training and who participate as training analysts, supervisors, and teachers. It has always been very difficult for Europeans to understand the insistence of the American Psychoanalytic Association on maintaining the medical requirement for entry into psychoanalytic training. The European view is that the diversity of background of analysts is stimulating and enriching.[1]

The topic of differences in psychoanalytic training is one highly loaded with emotion and irrationality, and it is only recently, at meetings of European training analysts that the ignorance and paranoia about training methods other than one's own have begun to be dispelled. There is, of course, a very natural tendency for every psychoanalyst to feel that the method by which he or she has been trained and now contributes to is the best one. When, as recently as 1980, I began work on a survey of European training methods, presented at the Pre-Congress on Training of the IPA in Helsinki in July, 1981, and published in the *International Review of Psycho-Analysis*, (9, pp. 286–398) I was profoundly shocked to discover my own very strong prejudices and my difficulty in digesting

---

[1] In 1938, a situation developed in which the only way that the American Psychoanalytic Association could be kept within the IPA was for the IPA to agree that the American Association would have full control over its admission policy and training standards. (*Note added later:* The franchise given to the American was rescinded in 1987 at its own request, and a number of Societies in the U.S.A. with nonmedical members, existing outside the American Association, are now seeking component status within the IPA.)

the information sent to me by the Education Committees of the different European Societies.

I found myself wanting to deride those methods which were different from those I was accustomed to, and it took me some time to overcome my culture shock and to accept, at an emotional level, the reality that there were outstanding analysts who have followed a different training route. It took me some time to work through these prejudices, which were certainly motivated by my own anxiety, and to realize and accept that there was a rationale behind each of the different training methods.

In order to highlight the differences in training procedures among Societies in Europe, I should like to describe in some detail how the training is undertaken in two extremely different Societies, which in a sense represent the opposite poles of a spectrum. The first of these is the British Society, which in its training is probably the closest to that followed in the Institutes of the American Psychoanalytic Association. Its training system is one which I have called "closed" (and which the organizers of this meeting refer to as lockstep). The second is the French Association, which follows what I have referred to as an "open" system of training. The "closed" system of the British Society is a custodial one. After a rigorous and careful selection procedure, in which only a small number of applicants—perhaps 10%—are accepted, the Society takes full responsibility for the education of the candidate. As a consequence most candidates graduate as Associate Members of the Society within a few years of starting lectures and seminars. In the open system, the responsibility for psychoanalytic education is entirely in the hands of the candidate. Admission criteria are far less rigorous, but the training takes far longer and many candidates fall by the wayside.

In the British Society there is a clear line of progression. The aspiring candidate for training will usually have a preliminary interview with a member of the Admissions Committee (a subcommittee of the Education Committee) in order to decide whether a formal application is appropriate. Applicants must have a university degree, have had sufficient work and life experience—applicants under 25 are thought to be too young to be accepted—and appropriate financial resources. Applicants over 40 are considered only in exceptional circumstances. Those who are neither physicians nor clinical psychologists can be considered only if they have sufficient experience in caring for individuals (e.g., as therapists, nurses, social workers, counselors). So the Admissions Committee of the British Society would not consider a philosopher for training who had not spent some time actually working with others in a caring capacity. Certainly university teaching on its own would not qualify.

The decision about acceptance is made by the Admissions Committee. I want to emphasize the care with which this committee sets about its task. The interviewers write up their interviews in great detail, independently of each other. The written reports are the distributed to all the members of the Admissions Committee, and discussed at length. The discussion plays a very great part in determining the decision of the Committee, as the members—who are used to working together—will be able to interact and comment on, for example, the relationship of the two interviews. Interviewers occasionally change their minds about the suitability of the applicant as a consequence of the interactive discussion.

I do not want to go into great detail about the admission criteria, except to mention a few points. The Admissions Committee is not particularly concerned with a formal psychiatric evaluation of the applicant, but is *very* concerned about the quality of his or her relationships, the amount and quality of affective contact which the applicant can make and the degree of analyzability of the problems presented. The interviewers are very alert to the changes which take place within the course of each interview, and the effect of the first interview on the second.

The evaluation is, of course, very much affected by the requirement that the candidate be in analysis throughout the training, *irrespective of any analysis the candidate may have had previously.* If accepted, analysis must be started five times weekly, for sessions of 50 minutes each, which a recognized training analyst acceptable to the Admissions Committee. If the candidate is in analysis at the time which an analyst who is not a training analyst, a change to a training analyst must be made.

There are three possible outcomes following evaluation of an applicant by the Admissions Committee. The candidate may be accepted, may be rejected, or may be advised (and assisted) to go into analysis with a training analyst, with a view to applying again later. Once accepted, the candidate is assigned to a progress adviser, who is a member of the Student Progress Committee. Following acceptance (which is always provisional) the candidate has to sign an undertaking to abide by the rules and procedures governing the Society's training. The candidate undertakes not to call himself or herself a psychoanalyst until elected as an Associate Member of the Society. Medically qualified candidates who have insufficient psychiatric experience are required to complete not less than 12 months half-time work in a mental hospital or a psychiatric outpatient clinic. Nonmedical candidates must obtain somewhat more substantial psychiatric experience. An individual program is arranged for each candidate.

After the candidate has been in analysis for a minimum of a year (quite often longer) permission to start lectures and seminars may be given by the Student Progress Committee (another subcommittee of the Education Committee) on the recommendation of the candidate's training analyst.

Lectures and seminars are given on three evenings a week, and last for a minimum of 3 years. There is a fairly well-defined curriculum, although the candidates have some choice in regard to which of the lectures and seminars they will attend. In the second and subsequent years they must attend weekly clinical seminars in addition to the basic courses on various aspects of psychoanalysis. There are about 40 course units to choose from (of five evenings each) from which a minimum of 26 must be attended before qualification.

It may be of some interest that throughout the first year there is a weekly seminar on infant observation. Each candidate is required to find a family with a very young infant, to arrange to visit weekly, and to present a regular report to the seminar. The report of the observations should emphasize not only the development of the infant, but also the interaction between infant and mother, and the way in which the members of the family relate to the observer. This course has been found to be extremely useful in that it throws a great deal of light on the candidate's capacity to cope with the anxieties aroused by the observation situation, and to deal with the transferences and countertransferences involved.

After about a year of lectures and seminars the Student Progress Committee will begin to consider the possibility of the candidate being given permission to start a first case under supervision. This is only granted after the training analyst has made a positive recommendation. The progress adviser will also participate in the decision regarding commencement of a case, having received full reports from all the lecturers and seminar leaders. The choice of supervisor rests with the candidate, the candidate's analyst and the progress adviser. The training case is selected by and is treated under the auspices of the London Clinic of Psychoanalysis. The case is seen five times per week and supervision has to be once weekly. This *must* be individual supervision with a training analyst. At this point the analyst will no longer be consulted about the student's progress, but after at least 6 months with the first case, a second case may be started, permission for this being given by the Student Progress Committee only on the first supervisor's recommendation and on the receipt of positive reports by the progress adviser. It should be added that the supervised patients pay low fees to the Clinic, the student receives no part of these fees and pays for his or her supervision.

Completion of the training course does not in itself represent qualification as a psychoanalyst. Qualification only occurs with the election of the candidate, once his or her name has been allowed to go forward, to Associate Membership of the Society. In order to be recommended, the training analyst, both supervisors and the progress adviser must indicate their agreement. The progress adviser will collate reports from lecturers and seminar leaders, as well as those which have been given by the analyst and supervisors.

While Associate Membership allows the candidate to be considered to be a psychoanalyst, he or she does not yet have full voting rights within the Society and may not be elected to certain administrative positions nor be given training analyst status. In order to become a Full Member the associate may, after at least 2 years of independent practice, present a paper to a specially constituted membership panel. However, there is an alternative route to membership through participation in a membership course lasting 2 years. This involves the discussion of two cases with a senior training analyst at monthly intervals, and attendance at weekly seminars and research meetings. At the end of the membership course, recommendation for election to full membership may be made by the Membership Course Committee.

It will be clear that this system of training, which is very representative of the closed systems, involves the Institute in a great deal of responsibility for the candidate. The candidate is constantly assessed, there is a great deal of support given, and every effort is made to help the candidate toward eventual qualification. Consequently the dropout rate does not exceed 10%, even though some students may take several years more than the minimum in order to qualify.

Within the British Society there are, as is well known, three different groups: the Contemporary Freudian Group, the Klein Group, and the Independent Group. While I do not want to discuss the different group orientations here, I should say that the Institute makes an effort to counter the natural tendency of the candidates to identify completely with one group or another.

Turning now to the open system, we find a good example in the French Psychoanalytic Association. Here the responsibility for the training rests primarily with the candidate.[2] It is his or her responsibility to find a suitable analyst. There is no special category of training analyst, but the analysis can be conducted by any full member of the International Psychoanalytical Association. The aspirant may start or even complete analysis without making any contact with the French Association at all. He or she may have asked the Association for a list of analysts, or may have signified to the Association an intention to commence an analysis with a view to training, but this is not essential.

Most analysts-in-training have an independent practice as analytically oriented psychotherapists or as analysts. This is thought to be desirable as it gives the aspiring analyst a feel for working with patients—a view diametrically opposed to that taken by the British Society.

In the French Association the initiative in asking for supervision is left entirely to the analysts-in-training. When they feel ready to take a case to be supervised, they contact an officer of the Association, who will arrange for an interview and will either recommend that the candidate enter supervision with the supervisor of choice, or dissuade the applicant from it. If the request is successful, he or she will enter supervision, and no further contact will take place between the supervising analyst and the Training Committee until the analyst-in-training applies for permission to have the supervised case "validated."[3] When supervisors agree to validate supervisions, they are required to present themselves to the Training Committee in order to discuss the cases of their supervisees. The reasons for this are twofold. First, it is thought that by not interfering directly in the supervisor–supervisee relationship the disruptive effect of being in

---

[2]Actually the terms "candidate" or "student" are never used in the French or Paris Societies. What we call a candidate is known in France as *analyste en formation* (analyst-in-training).

[3]Although the IPA stipulates a minimum frequency of four-times-a-week analysis for sessions of 45 minutes each, there has been a tendency in France, for a number of years, to conduct personal analysis and the analysis of supervised cases on the basis of three sessions a week. I shall return to this point later.

supervision will be reduced. Second, it is assumed that the understanding the supervisor will have acquired about the supervisee's patient will reflect the supervisee's capacities and quality of work. If the supervisor cannot communicate a clear understanding of the unconscious mechanisms at work in the patient, cannot give a reasonably clear idea of the core problems and the structure of the patient's disturbance, then it is assumed that this reflects a deficiency in the analyst-in-training.

After the "validation" of the first case, the analyst-in-training may or may not continue in supervision with the first supervisor, but can not take a second case with a new supervisor. The validation of the second supervision is submitted to a procedure similar to that which I have described for the first case, but now the analyst-in-training *and* the supervisor are interviewed separately, on behalf of the Training Committee, by an appointed commission of three analysts.

If the two supervisions have been validated, the analyst-in-training may ask to have the whole training curriculum approved. This curriculum includes far more than the two supervisions I have described. In the first place, there are many seminars conducted in France which have no formal connection with the Institute, and it is very likely that, before starting a first case, the analyst-in-training will have attended a number of these. If the applicant for supervision shows insufficient knowledge of psychoanalysis, difficulty may be encountered in finding a supervisor. However, after starting supervision, a considerable number of seminars held under the aegis of the Institute are also available. I want, however, to stress that there is no formal curriculum or organized teaching program. Any member of the Association may offer a seminar or some other event, and the Institute will simply function as a coordinating and information-giving body. The analyst-in-training is expected to make his or her own choice of seminars. Throughout, the responsibility for obtaining a thorough, well-balanced, and serious training is left entirely to the individual, and the process is, not surprisingly, a lengthy one.

When the analyst-in-training asks to have the whole training curriculum approved, the Training Committee will appoint a full member to have one or more interviews with the analyst-in-training, who will be evaluated on the basis of his or her qualities and abilities as an analyst. However, account will also be taken of professional experience, attendance, and participation in research and training activities, publications, active participation in scientific meetings, and so on. Following this, the report of the interviews will be presented for discussion to a meeting of full members, and the analyst-in-training will have to gain a two-thirds majority of votes in a secret ballot in order to graduate. Following graduation, application may be made for election as an Associate Member of the Association. It is worth noting that a significant number of "graduates" do not get to the point of election as an Associate Member. In order to be elected, the graduates must be able to convey their clinical experience to other analysts and should be able to report adequately on their practice in terms of analystical process, and be able to relate clinical findings to the theoretical psychoanalytic framework. They may demonstrate their skill by writing or reading a clinical paper, or may choose to refer to previously published clinical material. However, the essential criterion for becoming an Associate Member is the ability to practice analysis and to convey one's experience adequately to the Members of the Association.

Any Associate Member is entitled to apply for election as a Full Member. Besides the Associate's clinical ability to practice analysis, a number of further criteria are taken into account in determining whether the step to full membership can be taken. The Associate needs to have a substantial psychoanalytic practice (at least half-time) and to have had sufficient experience, that is, should have seen a sufficient number and a variety of patients in analysis. A capacity for and interest in scientific research should be demonstrated, as well as an indication of a wish and ability to participate in the administration and organization of the Association. There should be a potential ability to supervise clinical work, leading eventually to the status of supervisor. The Associate wishing to be elected will meet three senior analysts who report to the full membership, and after discussion of his or her abilities, a secret ballot is held, and here again a two-thirds majority is required.

The differences between the two Societies whose training programs I have described reflect not only differences in procedure, but fundamentally dissimilar approaches and attitudes towards training.

It is important to emphasize the fact that those analysts involved in the training in their Institutes devote a great deal of time and energy to appraising and reappraising their training procedures, even though the basic structure of the training may not be questioned. We can see some advantages and some disadvantages in all the approaches taken by the different Institutes. Each strives to find the best system for itself, but fall short of a totally satisfactory model. In France the whole concept of psychoanalytic education and the paradoxes involved have been seriously and intensely debated, and there are many differences of opinion. There is, however, one point of complete agreement, that is, that "education" is the wrong term for the "formation" of a psychoanalyst. The France, analysts take the view that there is a fundamental opposition between the analytic attitude and the authoritarian stance of those normally involved in providing education. It is felt that there is a danger in asking candidates to submit to a fixed or structured curriculum, as well as a danger that dependence on teachers, with consequent infantilization of the analyst-in-training, might be fostered. None of these issues around the concept of education, issues which have occupied French analysts for many years, has been of central concern in England.

Let me make a few personal comments at this point. In spite of the immediate appeal of the "open" system of training because of its flexibility, it is necessary to be aware of some of its disadvantages. One of these is that the aspiring analyst must inevitably suffer from lack of institutional support. The lack of involvement of the institution may lead to callousness and indifference towards the problems and difficulties of the "analyst-in-training." In this connection it is worth remembering that the "open" system is, in one sense, far less "student-oriented" than the "closed" system of, for example, the British Society, for the "open" system does not take responsibility for the individual in training.[4] In the "open" system, qualification is oriented much more towards the final product of the individual's total analytic experience. Much of this experience may have been gained even before the person had made the decision to try to become an analyst.

A further major disadvantage of the "open" system is, in my view, that there are serious and inevitable limitations to the process of evaluation for the final qualification. There is, in particular, difficulty in assessing the character structure of the applicant for final qualification. Although he or she must have had two satisfactory supervisions, the final report to the Training Committee is prepared by a single member of the Committee on the basis of a number of interviews. The two people involved may not have met previously. On the other hand, the "open" system allows for much opportunity for learning and for personal growth unhindered by the infantilizing effect of the training institution.

The "closed" system of training has the advantage of being relatively short. Once accepted into the training there is a high probability that the candidate will graduate. If the candidate runs into difficulties, there are always persons available to whom he or she can turn for advice and guidance. Yet there is no doubt that the feeling of being scrutinized and evaluated has an inhibiting and disturbing effect. It tends to hinder originality and creativity, and to encourage conformity. In contrast to the "open" system the candidate will graduate unless there are strong contradictions; and some, who have been mediocre students held back in their studies, will ultimately be graduated on "compassionate" grounds.

Taking Europe as a whole, it would seem that the models of psychoanalytic training range between the two extremes I have described. Most Societies and Institutes are preoccupied with keeping the training analysis as uncontaminated as possible, and for most the training of the candidate is kept totally separate from the analysis. However, in some Societies the analyst can veto a graduation.

A number of Institutes have a two-tier system of training. After some years of analysis the candidate is regarded as eligible to start a course of theoretical lectures and seminars. The theoretical courses will last some years and are followed by a form of further selection or examination. If the candidate passes this hurdle, entry into supervised clinical work and clinical seminars is possible. It is worth noting that most training systems in Europe tend to be the closed type.

---

[4]A great many of the "analysts-in-training" drop by the wayside but still call themselves analysts and continue to see patients, sometimes with worrying results for their patients, colleagues and themselves.

As a result of variations in psychoanalytic training in Europe it is not easy to recognize what is meant by a "candidate" in each Society. In many countries it may be that applicants only become candidates at the point when they are allowed to start attending lectures and seminars, even though they may have had several years of analysis with a training analyst. In other countries the term candidate may simply refer to someone who has been accepted by the Institute and has entered a training analysis. In others, the aspiring analysts are only regarded as candidates when they have at least one case under supervision. Clearly one has to exercise care in comparing the status of candidate in different Societies and Institutes in Europe, and in comparing European candidates with those elsewhere in the world.

It is important to try to place the training methods and preoccupations of any one Society within the context of the prevailing analytic climate in the country in which it is located. For example, in England psychoanalysis is a treatment regarded as appropriate for a large spectrum of disturbances. As a result, candidates have patients presenting severe character problems, borderline features or even psychotic pathology for their supervised cases. Few so-called "ordinary" neurotic cases are available. This reflects and is reflected in the emphasis in the whole of the British Society on those technical approaches which involve close scrutiny of the way object-related mechanisms show themselves in the here-and-now of the analysis, and on the central and crucial role of transference and countertransference. The particular view of psychoanalytic technique which has evolved in Britain places central importance on the work taking place within the relationship between patient and analyst, and as a consequence the regularity and frequency of sessions is given great importance. Thus psychoanalysis is clearly conceived of as a treatment involving five daily sessions of 50 minutes each. Perhaps paradoxically, the differences for many British psychoanalysts between what is regarded as analysis and psychoanalytically oriented psychotherapy is primarily related to the frequency of the sessions. In psychoanalytically oriented psychotherapy the analysts or therapists will attempt to tailor their analytic technique to the limitations imposed by the lesser frequency. Apart from this, psychotherapy is often conducted in a way which resembles psychoanalysis as closely as possible, given the specific circumstances of the therapy. The situation appears to be quite different in France where psychoanalysis is seen as a very different technique from psychoanalytically oriented therapy. The psychoanalyst takes a much more passive role than the therapist, and regards the primary task as being to facilitate and to protect the analytic process—what is known as the "trajectory" of the analysis. The patient produces free associations in the presence of the analyst whose active participation may be minimal. This is not to say that the analyst is completely silent; but his or her task is in large part to make connections and allusions which facilitate the emergence of unconscious material into the conscious awareness of the patient. In psychotherapy, in contrast, the therapist will be more active, will interpret more frequently and forcefully, and be more concerned with the present and with the patient's relation to current reality. On the whole, the view of the analytic process and of pathology current in French psychoanalysis appears to be much closer to Freud's views on the central role of psychosexual conflict, particularly oedipal conflict, than is the case in Britain. Psychoanalysts in France tend to see their main function as that of uncovering the infantile neurosis through the analysis of the transference neurosis, and helping the patient to unearth and understand the conflicts of the oedipal situation, the effects of the primal scene and vicissitudes of the sexual and aggressive drives, through the analysis of the way the infantile past is repeated in the present. It is often said that "good" analytic patients can work well with four or even three sessions a week of 45 minutes each, and that the definition of analysis is not tied to the frequency of the sessions. What makes the difference between psychoanalysis and the analytically oriented psychotherapy is not at all the frequency of sessions but the attitude of the analyst or therapist. I have heard French colleagues say that British analysts do five-times-weekly psychotherapy! The view is taken that in order to permit a truly psychoanalytic development of the unconscious material the analyst needs to be very cautious and careful not to interfere, through interpretation, with the flow of the patient's communications.

Certainly all the European Societies have been very aware of developments in psychoanalysis since Freud and the widening scope of psychoanalysis. But it must be evident that psychoanalysis in Europe is not at all a uniform procedure. There are many trends, many various emphases, and these in turn make their mark on the psychoanalytic education provided within each Society or Institute.

At this point it might be appropriate to comment on the attitude of Societies toward those who have not trained within the Society's own training system. All component Societies of the IPA have an agreement that colleagues from other IPA Societies may attend their scientific meetings as guests. However, this right of attendance is the only right available to IPA colleagues. After a guest has attended for some time, the Society may see fit to elect him or her to associate membership (or even to full membership), but this is entirely at the discretion of the local Society. No automatic recognition is given to the status the person has reached in another Society, even though the person may be a training and supervising analyst. Societies will, entirely at their own discretion, make use of various criteria to assess the suitability of guests for election to membership, and these criteria will vary from one country to another.

It is difficult for colleagues—usually psychotherapists—who have not qualified in a recognized component organization of the IPA, to become members without undergoing the full training at a recognized Institute. No Society affiliated to the IPA accepts someone as a member or associate member who has not had an "official" training, except very rarely, in special circumstances; nor is acceptance possible simply on the basis of the presentation of a paper to the Society. However, it should be said that there is some variation in what is demanded of such applicants by different Societies. Some require a few years of supervised work, and the presentation of a clinical or theoretical paper, while others expect the full training procedure to be followed, no allowance for previous training or even for previous personal analysis being given. In some Societies this is the case even if the applicant's analyst has been a training analyst in one of the component Societies or Institutes of the IPA.

In the British Society a situation arose some years ago related to this problem. A 4-year, full-time course, organized and headed by Anna Freud, had for many years been in existence for training in child psychoanalysis at the Hampstead Child-Therapy Clinic (now the Anna Freud Centre). The training course required a personal analysis, five times a week, with an appointed training analyst, for the duration of the training. The Hampstead course was in many ways organized as an intensive and high-level "closed" Institute for child analytic training. However, only child cases were treated analytically, and by agreement with the British Psychoanalytical Society, the graduates were known as "child therapists" and not as child psychoanalysts. Over the years a number of graduates of the Anna Freud course had applied to the British Society for training in adult psychoanalysis. If and when accepted, these candidates had been required to begin a new training analysis and had to attend all the lectures and seminars, without any allowance being given for their previous training. After prolonged negotiations, an agreement was reached some 15 years ago between Anna Freud and the British Society. Successful applicants from the Hampstead course would be allowed to start lectures and seminars immediately on acceptance for training by the British Society, and would not be required to attend the lectures on basic Freudian theory and on child development. This was the only concession given in regard to the years of strenuous study and work the candidates had put in beforehand. It was started, quite explicitly, that adult psychoanalysis has to be regarded as a very demanding specialty, distinct from child analysis, and that the previous training, though helpful in some ways, could be a hindrance in other respects. The new training in adult psychoanalysis would even demand a certain amount of "unlearning."

Finally, I want to express my gratitude to the organizers of the conference. Preparing this paper has helped me to reflect on the complexity of the various ways in which we transmit psychoanalytic knowledge, and has made me even more aware than before of the wide variations possible in regard to the training of psychoanalysts. One cannot fail to be impressed by the dedication, creativity, and true concern which has entered into the creation of appropriate training programs leading to the qualification of the candidate as a psychoanalyst; and one cannot but be aware that there is no perfect method, and that methods different from one's own have to be considered with respect.

7

Introduction: Institute and Alternative Training Models

Ester R. Shapiro

The session on *Institute and alternative training models* was designed to stimulate discussion of varieties of "open" and "closed" training programs, their costs and benefits, as well as potential integration of the two models. The presenters were in agreement as to the fundamental goal—to improve psychoanalytic education—and did not promote and artificial polarity between the two models of training. Rather, each paper addressed the tensions inherent in a variety of attempts to balance the support of *tradition* and the creativity of *innovation* in psychoanalytic education. How can we preserve the essence of psychoanalysis, and at the same time allow psychoanalysis to change and evolve?

Charles Spezzano, Ph.D., reviewed psychoanalytic training for psychologists in the United States, and proposed that because of their exclusion from the medical institutes of the American Psychoanalytic Association, psychologists have overemphasized the quest for psychoanalytic legitimacy, and have sought external authority modeled on the American Psychoanalytic to create this legitimacy. He argued that psychologists have invested too much of their energy in defining themselves as a guild, at the expense of addressing the major issues that confront the discipline as a clinical and a scientific activity. He proposed that the variety of interdisciplinary programs in New York represent the best example of the diversity which best serves the future development of psychoanalysis.

Marvin Hyman, Ph.D., is a psychoanalyst whose own training evolved through independent study with Siegfried Bernfeld and Richard Sterba, both original thinkers in the early psychoanalytic movement. This background allowed him to speak for the benefits of independent psychoanalytic study, without allegiance to a particular institution. Hyman noted that since the mid-1920s, it

59

has been widely assumed that psychoanalytic training is best conducted within an institution. Yet the early psychoanalytic movement, with its informal, individualized approach, generated valuable training experiences and exciting climate of creativity.

Hyman referred to Siegfried Bernfeld's 1952 presentation to the San Francisco Psychoanalytic Institute (Bernfeld, 1962) for a critical discussion of the history of psychoanalytic education, and as the foundation for his own vision of psychoanalytic training. The initial psychoanalytic circle, as Bernfeld described it, consisted of outcast physicians and the cultural avant-garde; in the early 1920s, Freud and his followers found that the psychoanalytic movement had become world-famous, and was of special interest to socialist reformers as part of a cultural revolution which challenged authoritarianism in government and in education. According to Bernfeld, psychoanalysts responded in two different ways to the growing cultural acceptance of psychoanalysis: The Vienna society, closest to Freud, continued to support an   independent educational model, and wished to offer training opportunities to the new movement so as to expand the application of psychoanalytic theory. In Berlin, the emphasis was on establishing the legitimacy of psychoanalysis by making it a medical specialty, and by structuring and restricting the educational process from admissions to graduation.

In addition to these political and historical developments, Freud was diagnosed as having cancer in the summer of 1923, and for some months it was believed he would die within the year. By the summer of 1924, it was clear that the cancer was under control and that Freud could live many years longer. Bernfeld felt that in the ambivalent response to Freud's death and resurrection, outbursts of id forces, for example in Rank's separation from Freud, were followed by reaction-formations which attempted to restrict heterodoxy and therefore safeguard the future of psychoanalysis. Bernfeld concluded that the repressed ambivalence toward Freud as a loved and hated father figure heightened by his illness, coupled with the political climate of the time, combined with a Prussian spirit of authoritarianism that characterized the formation of the Berlin Institute, the model for psychoanalytic Institutes since that time.

In his own paper, Hyman argued that Institutes which place educational responsibility on the institution rather than the students infantilize students, and give administrative needs priority over educational needs. He agreed with the model of psychoanalytic training which emphasized personal analysis, supervision of control cases, and coursework, but felt that the particulars of program, timing, and sequence should be determined by the individual student's unique educational needs. He described the Michigan local chapter's Center for Psychoanalytic Studies as an example of such an independent study program, in which the center offers a variety of courses, as well as informal advising on supervisors and personal psychoanalysts available to any student who wishes to pursue an individualized course of study.

Anna Antonovsky, Ph.D. argued that psychoanalysts, unlike other scientists and professionals, have to develop a unique capacity for psychic functioning which doesn't come naturally and which requires support and reinforcement throughout their professional careers. Quoting Widlöcher (1983), Dr. Antonovsky described a complex mode of thought, feeling, and relating in which primary and secondary processes are combined, and in which transference and countertransference are experienced, contained, and collaboratively analyzed. She suggested that a psychoanalytic Institute provides the supportive, collaborative community in which the difficulties of this psychic development can be shared, and in which a psychoanalytic identity can be formed and consolidated throughout one's analytic career. Antonovsky concluded by stating that psychoanalysis, from Freud's time onward, has struggled with the tensions and pulls over tradition and change, and has successfully integrated new theory and technique consistent with psychoanalytic principles.

In a discussion of the institute and open training models, **Milton Horowitz, Ph.D.**, agrees that it is important for Institutes to avoid punitive authority or discipline as part of training, because students may internalize compliance to rigid authority as part of their ego ideal. He described a point made by Lewin and Ross (1960) that role confusion or syncretism between two opposing functions—the candidate as student and the candidate as patient—restricts both the educational process and the personal analysis. He proposed that Institutes too often neglect the developmental needs of faculty and supervisors, who are under a great deal of pressure themselves in offering psychoanalytic training.

Susannah Gourevitch, Ph.D. responded to Hyman's paper, and pointed out his implicit assumption that the goals of psychoanalytic training and psychoanalytic treatment should be based on compatible values: self-determination, personal responsibility for training, acceptance of diversity and lively curiosity, in a relational climate of mutual acceptance without dominance or rigid hierarchies. She described a tension between this open outlook as an ideal on the one hand, and the question of maintaining standards or defining who is an analyst on the other. She concluded with a description of the Washington Association for Psychoanalytic Study, arguing that a structured curriculum can be taught, offering a systematic program of study and remaining supportive of individual creativity and an intellectually open mind.

In sum, the papers addressed the question of what kind of balance between tradition and innovation is most supportive of the development of psychoanalysts? These presenters suggested that an open model or independent study program promotes creativity and best acknowledges individual differences, while a closed model or requirements-oriented Institute training program creates a supportive community with clear expectations and affirmation of the psychoanalytic process as a difficult, shared experience. Requirements or standards need to be offered respectfully rather than harshly imposed, so that students do not internalize compliance to rigid authority as part of their ego ideals. Finally, these papers suggested that the balance of "open" and "closed" models is itself best left to the individual communities, taking into account differences in local circumstances, rather than established a priori and then arbitrarily imposed.

REFERENCES

Bernfeld, S. (1962). On psychoanalytic training. *Psychoanalytic Quarterly, 31,* 453–482.
Lewin, B., & Ross, H. (1960). *Psychoanalytic education in the United States.* New York: Norton.
Widlocher, D. (1983). Psychoanalysis today: A problem of identity. In E. Joseph & D. Widlocher (Eds.) *The Identity of the Psychoanalyst. New York: International Universities Press, pp. 23–39.*

8

A History of Psychoanalytic Training for Psychologists in the United States

Charles Spezzano

If we consider both the span of time and the number of characters involved, the history of psychologists trained in psychoanalysis in the United States is not the *War and Peace* of social sciences history. It covers a short span of time and, outside of New York City, a limited number of people. However, what I'd like to do is put this history in a broad and, I hope, interesting, perspective and to provide a factual recounting of what has actually taken place, rather than rely on sweeping generalizations or broad rhetorical statements.

Since the end World War II, psychologists have sought inclusion in psychoanalysis, not only as a clinical and scholarly enterprise, but also as a high-status guild within the broader psychoanalytically oriented subculture. Such trends do not exist in a social vacuum. This one is part of a tradition of credentialism that began over a century ago.

The first commentator on this trend was Mark Twain, who left us an account of the origin of credentialism among the pilots who guided boats on the Mississippi River (Fallows, 1985). Because many people could successfully be trained as river pilots, their number increased and salaries began to decline. So some of the pilots formed a limited membership association and demanded higher salaries than the rest. They claimed that they deserved these higher salaries because, through careful selection and demands for the highest standards of training, they represented the safest and most competent pilots.

At first, employers did not take this claim seriously, but then the members of the association got the idea of circulating, only among themselves, information they gathered about the latest river conditions, especially the location of such potential dangers as snags and sandbars, which changed frequently. Well, lo and behold, their original claims of greater competency began to come true.

"The outsiders began to ground steamboats, sink them, and get into all sorts of trouble, whereas accidents seemed to keep entirely away from the association men." Passengers and cargo shippers wanted these association pilots. Insurance companies demanded them. Nonassociation pilots could no longer find work.

The number of river pilots dropped because, to become a member pilot of the association, you now needed the recommendation of two association members. With that requirement in place, the association had acquired the power to regulate its own competition. The only problem was those higher wages. They kept getting higher.

Steamship owners had to comply with the constantly escalating demands of the association. They passed their increased costs onto commercial customers. The industry became overpriced, helping the new railroads to underbid and, thus, make obsolete, the entire steamship business.

As a more recent critic of credentialism, James Fallows, points out, "the economic logic that lay behind the pilots' association shaped the other organizations as well. They controlled entry into their fields, they often raised professional standards, and they sheltered their members from the more chaotic side of the marketplace."

The attraction of this kind of credentialing quickly took hold of the collective attention of the professions, but the public was slower to respond. "Before the First World War not a single state required that its lawyers have attended law school, and fewer than a third of all North American medical schools required even a high school diploma for admission." (Fallows, 1985). It was between the two world wars that credentialing got a firm foothold in public consciousness. And it was during this period that American psychoanalysts organized themselves.

The American, between 1911 and 1932, was an interest group for physicians. The spread of Institutes was, in part, related to the emigration of European analysts to the United States. As the Americans organized, they quickly restricted training to physicians and argued that the "strictness of the American law against quack treatment" (Oberndorf, 1926), made their stance necessary, but Fine has challenged this, arguing that, "if anything, the American laws against quackery have always been much looser than the European." (Fine, 1979).

In the end, the International Training Commission allowed each society to set its own criteria for admission. As Fine concludes, "In practice, this meant that the training of lay analysts was officially outlawed in the United States but permitted in all other countries" (Fine, 1979).

In fact, during World War II, the number of American psychoanalysts relative to the total membership of the International increased to a point where the Americans could clearly do what they wanted. At the same time, clinical psychology was making its appearance on the American professional landscape. During World War I, psychologists had demonstrated the value of their testing procedures. That involved them in the clinical enterprise and they gradually developed an interest in psychotherapy as well. World War II provided an opportunity for this interest to blossom into practice.

It is not surprising that this trend expressed itself in an interest in psychoanalytic training. Psychoanalysis was establishing itself in those days as the model for psychotherapy. In fact, Shakow, in a 1945 paper on clinical psychology training, suggested requiring an analysis as part of that training.

In the last 40 years, psychologists have pursued this interest in psychoanalytic training within three different educational traditions. Some entered the Institutes of the American as special candidates. Others studied privately. Finally, independent Institutes were created for the training of nonmedical analysts. These were mostly in New York, although recently they have also developed in Los Angeles, Michigan, Chicago, Washington, Florida, and Colorado.

Before reviewing these three traditions, it is worth noting that such a historical review suggests the following preliminary conclusions:

1. While the APA has been trying to figure out how to be less homogenized, psychologists have been trying to become more so; the American has been much more critical of what it has accomplished in its training efforts than outsiders are, and internal criticism often lays blame for the major shortcomings at the doorstep of the same rigidly controlled, homogenized national training model that psychologists often admire from afar;

2. Psychoanalysis has, more than any other practicing profession, had trouble satisfying its wish, common to all guilds, to keep its identity clearly positioned in the minds of potential consumers. Health care consumers, for example, are unlikely to allow someone who has not graduated from a dental school to perform a root canal on their tooth, but they regularly allow therapists who have not graduated from psychoanalytic Institutes to interpret their transferences. And, without such unambiguous acknowledgement from consumers, psychoanalysts have taken the quest for a firm identity within their own house to a degree unnecessary in the other professions who rely on a publicly established identity. They would like to be in the position of dentists and attorneys, but are, instead, in the position of philosophers. In fact, recent British Royal Institute of Philosophy Lectures discuss the problem of the identity of American philosophers in a manner that will be very familiar to us. The audience at one of the lectures had raised the question of why Thoreau was included in the list of American philosophers. The explanation was:

> If any words are vague, philosophy is. . . . Even the most skeptical and cautious philosophers tend to wax dogmatic on this topic and to insist that what they are doing is philosophy, or real philosophy, and what whoever is doing anything of a different stripe is not, and there is an oddity in this that bears noting. . . . Considering Thoreau as a philosopher helps us test and stretch . . . our conception of philosophy and of what is important in a philosopher . . . in the American

tradition there is ample precedent for including Thoreau, as an example of a non-academic, even anti-academic, way of thinking that certainly regarded itself as philosophical, and in an important way.

Furthermore, it was said at that meeting, many philosophers hold to the point that a real philosopher lays out and analyzes arguments in a particular way and when it is felt by a philosopher from tradition A that a person from tradition B neglects such argument, that person is "regarded as a remarkably penetrating sage rather than a philosopher." For "penetrating sage," we can substitute the left-handed compliment that someone, while not an analyst, is a remarkably skilled therapist.

In any case, although many analysts don't like it, even the Federal Office of Education has held that a broad range of heterogeneously trained professionals have the right to call themselves analysts and that many organizations have the right to train analysts—in essence, restating in principle the long-standing reality that American psychoanalysis has naturally evolved into a socially accepted system of like-minded groups of professionals gathering to study and train in ways they find congenial to their vision of the psychoanalytic enterprise. And it is as if, in the absence of sufficient public concern about who we are to generate a binding public definition, like other professionals have, we are left to argue with each other, *ad infinitum, ad nauseam,* and too often, *ad hominem,* about whose training grants mythological "genuine psychoanalyst."

3. As the previous argument suggests, my historical inquiry has left me with the conviction that psychoanalysis itself either enjoys or suffers, depending on your point of view, not so much a set of standards as multiple traditions. There is nothing about any subgroup of us that is generally recognized by our consumers as guaranteeing our greater excellence and authority. Instead, we have a situation in which some of us agree that others of us have the proper breeding for membership in the guild to which we want to belong. The strength of this argument was bolstered by the fact, brought to my attention recently by Dr. Pine, that the aspiring-to-be standards of Section 1 of our Division, although frequently justified on the grounds that they might open the way for a society of psychologists to be recognized by the International, are actually different from those of the International. In a series of published statements over the last three years, the International has made clear that its tradition is not personal analysis and control cases conducted at a rate of three times per week, but rather a minimum of four times per week. This significantly diminishes the drama of our Section 1 versus Section 5 religious wars. Can the three-times-per-week standard now be defended with the same vigor it was previously or must it be traded in for the four-times-per-week standard? If it is not traded, we are outside the tradition of the IPA. If it is traded, such an action proves that what was being defended before was, at least in substantial part, the wish to remain within the tradition of the IPA, and not some clearly defined definition of the psychoanalytic process.

Having taken enough of your time with the sweeping generalizations I promised to avoid, let me now present the historical facts, I promised to share. By far, the best documented of the three training traditions is that of the American Psychoanalytic Association. In 1946, the American's membership had approved a bylaw requiring that all new members had to be physicians. In 1952, Knight reported that, while "the training regulations of the American permit official training of nonphysicians for research in psychoanalysis . . . research students are excluded from clinical courses and from analyzing patients under supervision (Knight, 1953). In effect, he argued, this meant that they did not actually get training in the use of psychoanalysis as a research instrument and this, combined with the general lack of interest in research among medical analysts, was "drying up the supply of research psychoanalysts." Knight added that simply training more psychologists was not the answer, because "a number of psychologists who have been given full psychoanalytic training for research use have simply become practicing analysts, abandoning any pretense of research."

Knight expressed concern over another problem. The self-selection process of the 1920s and 1930s had produced a much different crop of candidates than the current system.

"Many training analyses were relatively short and many gifted individuals with definite neuroses or character disorders were trained. They were primarily introspective individuals, inclined to be studious, thoughtful, and highly individualistic and to limit their social life to clinical and theoretical discussions with colleagues. They read prodigiously and knew the psychoanalytic literature thoroughly. Many of these have become our best teachers, theoreticians, and clinicians."

By contrast, Knight lamented, the new crop of medical candidates were mostly "normal" characters, with what he called "normal character disorders." They were, as he described them,

Not so introspective, are inclined to read only the literature that is assigned in Institute courses, and wish to get through with the training requirements as rapidly as possible. . . . Their motivation for being analyzed is more to get through this requirement of training rather than to overcome neurotic suffering in themselves or to explore introspectively and with curiosity their own inner selves.

Had *New York* magazine been telling this story it might simply have said that the candidates changed from "hippies" to "yuppies."

In any case, a similar sentiment was echoed 20 years later in the APA's 1974 National Conference on Psychoanalytic Education and Research. A report of the conference (Emde, 1974) stated: "Because of our recent history, in which there has been increasing organizational structure, we may have suffered a loss in candidates' enthusiasm for learning, particularly where the scholarly atmosphere of Institutes in lacking challenge due to rigidity and dogmatism.

That recent history, it was reported, was that "From 1932 to 1946, the American was a Federation of constituent societies, and membership in a constituent society automatically conveyed membership in the Association. (American Psychoanalytic Association, 1952). A 1946 bylaws change centralized authority over local Institute training in the APA's Board of Professional Standards and, by 1952, the Board had "developed almost absolute authority over admission of new members and over approval of new Institutes."

By 1952, there was growing concern about the power that the Board had accumulated. Knight pointed out that the Board had unilaterally increased the required supervision hours from 50 to 200 and had unilaterally stipulated that training analyses and supervised analyses must be conducted at a minimum of 4 hours per week.

Much as we argue today, within the Division of Psychoanalysis, Knight pointed out that those favoring such rules argued for them on the basis of setting and preserving high standards of training, while those arguing against them cited the unwarranted assumption of powers by the Board and the callous denial of membership in the APA for students who had followed on good faith the training policies of their Institutes, whose policies did not now match the APA's admission requirements. Of interest to us, by way of precedent, perhaps, is the recommendation of the Committee that, when someone applied for membership in the APA, the Board should respect whatever minimal standards were in effect in that person's training institution at the time of completion of his or her training and should base deferral on general deficiencies of training "rather than to any rigid application of numerical requirements."

Also of interest to us is that in the same midwinter meeting of 1952, the Committee on Ethical Standards was dealing with the issue of analysts who supervised control cases outside the official training program of their Institute. The majority of the committee felt that national enforcement measures should be implemented. In 1951, the Committee on Ethical Standards passed the following resolution:

> Recognizing in principle that training in therapeutic psychoanalysis is the function of the authorized Institutes of the American and not of the training analyst as an individual, it is resolved that it shall be against the policy of the American for any member to train or supervise any individual except under the direct auspices of a recognized training Institute of this association.

The committee also recommended that psychoanalysts who violated this code after official warning would be subject to suspension or loss of membership.

Also in 1952, the Committee on Training Standards restated a 1947 resolution that had extended the 1938 prohibition on nonmedical training from psychoanalysis to psychotherapy. It defined the practice of psychotherapy as a medical function and prohibited member Institutes from admitting to training anyone engage in or tending to engage in the individual practice of psychotherapy who is not a physician.

In December of 1954, the Executive Council decided that

> In response to an inquiry from the Institute for Psychoanalysis in London, it was agreed that London should feel free to train an American citizen who had spent most of his life and had received all of his scientific training in Great Britain, since it seemed highly improbable that he ever would practice in the United States.

It must have been their thinking either that the English were hardy enough to withstand a lay analysis or else that they suffered from nonmedical neuroses.

At the May, 1957, meetings, the Board moved to allow an approved Institute to request specific permission of the Board for an exception to current training regulations in order to train properly qualified research fellows. Thus, the waiver was born.

Later that year, it was used for the first time in the case of Roy Schafer and, in the following 2 years, for Christoph Heinicke, from the San Francisco Institute, George Mahl, of the Western New England Institute, Rhona Rapoport of the Boston Institute, Jacob Levine of the New York Institute, and Gardner Lindzey of the Chicago Institute.

One must assume that the experience of being in training varied greatly form one Institute to another, contrary to the notion held by many psychologists that APA Institutes have strict uniformity of training from center to center. Even in such basic aspects of the program as the training analysis and supervision, there was enormous variation. The two graduates of the New York Psychoanalytic that year had averaged 1,352 hours of training analysis, while the seven graduates of the Chicago Institute had averaged 521. The five graduates of Boston Psychoanalytic averaged 162 total hours of supervision, in contrast to the 494 hours averaged by the two graduates of the Topeka Institute, one of whom was a research student.

In December, 1974, a conference which might be viewed as the ancestor of this one was held in conjunction with APA's fall meetings. It was the National Conference on Psychoanalytic Education and Research, referred to briefly earlier (Goodman, 1977). A variety of interesting questions were raised and observations made. Several reports stressed the need to enhance "a graduate school climate in which self-study and learning in an active way is, following analytic principles, the student's responsibility." Several reports suggested multiple training tracks within Institutes to accommodate the needs of a larger variety of students. The value of an integrated tripartite training model was reaffirmed in most reports with special emphasis given to the importance of the didactic curriculum. Contrary to some suggestions made currently about the possibilities for guided self-study combined with supervised clinical work as an alternative to participation in an ordered and sequential curriculum, the conference report argued that the didactic curriculum "alone is the difference between psycho-analytic training and psychoanalytic education." This distinction was made repeatedly in the context of a broader argument for an avoidance of a trade school model of training with an almost exclusive emphasis on clinical proficiency.

In December, 1980, it was reported that in the 20 years of the waiver program's existence, 111 had been granted. By May, 1985, the total was approximately 150 granted over the course of about 30 years for people from a broad range of professions, including actress Janice Rule.

A broadening of the waiver has been approved recently by the membership of APA. In December, 1984, the members of APA were informed of the formation of a special committee chaired by Dr. Herbert Gaskill to review the question of nonmedical training. They were also informed of the possibility of antitrust action against their organization. On March 5, 1985, the American and International Psychoanalytic associations, along with the New York and Columbia Institutes were served with a complaint by four psychologists for violation of the antitrust laws. At the December, 1985, meetings of the American Psychoanalytic Association, the Board on Professional Standards and the Executive Council both voted in favor of submitting the report of the Gaskill Committee, as revised in October, 1985, to the membership for a referendum.

Ballots were counted on March 28, 1986. The result was 68% in favor and 32% opposed. The Gaskill report suggests the board create another waiver committee to review nonmedical applicants "who have the potential for excellence as analytic practitioners." It further states that:

"As part of the usual selection criteria we expect in general that such individuals will have achieved a professional identity as human caretakers through therapeutic clinical activities of demonstrable excellence. Consonant with the goal of excellence, such applicants should very likely have demonstrated competence through scholarly publications, among other professional achievements.

The report concludes with an emphasis on the need to approach such change gradually. It urges the maintenance of the medical identity of the American and states that "Both the national waiver committee and the individual Institute selection committees should carefully consider the issue of a balance of medical and nonmedical candidates so as to maintain the current perspective of the Association."

The Committee on Nonmedical Clinical Training was established in May of this year. The members were working on setting criteria for granting of the waiver at the time of this report. To what extent these changes are reactive to the antitrust lawsuit or the diminishing numbers of psychiatric applicants to many psychoanalytic Institutes, is unclear, but the wording of the Gaskill report, the small number of waivers granted in the past 30 years, and the history of the APA's commitment to maintaining its medical identity, all suggest, at least for the time being, a conservative set of expectations with regard to the rate of granting of the new clinical waiver.

In addition, however, this conference unfolds within the context of the two other traditions of psychoanalytic training for psychologists that have evolved over the past 40 years. One is the private apprenticeship tradition, which was the training model before it was displaced by the Berlin Institute model, and which is sometimes referred to as sub rosa or bootlegged training. Discussing this model, Fine reports the case of a control analyst who returned $2,400 to his psychologist-trainee, rather than provide any record that he had supervised him. The other tradition is the New York tradition, which, I will argue, has grown into something much more than just a clone of the Berlin/APA tradition, and which has preserved the possibility of a vision of psychoanalysis not doomed to the homogeneity the American has come to regret about itself.

That tradition begins with three training centers: NPAP, William Alanson White, and the Postgraduate Center for Mental Health. Taken as a whole, this tradition has lowered the priority of the goal of protection of the guild in favor of the goals of diffusing and transmitting psychoanalytic knowledge and taking psychoanalytic insight out into the community. The collective attitude toward both training and practice has been similar to what Rustin describes as the "missionary" approach, an approach, that can be contrasted to what both Rustin and Kermode describe as the secret society approach. I believe that analysts from these Institutes, and the others to which these have given rise, do themselves a serious disservice when they underestimate the value of their own tradition out of infatuation with the tradition of the American, or even the International, which has shared, in no small way, a secret guild tradition.

The NPAP, founded by Theodore Reik, began with 12 members, including some physicians, in 1948. By 1979 there were 300 students in training. Inevitable disagreements within NPAP gave rise to at least two other training programs: the Institute for Psychoanalytic Training and Research (IPTAR), founded in 1958, and the New York Freudian Society, founded in the mid 1960's.

Those remaining loyal to the original NPAP see it as having evolved flexibly in response to new theories and individual differences among candidates in their needs and abilities. Those who have left it tend to see it as having rebelled against objective training criteria in favor of something more undesirably promiscuous in the granting of certificates.

From these two perspectives, NPAP, the New York Freudians, and IPTAR are routinely described along one of two continua: In one view, NPAP is humane in its attitude toward students, The New York Freudians are not overtly oppressive, and the only thing tougher than getting through IPTAR is becoming the social director of a South Bronx street gang, with at least one-third of the students who enter each year not making it all the way through, and only two to four graduates per year; in the other view, NPAP is too uncritical of both students and newer theories, while the New York Freudians and IPTAR preserve the genuine heritage of Freudian analysis in both training and theory.

Of these three historically related groups, NPAP is still the largest, with between 30 and 70 new students being accepted into training each year. My impression is that a larger proportion of these students are social workers than is the case at either of the other two Institutes and it is reported by NPAP that a large majority of the candidates are women. All the nonmedical Institutes have a higher proportion of women candidates than do the strictly medical Institutes. By contrast to NPAP, IPTAR accepts 8 or 9 new candidates each year. The New York Freudians also accept about 8 or 9 new students per year from among 15 to 20 applicants. About two-thirds of those accepted are social workers and one-third psychologists.

Another major historical force in determining the shape of the New York psychoanalytic tradition has been the William Alanson White Institute. Its history starts with the April, 1941, meeting of the New York Psychoanalytic Society, at which Karen Horney was disqualified as a training analyst. That led to the formation of the American Institute for Psychoanalysis in New York City.

This was at the beginning of the two-decade period of the most rapid growth of American psychoanalysis. Sixteen new societies of the American were created in the 1950s and 1960s. Then came the decline of the seventies. The Institutes of the American had classes of 10 to 15 candidates each year typically in all but the newest or smallest programs 25 years ago. Today, the most reliable estimates are that, even with the current rebounding, which some have suggested may be due to the general revival of interest in Freud, the more thriving APA programs start 8 to 10 new candidates per year, while in smaller cities such as Denver and Dallas, there is much more difficulty attracting students. Sometimes the whole program in such smaller cities may have only 11 or so candidates at one time and attempts may be made to start classes with 2 persons, or, one report suggested, even in the case of New York Psychoanalytic, not to start class at all if enough qualified applicants cannot be found.

But in the early 1940s, business was just beginning to boom, and Institutes were spreading. In April, 1943, at least in part over a dispute about Erich Fromm's standing as a nonmedical analyst within the American Institute for Psychoanalysis, 12 members resigned, including Sullivan and Clara Thompson, who founded White.

In the first two decades of its existence, using the membership of its society for approximate counts, White trained 70 psychologists and 100 psychiatrists. During the past decade, the total count of psychologists in the White Society increased to 112, while the total count of psychiatrists decreased to 95. Currently about 7 to 12 candidates begin training each year, with, typically, either equal numbers of psychiatrists and psychologists, or more psychologists than psychiatrists in each entering class, again reflective of the trend toward decreasing interest in psychoanalysis among the best psychiatry residents and a corresponding decline in the number of medical school graduates choosing psychiatry as their specialty.

As with NPAP, graduates of White have been instrumental in the founding of other training programs for psychologists, including those at NYU and Adelphi. Bernie Kalinkowitz, one of the founders of NYU's training program, and George Goldman, an early faculty member of the Adelphi training program founded by Gordon Derner, were both among the five psychologists in White's first matriculated class of candidates in 1948.

The NYU program, founded in 1961, has graduated about 290 psychologists. The number of candidates varies from year to year. The current class has 29 candidates, selected from 55 applicants. In the 2 prior years, however, the entering classes averaged 10 candidates. Candidates are required to see three patients in analysis three times per week with a minimum of 160 hours of supervision. Their own personal analyses, however, are conducted at a frequency decided on an individual basis one source, as some of you know, of recent controversies within the Division.

Adelphi University also accepts about 20 or 30 new candidates each year into its child- and adult-training programs out of a pool of about 50 applicants. About 150 people have graduated from Adelphi since its founding in 1963.

The third major root of the current community of psychologist-psychoanalysts in New York City is the Postgraduate Center for Mental Health. Partly because the founder, psychiatrist Louis Wolberg, was married to a social worker, the training in psychoanalysis at the Postgraduate Center has been open to social workers and psychologists since its inception in 1948. Through the mid-1960s each entering class had 3 students from each discipline. Class size was increased in the 1960s and now about 20 candidates enter each year. In recent years only about 1 or 2 of these new students have been psychiatrists and about half have been social workers, with the rest psychologists. Since 1948, the Postgraduate Center has graduated 192 Social Workers, 296 Psychologists, and 129 Psychiatrists.

Somewhat the reverse of NYU, candidates at the Postgraduate Center must be in analysis three times per week for a minimum of 400 hours, but have more flexibility in their control cases. Typically, one or two cases are seen three times per week, with the rest being seen once or twice per week. This, in part, seems to reflect the practical realities of running Postgraduate Center's large public clinic.

There are two ways to put this heterogeneous picture of training in New York together. From inside, there appears to be the usual amount of contentiousness and criticalness of everyone else's method of training. Looked at, as a whole, from outside, however, what emerges is the picture of a psychoanalytic community in the best sense of the phrase, with most interested professionals able to find an intellectual and clinical home that feels right.

This reading of its history has impressed upon me an irony about psychoanalysis. Psychoanalysis is unique in the history of ideas because it has been the most determined attempt to free us, in our behavior and our mental activity, from the tyranny of unnecessary and irrational authority. And those who practice it have been blessed by the fact that our society and its government don't care enough about what we do to want to set up external authorities to regulate and control us. Legally, anyone who can, in their state, practice psychotherapy, can see their patients as often as they want, using any kind of furniture, short of the rack, that they deem appropriate, all the while interpreting both transferences and ever transference neuroses, without fear of fine or imprisonment. The citizens of our society want protection from quack dentists and attorneys and electricians, but they apparently do not live in fear of a blurry distinction between psychotherapists and psychoanalysts.

Given such a noble enterprise and such freedom to pursue it, we have doggedly set about to strip ourselves of as much of this advantage as we are capable of doing. At any given moment in time, one faction or another of us are either petitioning the government to control us or else we are setting up institutional, local, national, or even international hierarchies and authorities to keep us in line and validate us from outside. We seem unable to get enough of this. Ignoring one of Freud's clearest messages, that our identity is ours to choose and that none can choose it for us, "as in the days of living gods and imposing fathers" (Reiff, 1959), as Philip Reiff has so elegantly put it, we devote as much energy and passion as we can spare for the work of arguing whose external authority is the one true authority, and having decided that, figuring out how we can force as many of the rest of us as possible to submit it.

All of us seem to find this enterprise seductive, at least from time to time. Our debate topics have ranged from such mundane and trivial issues as the true dividing line between "sub-rosa" and above-board training, to the awe-inspiring and critical for all mankind, who is a psychoanalyst? Hopefully history will not remember us for these debates. In addition to consuming far too much of the energy of this Division, they have historically never come to anything. Fortunately, psychoanalysis has proven robust enough to withstand the affectionate embrace of its inheritors. Our battles over dogma, standards, and identity, although assuredly intense and absorbing for a moment, become, in the broader sweep of history somewhat like the one between an American and Russian warship off the coast of California described by novelist Thomas Pynchon:

What happened on the 9th of March 1864," he wrote, "is not too clear. Popov the Russian Admiral did send out a ship . . . to see what it could see. Off the coast . . . the two ships sighted each other. One of them may have fired; if it did then the other responded; but both were out of range so neither showed a scar afterward to prove anything"(Pynchon, 1966).

The preparation of this chapter has left me with the nagging thought that we psychologists are apparently determined to repeat the organizational vicissitudes of the other APA. My hope is that the facts and ideas I have presented will push things at least slightly in another direction, both this weekend, and in our organizational efforts afterwards. That direction is, as best I can capture it, one of as little centralization of authority as is absolutely necessary to allow us to carry on the work to which we are all obviously committed.

Some kind of association among Institutes created by psychologists might well strengthen our identity, but I would prefer to see us nurture hundreds of small enclaves of our colleagues in their heterogeneously styled commitments to the psychoanalytic experiment and to create a national community of psychoanalytic societies curious about, not critical of, each other, rather than to structure ourselves into any kind of large national monolithic association homogenizing everything in its path with the seduction of national recognition. That path has been tried once already in this country, and, as Freud so often reminded us about the past, it really does not bear repeating.

REFERENCES

American Psychoanalytic Association Bulletin. (1952). Midwinter meetings report.

Emde, R. (1974). Report of the National Conference of Psychoanalytic Education and Research. *Journal of the American Psychoanalytic Association, 22,* 569–586.

Fallows, J. (1985). The case against credentialism. *The Atlantic, 256*(6), 49–57.

Fine, R. (1979). *A history of psychoanalysis.* New York: Columbia University Press.

Goodman, S. (1977). *Psychoanalytic education and research.* New York: International Universities Press.

Knight, R. (1953). The present status of organized psychoanalysis in the United States. *Journal of the American Psychoanalytic Association, 1,* 197–221.

Oberndorf, C. (1926). Discussion on lay analysis. *International Journal of Psychoanalysis, 7,* 142.

Pynchon, T. (1966). *The crying of lot 49.* Philadelphia: Lippincott.

Rieff, P. (1959). *The mind of the moralist.* New York: Viking.

9 Institute Training
and Its Alternatives

Marvin Hyman

I would like to take as my starting point for this presentation the now seemingly general agreement that one becomes a student and practitioner of psychoanalysis by studying it, by doing it, and by experiencing it as patient. For those who do not share the belief that this view of how one becomes a psychoanalyst has been empirically demonstrated, let me propose that, for purposes of this discussion, they accept the idea as axiomatic.

Since the mid-1920s, the idea has become increasingly entrenched that the best, and perhaps the only, way in which one can experience, study, and learn to do psychoanalysis is within the context of an Institute of psychoanalysis. Defining Institute as broadly as possible, it may be conceived of here as an organized entity consisting at least of a curriculum, a faculty, designated training analysts, designated supervising analysts, an administration, and last, and often least, candidates for training in psychoanalysis. Each of the foregoing components of the Institute has come into being for seemingly good reasons, and the successes of analytic training over the years seems to attest to the utility and value of them. Yet, despite the successes, it would be erroneous to take their merits and strengths as self-evident, and, therefore, to forgo questioning their weaknesses and deficiencies. I would like to urge that we not commit that error in our efforts at this conference.

One of the corollaries of the Institute conceptualization is the assignment of responsibility for the training of the psychoanalyst. From the administrative point of view, the merits of the structured and organized Institute and its program cannot be questioned. We can ask, however, what effects ensue from organizing training in a way that is admirable primarily for administrative reasons. One such effect is that the organization and its needs take priority over the needs of the teachers, trainers, and students, particularly the last. Examples of this are: classes that begin when there are enough students, rather than when the individual is ready to study the subject; the candidate who has to continue treatment with the assigned training analyst in order to continue in the Institute, regardless of evident mismatch between analyst and analysand; the disapproval by the Institute, for economic as well as conceptual reasons, of candidates pursuing part of their training outside of the auspices and organizational elements of the institute.

Another effect that can accompany the tightly organized Institute structure is the unhappy one that training becomes Institute-centered rather than student-centered, that the responsibility for training is centered substantially if not entirely in the Institute rather than in the hands of the student. The result is that the student is implicitly, and perhaps explicitly, infantilized; deemed incapable of participating in or making crucial decisions relative to his or her training; and is expected both by the Institute and by the student to await the bar or bat mitzvah of Institute graduation before thinking of oneself as an analyst.

Many Institute people believe that a psychoanalyst is one who has graduated ·from an Institute; there are some who believe that a psychoanalyst is one who has graduated from *their* Institute. It can be argued that this viewpoint, which is still another effect of an Institute-oriented conception of training, stifles the implementation and utilization of other (and perhaps better) definitions of who is a psychoanalyst. One such alternative definition is that a psychoanalyst is one who has persuaded representatives of his or her peer group (and, by extension, the peer group itself) that he or she possesses *and can demonstrate* the abilities, skills, knowledge, and other qualities the peer group believes are characteristic of the psychoanalyst. Were this definition of the psychoanalyst to become widespread, it might have the salutary effect of making Institute adherents more open to ideas from other training entities.

We are closer now than ever before to having the mechanism whereby we can define a psychoanalyst by what he or she *does* and how this is assessed by the profession at large. I refer to the development of the program for the Diploma in Psychoanalysis, which, when it comes into being, will relieve Institutes of the responsibility of defining who is a psychoanalyst and the possible inflexibilities that such definitional responsibilities may impose. I will try to demonstrate later the kind of flexibilities that can be made possible by this development.

Turning now to the component elements of the Institute model, I would like to consider some of the difficulties connected with those components. First, the training analyst and the training analysis: I would like to believe that we have gone beyond the idea that the training analysis is primarily or only an opportunity for the analyst-in-training to experience psychoanalysis from the "other side of the couch." We could argue further that if the training analysis is didactic in nature and scope, it cannot be analysis since intellectual, ideational, and educational considerations come to have precedence over the achievement of insight into and resolution of intrapsychic conflict. Perhaps it is time then, to modify the conception of the training analysis and to view it only and entirely as a therapeutic analysis. Incidentally, we might in this way make unnecessary the need for the two-analyses syndrome that is increasingly common: One for the Institute and one for myself.

To be sure, if we view the training analysis as entirely therapeutic, then we would have to forgo the notion that it can be used for the continuing evaluation of the analysand as he or she progresses through training. Such evaluation, to the extent that it is necessary, would have to be achieved in the supervisory situation, the seminar situation, and the myriad other encounters a student has with teachers, colleagues, and the psychoanalytic community.

The idea of the training analyst has an interesting history. It is my understanding that the need for training analysts arose when it was recognized that the analyst treating one's present and future colleagues could not also be the colleague's teacher, adviser, mentor, or friend. It became apparent that it is difficult to reveal one's private thoughts in the consulting room to an analyst with whom one has significant other contacts. Thus, Hans Sachs went from Vienna to Berlin to be the analyst of those who wanted analysis but were uncomfortable at the idea of revealing themselves to their Berlin colleagues. In that vein, Sachs eschewed the role of supervisor and teacher in the Berlin situation and limited himself to analyzing junior and senior psychoanalysts.

Over the years, the concept of the training analyst has changed, and in ways that I question are better. The training analyst is not now defined *only* as an analyst who keeps oneself appropriately aloof from other aspects of the analysand's life; the training analyst is defined as senior, special, elite, more competent than other analysts, and, most problematically, an agent of the Institute as well as of the analysand. In this last role, the training analyst is conceived of as one who monitors the candidate-analysand and reports (some say "rats on the candidate") to the training administration. And even if the training analyst does not so report, the assigned analyst does monitor, in the analysand, conformity with the orientation and prejudices of the Institute and its personnel. We have to ask if this is what we want to provide to those becoming psychoanalysts as a model for what analysis should be.

In a like manner, we have changed the definition of the supervising analyst from one who has more and/or different experience than the supervisee to one who is accorded special status by the Institute. As a special designee of the Institute, the supervising analyst is responsible not only for providing technical supervision for the case being supervised, but also for the conceptual and theoretical purity of the supervisee's work and thinking. To the extent that the supervising analyst works on behalf of the Institute there is a continuing risk that the supervisee's curiosity, talents, skills, and abilities will be directed, constrained, and organized to fit the preconceptions of the Institute rather than the needs of the individual in supervision. At the very least, the supervisee will be guarded against coming into contact with technical viewpoints other than those of the Institute.

In still another component area of Institute training, I don't think there would be much disagreement among us that the curriculum of an analytic training Institute is designed to impart the body of psychoanalytic knowledge to the developing psychoanalyst. Some Institutes conceive of that body of knowledge broadly; other more narrowly. Some see it as having a natural progression; others favor a more casual ordering of the curriculum elements. Despite these differences, all Institutes have to have in common the following: a definition of psychoanalytic knowledge that is Institute-determined, a sequence of courses or seminars determined by the Institute's conception of what should be taught when and how it should be taught, a faculty chosen by its commitment to the substance of the curriculum (rather than interest in all knowledge that can be considered psychoanalytic, however remotely), and a limiting rather than expanding notion of the body of psychoanalytic knowledge. One could ask the following questions about these commonalities: How do we know what should be taught when, for example, psychoanalytic therapy before or after psychoanalytic psychopathology? Object relations theory before, after, or instead of metapsychology? Dream interpretation before or after psychoanalytic technique? Freud before or after Jung? Jung at all—or Freud? Can we feel confident that seminars are a better way to learn than study groups, tutorials, workshops, and so forth? Will students in an Institute be forever contaminated or corrupted by exposure to a teacher from another Institute or of another theoretical persuasion? Too often we get the impression that the answers to these and like important questions are obtained not from empirical evidence, from carefully reviewed experience, or even from a desire to promulgate a certain conviction. Rather, they are determined by the administrative and organizational needs of the Institute, for example, since the Institute needs the students' tuition for reimbursement of faculty and for administrative costs, students are discouraged, if not forbidden, to obtain part of their psychoanalytic knowledge and education outside the Institute's auspices. And this proscription might include workshops, tutorials, study groups, or other educational experiences with universally recognized psychoanalysts from other Institutes or of other persuasions.

I would like to mention one other component of the Institute model that deserves scrutiny: the selection process. Does our current knowledge of psychoanalysis enable us to predict, with sufficient accuracy, who will or will not eventually become a psychoanalyst with whom we would want to be associated? And even if we could make such a prediction accurately, would we not be constrained in selecting students according to nonpsychoanalytic criteria, for example, possession of a doctoral degree, and such a degree in medicine, psychology, or social work? And, however we select, using whatever criteria, should not the substantial number of false positives and false negatives we currently observe in connection with Institute programs give us qualms about selection in the first place?

I hope that what I have offered for consideration up to this point, despite its schematic presentation, will have persuaded you that the Institute model, as it currently exists, cannot be taken for granted as an ideal. Rather the model should be continuously scrutinized and questioned, and alternatives considered. In presenting alternatives to the model and its components, I want to emphasize that I am not suggesting that Institute training be abandoned in favor of some other training schema. Rather, I am offering the conception that we view the Institute model as one end of a continuum of training possibilities; the other end of which continuum might be training in which there is no Institute, no organization, no structure whatsoever: something like the training that Freud received in his preparing to become a psychoanalyst. A training organization might choose, entirely, or in regard to any of its component elements, to place itself at any point along this continuum, according to that which best suits its needs and circumstances. And, it ought to be able to do so completely assured that the psychoanalytic community will be accepting of its decision. What might such a training program, and its components look like? I'd like to spend the remainder of my allotted time sharing some ideas about that.

In the first place, the program offering psychoanalytic training, or the individual seeking to give training to and get training for oneself, must be assured that their efforts will be accepted by the psychoanalytic community, that is, that the products of their efforts will be admitted to examination by their peers. It would be unfortunate and ironic if the mechanism by which we can achieve maximum flexibility and freedom in our training efforts were to become instead, rigidified and inflexible, a captive of one model or another of training.

Second, we would have to subscribe to the principle that psychoanalytic training is as much the responsibility of the individual seeking the training as it is the responsibility of those providing it (other than the individual). This principle, by the way, parallels the psychoanalytic treatment situation, in which the patient is as much responsible for the therapy as the analyst. In some instances, the individual might assume the total responsibility for getting training; in other instances, the individual might assign the responsibility totally to some training facility; and, in most instances, the individual would probably choose to share the responsibility with a facility, teachers, an analyst, supervisors, and/or peers. The crucial point here is the responsibility carried by the student for his or her own development.

With the responsibility for designating who is an analyst assigned to the community and its representatives, and the responsibility for the training placed in the hands of the student, all sorts of innovations become possible.

An organization might decide to limit its administrative responsibility to maintaining records of those affiliated with it in regard to training analyses, supervision, courses taken or other educational experiences fulfilled, papers presented, and so on. Or it could assume an evaluative function of candidates, supervisors, analysts, and teachers. Or it might limit itself to getting together students and teachers, analysands and analysts, practitioners and supervisors. Whatever the choices, they are made easier by having the standard of the Diploma in Psychoanalysis to use rather than some idiosyncratically defined (and therefore challengeable) criterion. Some organizations might take on the responsibility of recruiting faculty, offering courses, maintaining a library, sponsoring a treatment clinic, and performing the myriad administrative tasks attendant upon such activities. Others may choose to do none of these, leaving the responsibility to those who wish to be trained and encouraging them to make all the necessary arrangements to do so. Some individuals might choose to get training outside of some organized entity. Such individuals would be responsible for arranging their own training analyses, supervision, and course of study, using whatever means and resources are available. This would be a kind of apprenticeship training, a form of education and training that may be most suited to learning an art like psychoanalysis.

By tossing out these several possibilities, I am attempting to illustrate what becomes available as training alternatives when we agree that the profession at large will do its own certifying. You can see that I have an optimistic and perhaps unrealistically simplistic view of how the diploma process could work. Yet, I would argue that it doesn't have to be all that complicated if we approach it with a degree of open-mindedness. Essentially, all there has to be to it is that, once an individual has presented evidence that he or she has studied psychoanalysis, done it under supervision, and been psychoanalyzed, that individual will then be provided an opportunity to present his or her work, writing, and thinking to a group of diplomaed colleagues perhaps selected jointly in some way both by the examinee and the profession. Hopefully, these colleagues, even though they may not be able to define what a psychoanalyst is, will know when they see one, and will then go ahead to award the diploma to the individual or not.

Just as institutes or other organizations can thus become more innovative and flexible, so too can the component elements in training. The training analysis can be conducted by whoever has a diploma and by whomever the analysand selects. If an individual elects to obtain training through an Institute, he or she might select or have selected an analyst affiliated with that group. Or, if an individual does not so elect, the training analyst will be chosen by the individual on whatever basis the individual finds appropriate. Likewise, Institutes can be free to choose whether or not they wish to involve themselves in selecting and ordaining training analysts. They would be free to designate, from among their diplomaed affiliates, analysts who will remain aloof from the affairs of their analysands, the better to conduct the analyses of their colleagues-to-be.

Curriculum might also become less of an issue. My proposal would be that we can, as a community, define as broadly as possible what a psychoanalytic practitioner and/or student of psychoanalysis should know. We could even include knowing those topics and areas that, from our own points of view, we would argue vehemently are not psychoanalysis. In this way we might avoid that perversion of scholarly process which consists of not knowing that with which we categorically disagree.

Assuming then, that we specify the essential areas of psychoanalytic knowledge, we can then leave it to the student to acquire that knowledge in whatever way and from whomever he or she chooses. Knowledge can be acquired, in this more flexible format, from Institute teachers or from any knowledgeable person in the community and through whatever means is best suited and appropriate. All that we would want to expect is that the student has been exposed to the essentials of psychoanalytic knowledge and can use them adequately as this is demonstrated in discourse with colleagues.

As a mild digression, don't you all find it curious that the issue of curriculum in analytic training is nowhere on the conference program? It is as though we have all agreed (which we have not) what the curriculum is and that it needs no discussion or consideration. Perhaps our next conference will address that issue.

If one reads the memoirs of those trained in psychoanalysis before 1925 (the year of the founding of the first Institute in Berlin), and compares their careers with those trained in Institutes, one finds that individuals who were self-selected and casually admitted to training fared no differently in their psychoanalytic careers than those who were rigorously screened, assessed, evaluated, intensively and extensively interviewed, psychologically tested, and carefully selected. My point is that if we cannot predict who will be successful (whatever that is) in a psychoanalytic career, why bother. If we abandon the view that psychoanalysts are somehow special, and need, therefore, to be selected carefully, then we can leave it to the diploma process to screen out those who have attempted to become psychoanalysts and have not succeeded in the effort. Perhaps, then, we could use those resources thus made available to disseminate knowledge about psychoanalysis and to recruit more individuals to a psychoanalytic career.

The last part of my presentation will be a brief description of a training effort that incorporates some of the principles and ideas I have offered here and stands as one of the myriad possible alternatives to the Institute model. This Center for Psychoanalytic Studies, as it designates itself, adopted as its standard of who is a psychoanalyst the criteria for membership of the International Psychoanalytic Association. It would have been better, on reflection, if the Center had conducted a series of round-robin intercollegial encounters, thus enabling a designation by the psychoanalytic community itself of those whom the community considered psychoanalysts. When the national community adopts a diploma process, then that will undoubtedly become the basic standard for the Center.

On the basis of this standard, any analyst, in the local community or elsewhere, can be selected, by an individual seeking training and/or by the Center, as a training analyst, as a supervising analyst, or as a teacher of some aspect or other of psychoanalysis. Any analyst who meets the standard and wishes to offer a course in some aspect of psychoanalysis through the auspices of the Center is welcome to do so. The Center, in turn, will provide the minimal administrative backup necessary, for example, announcement of courses, collection of tuition, maintenance of records, and so on. If a course fails to obtain a sufficient number of enrollees, the teacher may provide a tutorial in the subject to any individual who wishes to pursue it.

Any individual may take any course offering provided by the Center. It is the individual's responsibility to decide if he or she has sufficient background for the course, which decision may be made in consultation with an analyst connected with the Center or with the teacher of the course. The Center has noticed that development of sophistication in psychoanalytic knowledge does not follow a particular progression through certain subjects, from easy to hard or from basic to advanced. Rather, it seems to come from immersion in psychoanalytic subjects and activities. Some individuals become deeply immersed, others just dip in a toe; all are encouraged to participate, at whatever level of intensity and sophistication.

Instead of curriculum, the Center provides a relatively detailed statement of what its analysts consider the essential areas of psychoanalytic knowledge that one should possess in order to function as a psychoanalyst. Because the community is relatively heterogeneous, the statement is rather broad in its range, suggesting that one ought to know about the theory and practice of all persuasions labeling themselves as psychoanalytic, even though an individual might decide to study only one such persuasion intensively.

For a time, the community thought it might develop a center for psychoanalytic treatment which would facilitate the referral of patients to analysts seeking supervised experiences. Liability insurance problems made this an impossibility, so the community uses an informal system wherein any individual who wants to treat such a supervised case can solicit referrals and indicate his or her own willingness to provide services at a lowered fee. When a patient is seen, the analyst provides a supervisor for himself or herself who can attest, if necessary, to the experiences of the analysand. Likewise, the Center will maintain a record of the process if it is so desired.

The Center does not have the resources to provide a library. A local psychoanalytic Institute does maintain one, and that library is supported by the community through donations to it. The library is available to any serious reader in psychoanalysis.

It is the hope of the Center that, as the diploma process comes into place, those in the community who wish to, will examine their background and experience and will decide whether or not they have the training analysis, the supervised analytic experience, and the knowledge of psychoanalysis to apply for examination. If the individual decides that that is the case, and the diploma process concurs, then the national psychoanalytic community will examine their psychoanalytic abilities and skills and will decide whether or not to accept them into the community.

In the presentation I have made today, I have tried to suggest that we leave ourselves free to include in today's view of training the casual and valuable training experiences that preceded the psychoanalytic Institute format in psychoanalytic history. I would hope that the psychoanalyst of the 1990s will have had the opportunity to participate in the kind of excitement and experiences that were characteristic of psychoanalysis in the 1900s. In that sense, if we cannot go back to the future, let us think about going forward to the past.

10 Institute Training

Anna M. Antonovsky

Introduction

I am grateful to Marvin Hyman for his statement, which I received about a week ago. I had a hard time getting ready for this conference. I knew that I wanted to say something about what a psychoanalytic Institute is and about psychoanalytic identity, but I wasn't sure how relevant it was to do this in the face of the dividedness in the Division with regard to the question of standards of training and with that, implicitly, about the definition of a psychoanalyst. Several specifics contributed to my unease. I participated in the Ann Arbor meeting on training in June of 1985. When I presented some remarks about how I and others, in the Education and Training Committee and in Section I, saw the nature of psychoanalytic experience, I felt that many people were in tune with what we were saying but, on the question of standards, we remained as far apart as ever. Then came the struggle over the formation of Section V. Though a compromise of sorts was eventually arrived at in that Section V was formally constituted as a "forum" for the discussion of clinical practices rather than as a Section underwriting a definition of a psychoanalyst according to training standards differing from the traditional ones, this formal resolution may indeed only cover the substantive difference which continues to exist.

The most recent reminder of our dividedness came within the last few weeks. The newly incorporated Board of Directors for the ABEPP Diplomate in Psychoanalysis—ABPsaP we're calling it—met on September 21, in New York, for its first formal full-scale meeting. It was a good productive meeting, starting us on the road to developing the steps needed to formulate and put into practice a diplomating process. I am still very hopeful that we will succeed in this endeavor but apparently not everyone present at that meeting felt comfortable with the direction of the discussion.

When Marv Hyman's statement arrived I saw that he was bypassing the issue of standards and was proceeding to his topic—Alternate Training Models—with the assumption that ABPsaP would set the standards and would thereby free individual training programs from this aspect of policy making. For reasons indicated I am not as reassured about this as he is, but I decided to follow his example and to go on to my few remarks about psychoanalytic Institutes, adding to them some questions about how conflict and dividedness have lived themselves out in the psychoanalytic movement.

Now, what is a psychoanalytic Institute? I would say it is a community that fosters the development of the analyst's identity and reinforces the continuing functioning of that identity. As a training institution it provides the opportunity for those who aspire to become psychoanalysts to have the kind of experiences which might lead to the formation of a working psychoanalytic identity. For those who have become psychoanalysts, it provides a setting for continuing reclarification and reaffirmation of a psychoanalytic mode of working.

Why is the continuing reclarification and reaffirmation needed? Chemists, presumably, don't do it and neither, probably, do historians. Perhaps it is needed because what the analyst qua analyst does is unusual, doesn't necessarily come naturally, and requires a special discipline in personal responding and relating. Psychoanalytic work never becomes a fixed skill. The psychoanalytic stance is an availability for a certain work-in-engagement with the other which at best will move along the process of knowing the other—and oneself—in a nontrivial way.

The French analyst Widlöcher (1983) has said that our identity as analysts "rests in fact on the discovery, which each must make on his own, of the psychoanalytic experience . . . and *the particular method of mental functioning* which it implies" (pp. 24–25; my emphasis). He stresses repeatedly the uniqueness of the "psychic work" which the analytic task "demands from us" (p. 31). Remarking that this experience tends to elude systematization (p. 25), he nevertheless makes a try at describing it:

> To arrange for a certain interhuman encounter, to encourage and to spot in this situation quite specific processes, to communicate certain of its elements so that the patient feels free and secure when facing the instincts and the internalization processes, seem to be three aspects of the task. (p. 27)

He elaborates that "to arrange for a certain human encounter" includes "to fight the enticements of the encounter," not to give in to a real relationship on the level of transferential regression (p. 31). "To spot in this situation quite specific processes" means to be aware of the patient's transferential holds and "to be capable of facing all these forms of hold" (p.32) with one's own analytic mental functioning.

It is in the personal analysis and, later, in supervision that the candidate may develop the needed capability, "a specific method of mental functioning which does not come naturally to us" (p. 32). It is difficult, says Widlöcher, to be an analyst. He is not referring primarily to countertransference interference.

> It can be said that the main aim of personal analysis, in analytic training, is not only to prevent excessive countertransference reactions and to facilitate insight, but to help the candidate live without fear and even with pleasure a complex method of thinking, one in which primary and secondary processes are combined, as well as instinctive and affective participation and an awareness of this participation. (pp. 32–33)

I myself feel that this new method of mental functioning which one acquires in becoming an analyst *can*, with immersion and experience, become a kind of second nature, but I certainly agree with Widlöcher that it is never reduced to an automatism (p. 32).

Where does the psychoanalytic Institute come in? The candidate's introduction to this new method of mental functioning is taking place in this vision, in the framework of the analytic Institute, in personal analysis and in supervision, with others around one—one's classmates and siblings—having similar experience and there being the opportunity to share this, to compare, to confirm, and to dispute. This last aspect—candidates in their being together—I have seen, certainly in the White Institute. I don't know what contact French candidates have with one another. I suspect it is a different system. Widlöcher does not specifically mention candidates associating.

He does, however, speak very pointedly of the role of psychoanalytic societies in reassuring each member about his or her psychoanalytic identity. The analyst, in this view, eagerly seeks out confirmation that he or she is not alone in the difficulty experienced in maintaining a specific method of mental functioning which does not come naturally to us. The intensive scientific activity of psychoanalytic societies may only rarely yield original contributions but it serves to remind and reassure psychoanalysts of their common experience of the psychoanalytic encounter.

Pontalis (1983) traverses the path from the nature of psychoanalytic activity to the need for psychoanalytic community in a somewhat different though related way:

> The paradox of the analytic situation is that another person—not another ego but a *neutral* person who is out of sight and relatively silent—is necessary for one's self-discovery. And this is true for the two protagonists alike, both analysand and analyst. That is why self-analysis is for the most part an illusion, and also why an analyst cannot function properly on his own for any length of time without detrimental effects. A friend said of an analyst one day: "He should have at least

one patient and one colleague.'' There you have the nucleus of the psychoanalytic community; and it is all we need especially if the patient and the colleague are both hard to please. (p. 283)

You can see from the path I have taken that I am not as likely to focus on the possibly dire effects of Institute training on candidates as Marv Hyman is. I do believe that an Institute is well suited to carry out the needed training function. The alternatives Marv Hyman has suggested are of course acceptable. Whatever suits a given person is the main consideration.

I will not now go into the ways in which Institute training procedures can be improved, or what the various procedures are—Marv has mentioned some but not others. I assume, perhaps incorrectly, that the various patterns of Institute training are familiar to people. Insofar as they are not, we can talk about that in workshops. But I do want to say here that of course psychoanalytic Institutes, besides having the clearly positive training function which I previously suggested, also have a lot of other things happening in them—the sort of things that take place in all institutions.

I mention this because there is a tendency to idealize psychoanalytic Institutes, together perhaps with an inclination to fear them. People are inclined to assume that the special understanding and ethos which analysts bring to their work with patients will similarly pervade their dealings with their colleagues and with their institutions. The revelation that in these settings analysts behave more or less as do other people gives a special curiosity value to exposés such as those that appear in the *New Yorker* or *New York magazine*.

The expectation of special conduct is not to be dismissed completely. There is an attempt, I believe, within psychoanalytic Institutes to do justice to people and to take the whole person into account but the usual motives of ambition, self-interest, and personal preference also enter in. There are power struggles. There is competition for appointments to positions of responsibility which confer status as well as access to interesting work. Institutes are places where careers are made, or not made. This too they have in common with other institutions and both those seeking appointments and those in a position to make them are likely to be subject to the usual human failings.

The candidates are of course aware of the fallibility of their elders and they may participate, in ways to open to them, in the possibilities for acting out. Split transferences in relating to analysts and supervisors, and sibling issues acted out in class groups and involving teachers-analysts-supervisors are not uncommon.

The committee structures established by Institutes and the powers assigned to them—Training Committees, Executive Committees, Councils and Senates—provide some system of checks and balances, to see to it that fallibility does not lead to major abuse. Ultimately one relies on the awareness, goodwill and good judgment of one's colleagues on the faculty, and on the efficacy of psychoanalytic exploration when the various issues are brought into the analyses of the candidates.

Having made some comments about the nature of psychoanalytic work and its need for a psychoanalytic community or Institute, and about the nonidealized reality of psychoanalytic Institutes which may nonetheless be adequate environments for the working-through of projections and transferences, I would like to close with a few words about the everpresent issue of tradition and change in psychoanalytic ideas and practices.

Freud was the first innovator with regard to his own theory. He changed it significantly more than once. At one great turning point, when he introduced the death instinct, most of the psychoanalytic movement did not go with him. He did not on that account change his mind. He stayed his theoretical course. He was also forthright in admitting that he was not able to give the same open consideration to other people's ideas as he gave to the sometimes radical turnings of his own mind. In 1924—Freud was then close to 68 years old—he wrote to Ferenczi:

> I know that I am not very accessible and that I find it hard to assimilate unfamiliar thoughts that do not quite correspond with mine. I need quite a time to form a judgment and in the meantime I have to suspend judgment. (Grubrich–Simitis, 1986, p. 267)

In this letter, Freud encourages Ferenczi to pursue his own ideas, confident that neither Ferenczi nor Rank would in their "independent excursions" abandon the terrain of psychoanalysis. "Why then," he wrote to Ferenczi, "should you not have the right to try and see if things don't work differently from what I had thought?" (p. 267).

We know things didn't work out amicably. The break with Rank came 2 years later, and though there was no official break with Ferenczi, Freud found it necessary, in 1931, to condemn Ferenczi's technique of exchanging physical tenderness with his patients to help them resolve the effects of their childhood traumata. On this excursion, Ferenczi had indeed wandered beyond the terrain of psychoanalysis.

In light of this sharp separation from Ferenczi I found it all the more interesting to learn, from Riccardo Steiner's (1985) well-documented account of "the controversial discussions" between Freudians and Kleinians in the British Psychoanalytic Society, how Freud dealt with the disputes on early child development and child analysis between Melanie Klein and her followers, among them Ernest Jones and Anna Freud. Though Freud was clearly very much perturbed by the attacks on Anna, particularly the personal slur that she was not sufficiently well analyzed—and tended to come down on her side of the argument, he nevertheless suspended final judgment and left the verdict to "further experience." Steiner writes of "Freud's fundamental faith in the judgment of history" (p. 36). "In the last resort, something seems to have restrained him from delivering the definitive anathema" (p. 57). We know, with hindsight, that the British Psychoanalytic Society, with its subsequent subdivision into Freudians, Kleinians, and a Middle Group, splendidly survived these controversies, and that in the psychoanalytic world of the 1980s Kleinian concepts have become household words.

What impresses me is that while the history of psychoanalysis is replete with ideological schisms, organizational and institutional splits—not all of them claiming to have an ideological referent—the body of psychoanalytic theory has flexibly grown and an implicit consensus about the parameters of psychoanalytic practice has maintained itself over the years. And this is an ongoing process. Not only have "depressive position" and "projective identification" become part of our vocabulary, I believe "self-object" and "self-object transferences" are also here to stay, though I don't think the same holds true for Kohut's notion of drives as disintegration products or for the grand scheme of self-psychology replacing drive or ego psychology.

The extension of and shifting emphases within the "received" body of psychoanalytic knowledge are achieved at great effort and with much upheaval. I believe Steiner is wise to urge us toward an awareness of the neurotic and possibly even psychotic anxieties which may be stirred up in us when we are confronted with a major challenge to our deeply invested psychoanalytic approaches. He also tells us that a positive resolution—a recasting of our thinking—is possible, aided by the ability to tolerate ambivalence and to make room for the thought of another, qualities which Steiner associates with the (Kleinian) depressive position.

Which is not to say that all new proposals should become part of the psychoanalytic terrain Freud spoke of. I will not now attempt to define in any detail the elastic reach or boundary of what may be considered psychoanalytic thought or practice, but I would like to indicate my own understanding and commitment regarding an overall criterion of differentiation.

Coming back to the definition I started with of psychoanalytic identity residing in a particular mode of mental functioning engaged in by the analyst-at-work, I would say that the legitimate limit of change in psychoanalysis is reached when proposed ideas or practices would undermine or be incompatible with that mode of functioning. It seems to me, for instance, that the choices made in the two occurrences I have mentioned—Freud's ruling out the last development of Ferenczi's "active technique" but leaving Melanie Klein's ideas to the judgment of time—lend themselves to being differentiated by the criterion I've proposed.

To recap, then, with regard to Institute training: Psychoanalytic Institutes are complex places. They offer specific training procedures but also an overall atmosphere which interacts with the training. People in psychoanalytic Institutes are likely to:

1. Always try very hard to teach and reclarify with one another that serious, difficult and perhaps ineffable method of mental functioning which defines psychoanalytic identity or the psychoanalyst at work;
2. Often disappoint and disillusion themselves, their peers and their charges

by running their organizational affairs in ways that fall short of their implicit ideals, and;

3. Struggle—usually with a good measure of passion—with the tensions and pulls over tradition and change which seem be to a continuing presence in psychoanalysis.

In other words, Institutes are lively and somewhat mad places, intellectual and emotional hothouses, a cross between a rational professional school and a church or synagogue devoted to the worship of the one true brand of psychoanalytic doctrine. At best they are both serious and fun. At worst they are earnest and dreary. But isn't that true of a good many other places as well?

REFERENCES

Grubich–Simitis, I. (1986). Six letters of Sigmund Freud and Sándor Ferenczi on the interrelationship of psychoanalytic theory and technique. *International Review of Psychoanalysis*, 13, 259–277.

Pontalis, J.–B. (1983). Reflections. In E. D. Joseph & D. Widlöcher (Eds.), *The identity of the psychoanalyst*. New York: International Universities Press, pp. 277–287.

Steiner, R. (1985). Some thoughts about tradition and change arising from an examination of the British Psychoanalytic Society's controversial discussions (1943–1944). *International Review of Psychoanalysis*, 12; 27–71.

Widlöcher, D. (1983). Psychoanalysis today: A problem of identity. In E. D. Joseph & D. Widlöcher Eds. *The identity of the psychoanalyst*. New York: International Universities Press, pp. 23–39.

11

Institute and Alternative Training Models: A Response

Milton J. Horowitz

I was delighted to be invited to respond to the papers by Drs. Antonovsky and Hyman, but it was no easy task. I did not see Antonovsky's paper until last night. A few weeks ago, Hyman sent a note to say that he was going to rely heavily on points made by Siegfried Bernfeld (1962) in an article on psychoanalytic training. I read the article with great interest, immediately realizing why Hyman saw it as such a seminal contribution. But on receiving Hyman's paper about 10 days ago, I realized that it was Hyman and minimally Bernfeld. So, I adapted my prepared remarks on Bernfeld to the paper by Hyman. I hope to suggest a few key issues for workshop discussion. These suggestions seem to fit well with Anne–Marie Sandler's remarks last night, particularly her accounts of the open and closed versions of training, and with the paper this morning by Anna Antonovsky on the special qualities of Institute training.

Hyman accents what are perhaps Bernfeld's two principal messages: (1) We need to pay more attention to the processes of teaching and learning and less to the organization of training; and (2) Psychoanalytic education must remain student-centered rather than focus on the committees or teachers who offer this education. Bernfeld notes that once Institutes are founded, a new set of motives keep them going, quite different from what had brought them into being at the beginning. Parkinson's Law much before its time.

Dangers are immediately apparent: Institute leaders become too involved with matters of authority and discipline and ultimately with the exercise of power. Bernfeld cautions against having analysts in training develop these qualities as part of their ego ideal. In authority-oriented systems, candidates may become identified with power but also interested in showing compliance. Similarly,

Hyman warns against Institute-centered responsibility and against infantilizing the student.

Hyman notes that Hans Sachs, who is sometimes described as the first training analyst, withdrew from all offices in his Society and Institute. In writing about this, Bernfeld noted:

> Dr. Sachs saw clearly that the position of training analyst is incompatible with any involvement in society or institute politics. If the training analyst combines the transference authority of a father with the power and authority of office, his job as analyst becomes very different indeed. (1962, p. 464)

The combination of roles and functions presents a major problem to psycho-analytic Institutes. In their book *Psychoanalytic Education in the United States* (1960), published some 8 years after Bernfeld's address to the San Francisco Psychoanalytic Society, Lewin and Ross focus on this pivotal issue. They present the concept of syncretism-problematic combinations of roles and functions. The dictionary defines syncretism as an "egregious compromise—illogical, leads to inconsistency; uncritical acceptance of conflicting or divergent beliefs and principles." Lewin and Ross note:

> Psychoanalytic education as a concept is a syncretism—the two models: the "psychoanalytic patient" and the "student" complement, alternate with, and oppose each other. A psychoanalytic treatment is *sui generis*. The education introduces a parameter for the therapeutic procedure, and the analytic procedure an even larger one for education. The institutes are unavoidably trying to exert two effects on the student—to "educate" him and to "cure" or "change" him. Hence, the student as phenomenon fits into two conceptual frameworks—he is the ped-agogic unit or object of teaching and the therapeutic unit or object of psychoanaly-tic procedure. (1960, p. 47)

I would agree with Lewin and Ross that it is an Institute's responsibility to help protect the treatment from influences outside it. The work of analysis, as we know, is difficult enough without having the analyst play decision-making roles in the candidate's professional life. Whatever its model, each Institute must keep the individual analysis as free as possible of man- or woman-made contaminants. This issue is addressed in various studies of psychoanalytic education, in addi-tion to the one noted by Lewin and Ross, including Goodman (1977) and Wallerstein (1981) (particularly the discussion by Howard Shevrin in the latter), and Shevrin (1978).

Hyman properly warns us about the dangers of contaminating the role of the training analyst. (Incidentally, I believe most of us would agree that a training analysis is essentially a therapeutic analysis.) Even in the beginnings of his work, when Freud conducted training analyses which were truly didactic and where he was eager to demonstrate psychic mechanisms to his analysands, Freud, according to Bernfeld:

> Kept his didactic cases absolutely free from interference by rules, administrative directives or political considerations. . . . He acted as a psychoanalyst should . . . continued this long after the establishment of institutes . . . to the dismay and embarrassment of "the authorities" as he sometimes, and a little ironically, referred to them. (1962, p. 462)

I would agree with Hyman that it is not the training analyst's function to evaluate the candidate in analysis in relation to progress within the Institute. Courses, seminars, and supervision provide opportunities for that. In our Institute, for example, if the training analyst happens to teach a course which his analysand attends (and very few of our analysts elect to do so), the analyst does not submit an evaluation of the candidate's performance in that course. Obviously, the evaluation could add complications to transference and countertransference issues. I would hope, along with Hyman, that training analysts do *not*, as he says, *monitor* and *report* to the Institute, nor evaluate, whether the candidate conforms with the orientation and prejudices of the Institute and its personnel.

A *must* question for our workshops is whether it is possible for the analysis of the individual candidate to proceed without contaminants entering the process from the organization and policies of the Institute. Can the analytic process (what goes on privately between student and analyst) and the educative process (what happens elsewhere in the student's training) move along, both separately (from the administrative viewpoint) but also, ultimately, in a functionally integrated way in the student's total development? These questions are especially critical for the Institute that sees itself as truly committed to emphasizing aspects of the teaching-learning process while also respecting the development of the individual candidate.

Fortunately, Hyman is not proposing to do away with Institutes. But he does raise a central question: Can they exist if they truly accept a student-centered philosophy? He sees a continuum—at one end is the Institute model; at the other, there is no Institute or structure whatsoever. Hyman argues that if students can be assured their efforts will be accepted by the psychoanalytic community (assuming the psychoanalytic community and it representatives have the responsibility for designating who is an analyst), then responsibility for training can be placed entirely in the hands of the student. Ultimately, Hyman asserts, the student can follow any desired pathway, with any admixture of analyst, courses, supervision, and so on, from within given Institutes or outside of them. At the extreme, Institutes become little more than record keepers or purveyors of library cards.

I am not for eliminating Institutes, either. Nor do I even want, here, to try to imagine what it might be like to offer psychoanalytic training without them. We are here concerned with trying to help Institutes become better—for example, working toward augmenting aspects of the teaching-learning process and moving toward greater flexibility regarding student-centered programs.

In the time remaining to me, I want to say a few words about how I believe Institutes can become better. These are matters, it seems to me, that we will want to discuss in our workshops.

The first concerns the subject of supervision. I know we will be focusing on the topic later today.

(1) Early in his paper, Hyman clearly underscores that psychoanalysis is something that one *does*. Fleming and Benedek, in their study of psychoanalytic supervision, describe psychoanalytic training as *experiential learning* (1966). Analysts become analysts by learning to *do* analysis. The supervision of a candidate's early cases plays a pivotal role in the development of the analyst and in the sense of oneself as analyst. The period of time in which the student is trained by an Institute is obviously very short in comparison with his or her total development as analyst. Supervision of the first few cases provides an unusual opportunity to influence longer-range attitudes in addition to helping develop knowledge and skills. In a survey of graduates of our Institute, we learned that their experiences in supervision influenced their attitudes toward themselves as well as toward their work in very significant ways.

But what have our Institutes done for supervisors lately? We appoint them and hope that the individual supervisory sessions will do their magic. We have learned much about supervision in the last 30 years—and though Bernfeld says much about many aspects of psychoanalytic education, nary a word about supervision. Since the early work by Ekstein and Wallerstein (1972), several major works on psychoanalytic supervision have appeared, including the earlier reference to Wallerstein (1981) which contains a major contribution by Herbert Schlesinger, one of our speakers this afternoon. If there is something that can be learned about supervision, there is also something that can be taught. I know our workshops will address the subject of supervision, including what might be done for the training of supervisors.

(2) At this time, we are more or less accepting a training model where courses and seminars, personal analysis, and supervision represent the three essential ingredients of psychoanalytic training. Each Institute, in its way, through its offices, committees, committee chairpersons, tries to implement a training program in which all three ingredients are given room for full development. This is not an easy task. On the one hand, we attempt to keep intrusions or impediments from disturbing the work of instructors, analysts, and supervisors. On the other hand, we try to offer leadership, to provide organization and direction and to facilitate the development of the individuals involved, including the faculty. As my second point, I want to stress an Institute's responsibility to faculty, including supervisors. As we work toward developing student-centered programs, we

may neglect responsibilities to the teachers. They are, after all, also involved in the teaching-learning processes. As we recruit faculty, we also need to consider how best to help them. Faculty want to grow, they want to be better teachers and supervisors, they also cast covetous eyes in the direction of becoming training and supervising analysts. They very much get caught up in the conflicts of having multiple roles and functions—analysts, supervisors, instructors, committee persons. They need as much attention, sometimes more, than the candidates.

(3) My third point concerns the subject of selection. Yes, Hyman reminds us, we have reason to question whether we can predict "who will or will not eventually become a psychoanalyst *with whom we would want to be associated.*" It is the latter phrase to which I will return later. Students, after all, *preselect* Institutes—or in Hyman's view of the non-Institute training model, students preselect becoming analysts *outside* of Institutes. They select the professional specialty but without selecting an institution through which to prepare to become that specialist. An interesting turn of events.

I would prefer a situation where a group of colleagues could make educated guesses whether a candidate would eventually become a psychoanalyst with whom they'd want to be associated. It may not be the whole ball game, but at least provide a feeling in the first few innings how the game might go. Our Institute has the usual applications process, including an interview with an Admissions Committee. But 2 years ago, we began to offer a yearlong course on psychoanalytic theory and therapy to a group of practitioners in the community. Three members of our faculty serve as instructors, and the course is limited to 15 carefully "selected" persons. The day-to-day interactions with these students during the year provide a valuable vehicle for us to find out about these students and for them to learn about us. A few excellent candidates have come forth from these groups. It is a process of mutual preselection.

I doubt that our decision to offer this course was influenced by Bernfeld's article. You can imagine my pleasure, therefore, in reading his description of what he calls "the most natural way of selection." Permit me to quote him:

> If I met someone who impressed me as interesting, talented, passionately interested in psychoanalysis, I would try to keep an eye on him. I would see him in seminars or at a party given by one of my colleagues, and I would have an opportunity to hear how he is doing with his . . . cases . . . (after a reasonable length of time, I would invite him to come as a guest to the scientific meetings of the Psychoanalytic Society. I would introduce him to friends and members in the Society. . . . We (might) invite him to give a paper or participate in discussions. . . . If he is a therapist, we would offer to control some of his cases. Since he is interested in psychoanalysis, he will probably be eager to be analyzed himself. Depending on my time and my countertransference, I would take his for analysis myself or suggest he get on someone else's schedule. . . . Let us say after one or two years, he will have established some social and professional contacts in addition to his meeting the group and to working with control analysts. (Most) of the group will

know by this time pretty well whether they like him and whether they think he is or will be a good analyst or not. Accordingly, one day the group will vote him in or out. (1962, p. 475)

Whatever else we may think about this proposal, to Bernfeld and others it touches on a very basic aspect of the selection process—that is, finding a way, by means of *actual* experience and *direct* contact, to come to some answer to the question: *Does the person interest me?* The method comes close to identifying what someone seems to want, what they seem able to do, and how well we seem to interact. Perhaps it sounds a bit seductive, both ways. But it gives some clues, early on, to an important part of Hyman's question: Is this person likely to become the psychoanalyst we would want to be associated with?

(4) My final comment is related to my interest in selection—it has to do with *evaluation*, a topic that is rarely given attention in discussions about Institutes. Few of us would argue with the notion that all evaluation procedures should ultimately be used as positive learning experiences. From the first admissions interview, through evaluation for readiness for the first control case, to the final case presentation before graduation from an institute, the ways in which these assessment processes are conducted can make quite a difference in what students take from an Institute, especially how they learn to feel about themselves. Evaluation procedures must ultimately be helpful to each candidate. The procedure is used by faculty to judge progress, to the candidate it becomes part of his or her growth. These processes also reflect benchmarks along the way about our selection procedures.

In my opinion, the selection process is not a one-shot experience. It continues throughout the candidate's education. We are learning more and more, each year, about the likelihood that he or she will become the analyst we hope they can be and one we want to be associated with.

Our Institute now has the policy of having two interviews for evaluating a candidate's progress in doing control analysis—the first before approval to start the first case, the second after the candidate has completed supervision with the first two cases. The idea is to follow the student's progress through the major work of two analyses. It should not surprise the experienced psychoanalytic educator to hear that candidates do experience a variety of problems in the course of their work even at later stages. These problems should be reviewed as part of an evaluation process, but these discussions can become helpful learning experiences.

To summarize: Whatever our institute model, or our theoretical bias, our principal missions are to select the best possible candidates and to help educate them, keeping in focus the relative contributions of coursework, personal analysis, and supervision. As parts of these processes, several major points emerge for workshop discussion.

1. Once Institutes are founded, a new set of motives keeps them going, different from what had brought them into being in the first place. There are dangers to the use of authority and discipline.
2. There is a significant problem in seeing the individual candidate both as a pedagogical unit, the object of teaching, and as a therapeutic unit, the object of analytic procedure. Each Institute must reconcile its position in trying to exert both effects on the student, particularly in protecting the individual's treatment from influences outside it. Role confusion for students and faculty is to be evaluated and minimized.
3. Institutes often do not recognize their responsibilities to faculty in providing guidance, as in the area of supervision, or in helping faculty members with their desires for growth and recognition. Even if the Institute is seriously committed to furthering the teaching-learning process, it may only pay lip service to the development of faculty.
4. Evaluation is a part of the continuing educational process and, wherever possible, should contribute to the candidate's total learning. All parts of the educational enterprise have, as their ultimate consideration, whether and how they contribute to each analyst's total development.

REFERENCES

Bernfeld, S. (1962). On psychoanalytic training, *Psychoanalytic Quarterly, 31*, 453–482.

Ekstein, R., & Wallerstein, R. (1972). *The teaching and learning of psychotherapy.* New York: International Universities Press (reprint).

Fleming, J., & Benedek, T. (1966). *Psychoanalytic supervision.* New York: Grune & Stratton.

Goodman, S. (Ed.). (1977). *Psychoanalytic education and research—The current situation and future possibilities.* New York: International Universities Press.

Lewin, B. D., & Ross, H. (1960). *Psychoanalytic education in the United States.* New York: Norton.

Shevrin, H. (1978). The Training analyst: A contradiction in terms. *Contemporary Psychology, 23*, 929–930.

Wallerstein, R. (Ed.). (1981). *Becoming a psychoanalyst: A study of psychoanalytic supervision.* New York: International Universities Press.

12

Discussion of Marvin Hyman's Paper: Institute Training and Its Alternatives

Susannah Gourevitch

I am going to be responding to Marvin Hyman's presentation, since that is the paper I received prior to the convening of the conference.

What is most striking in Marvin's paper is the continuous reference, sometimes explicit, sometimes implicit, to values in psychoanalytic training. While he shows a tolerance for a variety of values in training, it is clear where his own preferences lie and what he holds dear, namely self-determination, self-responsibility in training, openess in outlook, curiosity about the views of others, and open acknowledgment that there can be a wide range of knowledge, skills, and depth of training in psychoanalysis. He thinks that people can affiliate for common purposes and around common interests without necessarily dominating or controlling each other or establishing rigid hierarchies.

There appears to be an underlying assumption that the goals of psychoanalytic training and psychoanalytic treatment should be based on compatible values. In its broadest sense, psychoanalytic treatment promotes as a value a sense of well-being based on profound self-knowledge and self-acceptance, as well as maximum integration of the psyche and the release of creative potential. Psychoanalytic treatment takes place in an atmosphere of tolerance for free speaking and it values the individual per se. Psychoanalytic treatment does not aim to turn out a standard product and, at its best, promotes heightened differentiation of the self, as well as the capacity for intense inner-relatedness. Marvin seems to imply that psychoanalytic *training* ought to set an atmosphere that is relevant to and consonant with the values and goals of psychoanalytic *treatment*. He notes that unfortunately, that is not always the case.

There seems to be an unspoken tension running throughout his discussion, as there is throughout our field, between the emphasis on self-determination and openness in the ideal training model on the one hand, and the question of maintaining standards in psychoanalytic training and controls over the right to represent oneself as a psychoanalyst, on the other. There is a pull between the stress on intellectual freedom and toleration of new ideas versus the need for a common understanding of the meaning of the terms "psychoanalysis" and "psychoanalyst." It is this pull that accounts for the development of "schools" of psychoanalysis and endless controversy over who is and who is not an analyst.

Marvin expresses concern and dismay over that aspect or form of psycho-analytic training that intimidates the student of psychoanalysis and teaches conformity to the views of authority. I myself remember with both amusement and shock when I asked a candidate at the local Institute what he thought of Kohut's latest book and he said he hadn't read Kohut yet because "they" hadn't decided where Kohut fitted in with psychoanalysis. His nervous tone of voice suggested that he wasn't *going* to read Kohut until they *did* decide. Unfortunately, what Marvin says about the negative side of classical Institute training is true in our community too.

Marvin's solution to the problem of intimidating one's trainees by making conformity a condition for graduating is to put the anointing agency at a distance, namely a national examination in psychoanalysis. He thinks he may be "optimistic" in expecting such an examining body to show tolerance for many viewpoints and training methods. But at least the examining body won't consist of your analyst, your supervisor and the local colleagues with whom you must get along.

A national accreditation in psychoanalysis might indeed particularly meet the need of those who have trained outside the Institute channels. This group includes pretty much every psychologist-psychoanalyst-clinician outside of New York and a few other cities that have training Institutes for those who cannot meet the waiver requirements for nonmedical applicants. It would help with the problem of standards and self-identification as a psychoanalyst *if* such an accrediting body agreed with Marvin that superior, or at least acceptable training, could be attained outside of psychoanalytic Institutes of the traditional type. Such a credentialing body might also free those who are trained in traditional Institutes if the candidate could take the exam in the absence or refusal of graduation. The candidate's failure to focus on the resolution of the Oedipus complex in the candidate's analysand might still be a barrier to graduation at some Institutes but might not prove to be a barrier to taking a national exam in psychoanalysis. Moreover, displeasing one's supervisor or questioning what one is taught in class again might not prevent one from taking such an examination. Thus, having accreditation at arm's length from one's training institution might indeed make training both inside and outside of Institutes a more stimulating and freeing experience. All this assumes that such an accrediting board actually maintains a wide view of psychoanalysis and psychoanalytic training.

It is interesting that Marvin's concern with the values promoted by different kinds of training leads him to a model of training similar to that which has spontaneously grown up all over the country where there are psychoanalysts willing to supervise but where nor formal Institute training is available to nonmedical therapists. In Washington, D.C., for example, there have been many mental health professionals who have found teachers to lead classes in psychoanalytic literature, supervise clinical work and provide analytic treatment. This extrainstitutional use of local psychoanalysts and scholars has been going on for 40 years or so and has produced a large cadre of therapists very well versed in psychoanalytic theory and practice. This form of training used to be referred to as "bootleg training" but we now proudly call it the "open model." It operated for years in much the same style as Marvin's Center.

People learned whatever they were interested in learning at the moment, sought supervision and consultation from whomever they chose and sought analytic help in obtaining insight into their character problems from the various local practitioners. The main difference from the Center that Marvin describes was that each person had to figure out how to do this, whom to go to, all by trial and error, a particularly difficult enterprise for the newcomer in town. Having this history of self-initiated training, I think we became very attached to our freedom to think for ourselves. Thus, the Michigan group and the Washington group seem to have come to a similar set of values in training by somewhat different routes, one by thoughtful intention, the other by sheer necessity.

I would like to describe how one recently formalized Washington open model now works. The Association for Psychoanalytic Study provides course work, since that is what has been lacking in a consistent form. Since Washington has such an unusual plethora of highly trained analytic practitioners who are delighted to find a genuine analysand, we feel no need to provide training analysts to our students, although we might offer suggestions if asked. Supervision is a different issue but is widely available if correctly approached. Rather than duplicate the many study groups and open classes already available, we have designed a 4-year course of study for those whose professional training is already of considerable depth. One might say we teach classical psychoanalytic literature in an unclassical way.

A critical approach to discussion of the literature does not need to be encouraged in our group, as our students are experienced enough and quite untrammeled by institutional dogma or burdened by excessive respect for authority. While the faculty have their theoretical convictions, they aim for thorough treatment of every text selected. We tend to think of our program more as education than as training, since the apprenticeship aspect or supervision, is sought outside our program. Unlike a totally open model, students must, on entering, commit themselves to the entire 4-year program. One of *our* values is to form a cohesive group that can work hard and consistently together in the mastery of complex and contradictory material. Since we have a continuing case presentation running parallel to the course work, we enjoy the freedom of presenting all the ups and downs of a genuine psychoanalytic endeavor to known and trusted colleagues.

The longer I work in the field, the more strongly do I believe that one's values deeply affect one's work and one's vision of how both psychoanalytic training and psychoanalysis should be carried out. I am grateful to Marvin for having raised this issue in such a forthright and honest manner. I share his hope that psychoanaytic training in 1990 will be as exciting and innovative as it was in its very beginnings.

13

Introduction: Components of Psychoanalytic Training: Personal Analysis and Supervision

Ester R. Shapiro

The session on *components of psychoanalytic training: personal analysis and supervision* addressed the fundamental question: How does a candidate learn to become an analyst? Everyone agreed that a candidate needed both a personal analysis and supervision of analytic cases, but what is the relationship between these two aspects of training? While each paper differed in the particular problems of the training analysis or supervision which it addressed, the conclusions were remarkably consistent: when the candidate's personal analysis becomes the central place in which to learn how to conduct analysis, the entire educational process is seriously compromised.

Murray Meisels, Ph.D., referred to Schecter's (1979) critical review of the literature as background reading to his presentation on the training analysis. Schecter pointed out that from the organizational beginnings of psychoanalytic training, especially in the history of the American Psychoanalytic Association, control struggles over the right to appoint training analysts have dominated psychoanalytic education. She described the training analysis as creating a "syncretistic dilemma," in which two contradictory, irreconcilable goals, the therapeutic and the institutional/didactic, are simultaneously expected. Because the training analysis confuses real dependence and transferential dependence, Schecter and others argue that analytic candidates are more vulnerable than any other patients to unresolved infantile dependence on their analyst. In contrast, Fleming and others insist that the training analyst has a responsibility to the Institute and to the community to make judgments about the candidate's progress. Schecter countered that this "parental" attitude encourages the shallow goal of analysis by identification with the analyst. She concluded that any institutional involvement in the candidate's personal analysis interferes with its

107

essential goal, to provide intensive, experiential learning of psychoanalytic process.

Expanding on Schecter's discussion, Meisels proposed that the training analyst, in addition to being part of institutional politics and processes, suffers from a particular "typical" countertransference, in holding a strong set of values about what another analyst should be like. Training analysts act on, and act out, this countertransference by experiencing a strong sense of responsibility to the profession, to the Institute, to their own careers, or to future patients of the analysand. Meisels concluded that these realistic or "typical" transference and countertransference problems can be addressed directly in psychoanalysis, and need not undermine the psychoanalytic process. Meisels proposed that the training analysis continues to have an unfavorable reputation, because analysts often return to analysis after graduation. He suggested that practicing professionals pursue additional treatment for positive therapeutic and professional goals, rather than because their first analysis was necessarily a failure.

John Gedo, M.D. referred readers to two essays as background to his presentation on the training analysis (Gedo, 1984). In these essays, Gedo argued that psychoanalysis has become primarily a professional school oriented toward training competent clinicians, to the detriment of the intellectual and scientific development of psychoanalysis. He proposed a model for an intellectually rigorous interdisciplinary program based on independent study achieved through individualized tutorials. The high caliber of students who would be attracted to such a program will not need requirements, because they will want to master the fundamentals of psychoanalytic study as a matter of course. Gedo suggested that there is a conflict of interest between psychoanalytic educators and scientists, who are interested in training the broadest interdisciplinary group, and practitioners who temporarily benefit economically from the restriction of psychoanalytic training to physicians. He argued that the limitation of psychoanalytic education to physicians has led to a deterioration of the therapy as well as the science. Increasingly, psychoanalytic practice has become a ritualistic healing technique in which failures are attributed to failures of technical purity or failures of the patient's character, rather than to scientifically examined qualities of outcome.

In his presentation at the conference, Gedo focused on the problems generated by making the training analysis an institutional requirement. In an intellectually rigorous educational environment, students will themselves independently seek out a personal analysis as a means of expanding their self-knowledge. The institutional requirement, motivated as it is by competition for theoretical dominance or economic self-interest on the part of the training analysts, interferes with the original goal of providing the analyst with a living experience of the analytic transaction. Even in institutions with a nonreporting policy, training analysts are prone to make insidious, "off-the-record" statements that their analysands are doing well and are excellent recruits to the analytic cause.

Further, attempts at addressing countertransference problems which come up in supervision are rejected by both candidates and supervisors alike, so that both the training analysis and the supervision conform with the lowest common denominator as a standard.

Sabert Basescu, Ph.D. began by stating that the definition of analysis as requiring a certain frequency of sessions, as suggested in Meisel's paper, or analysis as requiring a regressive re-experience of childhood trauma as suggested by Gedo, is not to be presumed but examined (Gill, 1984). He agreed with Gill that analysis should be evaluated by intrinsic, rather than extrinsic, qualities. He suggested that the training program should intervene in the candidate's personal analysis as little as possible, and that the proving ground of the training process should be the candidate's work as an analyst. The great majority of the students at the interdisciplinary Institutes where he teaches are highly motivated, have had treatment prior to entering the Institute, and do not need the program to establish requirements for personal analysis. These Institutes suggest guidelines for a certain level of experience but leave the choice of the personal analyst to the candidate. If the candidate's analyst is on the Institute faculty, he or she leaves the room when their analysand's educational progress is discussed. These Institutes do require that at least some part of the personal analysis be concurrent with the period of psychoanalytic training, because of the enormous personal impact of psychoanalytic training itself.

Ava Siegler, Ph.D., described four educational models implicitly applied in psychoanalytic training: the religious or monastic model, the guild or trade union model, the art academy model, and the university model. Analysts would like to think that their training programs integrate the artistic and intellectual models, but more often they resemble taking the vows of a religious order, or undertaking a guild apprenticeship. Siegler warned against use of the personal analysis for the purpose of teaching the analysand how to conduct an analysis, because this creates the danger of trapping generations of young analysts in an unconscious infantile identification with an institutionally approved ego ideal. She saw supervision as the opportunity for the candidate to integrate the scientific, artistic, and therapeutic aspects of psychoanalysis, examine the clinical data, explore and test hypotheses, develop the artistry of a well-timed intervention, and become deeply fascinated with the complexity of the human mind, from which effective therapy emerges. She described supervision as a developmental experience which needs to be attuned to the particular candidate's developmental situation.

Herbert Schlesinger, Ph.D., noted that the personal analysis has come to be considered the most important aspect of a psychoanalytic education. Many programs proceed as if the training analysis needs to be protected from undue interference by other aspects of training, especially from supervision, as if the training analysis is fragile and easily distorted. Schlesinger argued that a training analysis is necessary but not sufficient in teaching candidates how to analyze patients, and that its primary function should be to support what the candidate is able to gain from supervision of control cases. Candidates do learn how to conduct an analysis from identification with their analyst, often unconscious. He suggested that these unconscious identifications as they are manifested in the candidate's analytic work with controls should be directly addressed in supervision. The training analysis should lay the groundwork for the candidate to attain a psychoanalytic education, by analyzing personality barriers that interfere with the candidate's capacity to analyze patients.

In sum, the presenters agreed that it is useful to make a conceptual distinction between a "personal analysis," which every candidate in psychoanalytic training should experience, and a "training analysis," is burdened as it is with institutional conflicts and goals that interfere with the personal analysis. The most significant problem of the training analysis is the use or the training analysis as a means of conveying what a good analyst should be like, with the conscious coercion that the training analyst could interfere with the candidate's realistic educational process, and the unconscious coercion to become an analyst in the image of the training analyst or the institution. Supervision of analytic cases, which should provide the opportunity to integrate coursework and personal learning in the analytic work itself, has suffered by being relegated to secondary status so as to protect the training analysis. Although there is a great deal of agreement in the psychoanalytic literature, as well as among the speakers, concerning these conclusions, many Institutes are still directly involved in the candidate's personal analysis, because of the economic advantage or personal power accrued with training analyst stature.

REFERENCES

Ekstein, R., & Wallerstein, R. (1972). *The teaching and learning of psychotherapy.* New York: International Universities Press.

Fleming, J., & Benedek, T., (1966). *Psychoanalytic supervision.* New York: Grune & Stratton.

Freud, S. (1910). The future prospects of psychoanalytic therapy. *The standard edition of the complete psychological of Sigmund Freud* (Vol. 11, pp. 141–151).

Freud, A. (1971). The ideal psychoanalytic institute: A utopia. *Bulletin of the Menninger Clinic, 35,* 225–239.

Gedo, J. (1984). *Psychoanalysis and its discontents.* New York: Guilford Press, Chaps. 11 & 12.

Gill, M. (1984). Psychoanalysis and psychotherapy: A review. *International Review of psychoanalysis, 11,* 161–179.

Schecter, D. (1979). Problems of training analysis: A critical review of current concepts. *Journal of the American Academy of Psychoanalysis, 7*(3), 359–373.

Schlesinger, H. (1981). General principles of psychoanalytic supervision. In R. Wallerstein (Ed.), *Becoming a psychoanalyst.* New York: International Universities Press, pp. 29–38.

Wallerstein, R. (1985). *Becoming a psychoanalyst: A study of psychoanalytic supervision.* New York: International Universities Press.

14 The Personal Analysis

Murray Meisels

SUMMARY

The analytic literature is filled with despair about the training analysis, many viewing it as compromised and doomed because the analyst reports on the analysand and others trying to rescue it from doom by arguing for the elimination of the reporting function, while in fact the graduates of one reporting and one nonreporting Institute overwhelmingly regarded their analyses as successful treatments. Many of us have heard horror stories about destructive training analyses, about analysands who do not tell their training analysts about certain life experiences, or about analysts who are only interested in certain aspects of the analysand, and many of us hold the training analyses in ill repute. Yet, survey studies indicate that countertransference-ridden analyses are in the minority and that most treatments are helpful. If so, why do two-thirds of Division 39 members pursue more than one treatment? Does the pursuit of a second analysis mean that the first analysis was a failure, or might the first analysis still be a success? It is the writer's point of view that much of the literature and controversy about the role of reporting is a deflection from the more penetrating issue of why multiple analyses are so commonplace and whether this fact compromises the robustness of psychoanalysis as a psychotherapy.

The history of psychoanalysis is replete with phenomena which were at first thought to be antianalytic but which were later incorporated as fundamental features of the enterprise. Transference was first viewed as a hindrance, and so too countertransference. The writer posits that the personality of the analyst defines the limits of the transitional space in the treatment and thereby restricts the possibilities of the transference, that some analysands may need more than one treatment anyway, that a second analysis does not necessarily mean that the first was ineffective, and that multiple treatments do not mean that psychoanalysis is compromised as a therapy.

Several definitions are offered. The *training analysis* is defined as that required by an organization, while the *personal analysis* is the total history of personal treatments of an analyst. The *pathological countertransference* is defined as the training analyst's own personality reaction, and it is the major factor associated with unsuccessful treatments. The *typical countertransference* is defined as the analyst's strong set of values about what another analyst should be like, and is connected with reporting and other breaches of confidentiality, although it is not connected to unsuccessful outcomes. A *typical transference* is associated with the analyst's actual control of the real-life career of the analysand. These typical transferences and countertransferences are seen to arise inevitably in a training analysis and, like fees and other reality issues, it is likely that they are best dealt with by open and frank discussion between the participants.

THE PERSONAL ANALYSIS

The analysis of the analyst was originally termed a "didactic" analysis, then a "training analysis," and is now often referred to as "personal analysis." The idea of analyzing the analyst has been long established as the most direct route to the analyst's subjective apprehension of the reality of psychoanalytic phenomena, especially of unconscious processes and transference. The term that describes this analysis is important, and different terms yield different implications. Thus, to call it a didactic analysis emphasizes the knowledge aspect; to call it a training analysis emphasizes its role in a training program; and to call it a personal analysis emphasizes the personal quest of the analyst an analysand. Since the personal analytic histories of analysts are usually far more extensive than the requirements of Institutes, it is useful to define the training analysis as that required by a training organization while the personal analysis can be defined as the total history of personal treatments of an analyst.

There are various problems connected with training analyses, and I should like to review these under four major headings. These are: first, splits in Institutes associated with designating who is and is not a training analyst; second, the special analytic issues particular to training analyses; third, the problem of reporting; and last, a typical transference-countertransference configuration particular to training analyses.

PROBLEMS WITH THE TRAINING ANALYSIS

1. Splits in Institutes

In her paper on training analyses, Schecter (1979) highlights two significant problems, and the first of these is the often stormy and bitter issue of who becomes a training analyst. Schecter (1979) cites such writers as Arlow and Fleming, who state that the major conflicts and splits in Institutes of the American Psychoanalytic Association have focused on the issue of who shall and who shall not be a training analyst. The warning here is clear enough: Training programs that designate training-analyst status invite the likelihood of conflict and the possibility of a split. In the greater New York area there have apparently been splits in psychologists' Institutes which has taken the form of spin-off groups, such that a subgroup dissatisfied with the lack of training-analyst status may establish a new Institute and thereby designate themselves as training analysts. However, no one in the literature calls for the elimination of the designation of the category of training analyst, that is, there seems to be agreement that only certain, presumably more qualified, analysts should train. One possibility here is to designate as training analyst anyone with, say, 5 years of experience after completion of a training program. Such a policy might derail and defuse the political tensions associated with this issue.

2. Special Issues

Many writers have considered that there are special features of a training analysis which make it problematical. As illustrative of this material, I shall summarize two presentations that were made at a panel on the training analysis that was presented at recent meetings of the American Psychological Association in Washington. Ernest Wolf (1986), a self-psychologist, argued that the very admission to an Institute and the start of a training analysis may activate such intense self-aggrandizement that the ensuing idealizing transference, and corresponding idealizing countertransference, may compromise the work of the analysis. A second presentation, by Allan Cooper (1986) an interpersonalist, outlines several special problems. These included: (1) That the analyst is not anonymous since the patient-candidate may know a great deal about the analyst, this occurring through direct observations at meetings and classes, by reputation, and by gossip; (2) That because of this reality, certain transferences may never develop—he gives the example that a patient with a "weak" father may never develop a father transference to his world-famous "strong" analyst; (3) That patients may be less revealing of personal pathology; and (4) That the analyst's countertransference is stronger for a candidate than a noncandidate analysand, because the training analyst will usually have a strong set of values about what an analyst should be like, and because the success of the student may have real-life importance to the analyst.

Neither of these writers, however, considered that these special features made analystic work impossible. Just more difficult. For example, from a self-psychologist's point of view, Wolf (1986) emphasized the importance of the analyst's maintaining a proper ambience in the treatment and from an interpersonalist view Cooper (1986) stressed the necessity for the analyst to bring into the treatment obvious reality matters if the patient does not do so.

3. Reporting

The effect of reporting on the integrity of the analysis is a problem highlighted by Schecter (1979) and many others. The problems here are usually viewed as serious and, to some, presents an unresolvable dilemma. The analyst, for a particular patient, is not simply an analyst, that is, someone who tries to understand, but is also a judge and jury, someone who has control of the real-life career of the analysand, a condition which may induce dissimulation, defense, conformity, idealization, or other reactions which are widely held to interfere with, even to preclude, genuine analytic involvements. Some have described the training analysis as necessarily more of a didactic experience because of these reality factors, so that the analysand must go on to a second analysis for a genuine experience. In summary, there is a strong theme in the literature on the training analysis that it is not a good analysis, that it produces conformity, and that a second analysis might be called for. The argument, however, is somewhat circular here: One reason for concluding that training analyses are not successful is precisely because psychoanalysts frequently pursue more than one personal analysis. Typically, the second analyst is also a training analyst. (It would be of great interest to study the perceptions of second analysts regarding what transpired in the prior analysis; and it would be of even greater interest to compare that perception with the view of the first analyst and, for that matter, of the analysand.)

To sketch a summary of much of the literature on training analyses, it seems that the reality of reporting is seen as the major factor which prevents full involvement on the part of the analysand so that a genuine analytic process may not occur. This is a point of view that would particularly appeal to Robert Langs and his followers, who argue that any disruption in the analytic frame precludes successful work until the frame is rectified. Well, this frame would appear to be easy enough to rectify, and many have in fact argued for the elimination of the reporting function, and the historical trend is toward nonreporting. In fact, according to a 1982 article by Orgel in the *International Review of Psychoanalysis*, 17 of 24 Institutes of the conservative American Psychoanalytic Association have nonreporting policies, so the issue of the significance of reporting versus nonreporting may be largely academic.

4. The Typical Transference-Countertransference Configuration

I define the typical transference of the candidate as reactions to the analyst's actual control of his or her real-life career, and I define the typical counter-transference as the analyst's strong set of values about what another analyst should be like. Those writers who advocate reporting, such as Fleming (1973), have, to my mind, articulated and acted on (acted out?) this typical counter-transference. Thus, training analysts experience a strong sense of responsibility not just to their analysands but also to the profession, to psychoanalysis, to their Institute, to their own careers, and even to the future patients of their analysands. This is an important issue to the analyst, and the moral absolutism in the writings of Thomas Szasz on the subject (e.g., 1962) lose immediacy and impact precisely because they sidestep this strong sense of professional responsibility on the part of the analyst. I view this sense of responsibility as a typical countertransference.

The responsibility of the training analyst and the institute toward psycho-analysis is often experienced as an immense one—after all, these are the trainers of generations of analysts. Like any countertransference, if it is not handled appropriately it may be acted out, that is, is may prevail even if the Institute prohibits reporting. I want to document this assertion. In two recent articles published in *Psychiatry*, Dulchin and Segal (1982a, 1982b), two sociologists, studied the communication network at an Institute whose historic and explicit policy was not to report. This Institute, called Eastern Institute by the writers, developed a procedure in which the injunction not to report was systematically violated. What happened was that the training analyst would sit in on meetings at which the candidate-analyst was discussed, and would make non-verbal sounds or gestures if the Education Committee seemed to be reaching a conclusion contrary to the training analyst's opinion. Or, a proxy of the training analyst would inform the Education Committee about which direction the decision had to take. And, material learned about the candidate from other confidential sources, such as through analyses of the candidate's spouse, relatives, and fellow stu-dents, such analyses being performed by other senior analysts at the Institute, was also used anonymously in evaluations by the Education Committee. Further, in one controversial case that had long been debated by the Education Commit-tee, actual material from the training analysis was openly discussed at the Education Committee. I remind the listener that all of this took place at an Institute whose historic policy was antireporting. Thus, it is reasonable to draw two conclusions from the sociologists:

1. A nonreporting policy may not stop analysts from reporting, or, stated differently, the injunction to preserve the confidentiality of candidates loses in the struggle for professional integrity.

2. The analyst's value system is an important ingredient in the analysis.

I have chosen to label the analyst's value system as a countertransference reaction for a variety of reasons. First, those writers who advocate reporting seem to argue from a position of objectivity, as if the world is that way: They write without due recognition of the subjectivity that is involved, of the emotions and even irrationality of the analyst's position. Second, by labeling the value system a countertransference it can be placed in the network of analytic understanding, that is, it is part of that aspect of analytic work connected with the analyst's apprehension of his or her own subjectivity. Like any countertransference, it varies in intensity from patient to patient, varies in intensity from one phase of analysis to another, and may have particular subjective meanings to the analyst, meanings which may be quite different from apparent issue. Further, the countertransference may speak directly to the problems of the patient. This last countertransference form was called by Winnicott (1975) the "objective countertransference." Third, labeling the value system a countertransference makes it another factor to use in analytic work.

SOME COMMENTS ON THE LITERATURE

There are four observations that I should like to make about the psychoanalytic literature in this area. First, the training analysis is widely viewed as a lesser analysis and the reporting function is largely held to be the cause of this. Second, there is almost complete unclarity about what reporting means. Reporting has been defined along a continuum to include: (1) Reporting the material of the analysis; (2) Reporting on the readiness of the candidate for major steps, especially starting coursework, starting controls, and graduation (but not reporting on the material); or (3) Only reporting that the candidate has completed the analysis. Nonreporting has been held to mean such diverse matters as: (1) Absolutely no reporting of anything to anyone (which in the extreme means no verification that the candidate was analyzed); (2) Reporting that the analysis is favorably concluded; and (3) Sitting in on meetings of the Education Committee and not speaking. The third observation, noted by Weinshel (1982) and others, is that material about training analyses is not published because of the confidentiality issue, so that abstract discussion replaces clinical history, and the whole matter spins off into speculations that are simply not backed by any data—not by systematic data, not by clinical data, not even by vignettes. It also seems to me that the whole discussion starts off on the wrong foot, and seems to stay there. The point of view in the literature is always that of the Institute, or of the training analyst, or of the second analyst, but never the view of the analysand: the analysand, and his or her perception and experience of these analyses, is almost never referred to. On the whole, it is a "superego literature," and the analysand's ("id") motives are deemed suspect.

SURVEY STUDIES

This is particularly peculiar since there have been some survey studies on the effect of the training analysis on candidates at Institutes. There are three surveys that I am aware of, in addition to some material that I have collected that is pertinent. The earliest study was by Thomas Szasz (1962), who conducted a survey in the late 1950s of the American, British, and Canadian psychoanalytic associations. One of his questions was whether training analysts should report, and 71% of the American respondents said yes. Of these, a fair number were "yes, but . . . " responses, such as (paraphrasing), "Yes, but only as necessary." Of the "no" responses, many of those were, "No, but . . . " responses, such as (paraphrasing), "No, unless it is necessary," so that many of the "yes" respondents actually favored minimal reporting and many of the "no" respondents actually favored some reporting, and consequently the actual number favoring some reporting would be far higher than 71%. Szasz's view of these findings can be aptly described as a moralistic one, since he asserts that psychoanalysis can only occur with absolute confidentiality.

What is rather clear to me is that his findings indicate that at least 71% of a group of psychoanalysts believe that reporting is a reasonable activity, a conclusion they would likely not reach if they viewed it as destructive of the analytic process. In other words, they apparently believed that the damage that might be done by reporting would not be such as to destroy the analytic process. It really could not be otherwise, or else the entire training analysis would long since have been banished.

The second study was reported by David Shapiro (1974, 1976) and is based on a 1970 questionnaire of 123 graduates of the Columbia Psychoanalytic Institute, an affiliate of the American Psychoanalytic Association. At the Columbia Institute, the training analyst was described by Shapiro as reporting since he or she gave recommendations about readiness for controls, about readiness for coursework, and about readiness for graduation. Shapiro seemed to be appalled to find dissatisfaction with the training analysis to the extent that some treatments were unsatisfactory to the candidates—now analysts. Shapiro states (1976, p. 22) "The extent to which difficulties were attributed to the training analyst was both unexpected and disappointing to me," since one-fourth of the respondents, 32 individuals, ascribed major or severe problems to the training analyst, which means that the analysts weren't such good analysts (this, despite the designation of training analyst). It makes sense to me that an analysis will not yield good results if the analyst is grossly disturbed or in the grip of what Racker (1968) called a countertransference neurosis. It does not make sense to me to assert, *ex cathedra*, that all training analyses are necessarily bad because of the analyst reports, since this does not specify the mechanism which produces the effect. The conclusion that 25% of a group of analysts may manifest countertransference problems should not be surprising when we recollect that Chief Justice Warren Burger of the United States Supreme Court stated that 50% of trial attorneys are not qualified to represent their clients.

There seems to be a narcissistic issue here. The idea that training analysts may be beset by personal pathology and severe countertransference problems, and that graduates from Institutes may continue to be troubled by serious psycho-pathology, may be experienced as a narcissistic injury to the extent that one entertains an idealized, grandiose view of psychoanalysis. Shapiro is downcast. He writes: "The general impression may be accurate that training analyses tend to be pallid as compared to the emotionally heated transference reaction that often arise in analysis under nontraining conditions." He does not quite believe another of his own conclusions, which has great bearing on our discussion, that, after all, 75% of the respondents did not find that the analyst's reporting was a problem or, if so, then only a slight problem. Let me summarize Shapiro's results:

Finding No. 1: 104 of 122 graduates, 86%, found the training analysis to be highly satisfactory or generally satisfactory, while 18 graduates, or 14%, found the training analysis to be somewhat unsatisfactory or very unsatisfactory. My conclusion: training analyses are generally experienced as satisfactory.

Finding No. 2: 31 graduates, or 25%, found that the analyst's counter-transference was a significant problem during training, countertransferences not related to the analyst's dual role (i.e., training and evaluating functions). My conclusion: countertransference problems in the training analyst are common.

Finding No. 3: 17 of the 18 graduates who rated their training analysis as unsatisfactory ascribed severe or major problems to the training analyst. My conclusion: Poor analysis yields unsatisfactory results.

Finding No. 4: Overestimation or excessive identification with the training analyst was a severe or major problem for 13 graduates, 11 of whom reported satisfactory results. My conclusion: Global identifications with the analyst are not usual occurrences, and are typically workable analytically.

To summarize my conclusions from Shapiro's survey, I would say that most training analyses are experienced as successful, that countertransference prob-lems are widespread but usually ironed out in the treatment, and that unsatisfac-tory results are connected to pathological countertransference problems. I imag-ine, I hope that these conclusions would also apply to any set of analysands, and I would view the training analysis like any other analysis.

PERSONAL ANALYTIC HISTORIES

Before trying to explain the bad reputation of training analyses, let me summa-rize the results of one other study, and of my own data and observations. The third study was by Sidney Goldensohn (1977), who surveyed graduates of the

William Alanson White Institute in the early 1970s, and found that graduates were very positive about their education and training. He found that 89.5% considered their training analysis to be very helpful or somewhat helpful, a statistic which is remarkably close to Shapiro's 86% finding for the Columbia Institute. Still, almost 55% of the White graduates went on to further treatment. Fully 38% of the respondents reported an additional psychoanalysis with someone who was not a training analyst at the White Institute, and these analyses were judged even more helpful than the training analysis. (Goldensohn used a 4-point scale in which 4 is very helpful: the training analysis was rated 3.49; the second analysis was rated 3.73.) Goldensohn notes that the survey item only asked about second analyses by analysts who were not at the White Institute, so that the 38% who pursued further analysis excludes those who returned to their own training analyst or to another analyst at the White Society. According to Goldensohn, the comparable figure for Columbia graduates was 20%.

In addition, 43% of the White graduates, or 59 individuals, used other psychotherapeutic modalities after graduation. These 59 graduates had 80 treatment experiences, including group therapy, family therapy, and couples therapy, and these were also rated as very positive experiences (for example, group therapy was rated at 3.59). All told, at least 55% of the White graduates had pursued further treatment, and at least 20% of the Columbia graduates did so.

The data that I collected were part of the 1980 membership survey of the Division of Psychoanalysis (Meisels & O'Dell, 1980). 327 of the then approximately 900 division members returned the questionnaires. The pertinent questionnaire item read: "Have you had a personal analysis or personal therapy?" If the respondent checked yes for analysis, he or she was asked how many hours and how many analysts; and if the respondent checked yes for therapy, he or she was asked how many hours and how many therapists. The results were that 84% of the respondents had been analyzed, 13% had therapy but no analysis, and only 3% had not had a personal treatment experience. The median number of analytic hours was in the 800s for those who only reported analytic experience, in the 500s for those who reported both analytic and therapeutic experiences, with an additional 200 therapy hours, and those who only had therapy reported a median number of hours in the 200s.

The results of the survey of the Division of Psychoanalysis indicated that multiple treatments were the rule, not the exception, since approximately two-thirds of the respondents reported more than one treatment experience. I wrote:

"These results, that two of three seek more than one treatment, are very striking. And humbling. If we surrender the image of the perfectly analyzed analyst we can at least satisfy ourselves with the notion of 'good-enough analyzing'. Yet, if we analyze other professionals, it is more than likely that they will seek re-analysis . . . and, even if we do the second analysis, there still appears to be a one in three chance that the analysand will seek yet a third treatment. (p. 5)

I suggested that ". . . we might give up the idea of "good-enough analyz-ing" and substitute the idea of a holding environment or container" (p. 5). In that paper, I also cautioned that conclusions drawn from analyses of profession-als may reflect but one aspect of the analysand's analytic history. The fact is that the training analyst is aware of but one phase of what may be a lengthy personal analytic history of the analysand.

I want to spend a few minutes talking about such histories. The data that I have to report here are unfortunately not systematic. Rather, these are impres-sions that I gathered by reviewing the personal analytic histories of hundreds of Division 39 members, material that I was privy to because I as a cochair a few years ago, of the Membership Committee of Section I, Psychologist-Psychoanalyst Practitioners. At the time, 1983–1984, Section I had just devel-oped a membership application form, and applications flooded in, and I reviewed all of them, hundreds of them. My overall impression, not backed by recorded data, is that approximately two-thirds reported multiple analyses, that the median number of years of analysis reported was probably 7 or 8, and that the median number of hours of analysis reported was probably nearly 1,000. My recollection is that approximately one-quarter to one-third had more than 10 years of treat-ment and that perhaps 10% had 15 or more years of treatment and 2,000 or more hours. I well recall meetings of the Membership Committee at which these extensive personal-analytic histories were reviewed. I was fascinated to find histories such as the following, which are schematic and not actual histories: Someone's first analysis started in the 1960s, lasted 7 years ending in 1974, and that a second analysis started in 1975 and was still continuing in 1983. Or, someone had a 6-year analysis with an analyst, then returned after a 2-year hiatus for an additional 4 years with the same analyst. Or, a 4-year analysis and then a 5-year analysis. Or a 10-year analysis and a 5-year analysis. It seemed to me that a fairly high percentage, perhaps 10% of this senior cadre of analysts, were still in analysis. At the meetings of the Membership Committee, I would often stop and ponder these matters, although I confess that they seemed to be more striking to me than to other committee members. First of all, since we discouraged applicants from reporting nonanalytic therapeutic encounters, it was entirely possible that their personal therapeutic histories were in fact far more extensive than the analytic histories that we as a Section I Membership Committee were interested in. In fact, we had to change the application form to discourage applicants from telling us about all of their therapeutic experiences—we had to put in bold type: "Only report 3 times-a-week treatments"—but even then applicants kept reporting about one-time-a-week and two-times-a-week treat-ments (a finding which suggests that many applicants viewed those experiences as analytic, else why report them?). What impressed me so were a host of questions: What transpired in the first analysis? A year or two or three after termination, the psychologist started a second analysis. What was happening then? How does the psychologist rate the results of the first analysis? Of the second analysis? How does the psychologist rate the first analyst? The second analyst? What was the role of countertransference in these analyses? Was the one analyst male, the other female? Was one classical, the other object-relational? Did one focus on oedipal issues, the other on pre-oedipal issues? Was one a training analysis, the second a nontraining analysis? Another question: In the psychologist's view, was the training analysis, if he or she had one, different from the nontraining analysis? It seemed to me then and it seems to me now that we have a wealth of information about psychoanalysis contained in the personal analytic experiences of our own cohorts, and that we could likely learn a great deal about the therapeutic action and effects of psychoanalysis by systematically studying ourselves.

At this point, I should like to draw a picture of the training analysis that is different from the negative image presented in the literature. I think that the bad press given to training analyses derives from two sources: First, a certain number of such analyses do indeed fail. Second, large numbers of analysands pursue second analyses and/or other treatments even when the training analysis was successful. Some may perceive the pursuit of a second analysis as directly meaning that the first analysis failed. After all, if the transference neurosis is resolved, there should be no need for a second analysis. The perceived failure of the training analysis is then attributed to an unfortunate but unavoidable circumstance that the analyst reports to the Institute. The reporting function, which has been much discussed, debated, defended, and vilified in the literature, may, in my view, be a distraction from the real issue of why analysts seek multiple analyses, and whether this means that psychoanalysis is less effective than thought.

However, the fact that 86% and 89.5% of graduates of two Institutes found their training analyses to be helpful or satisfactory is a very strong statement that the training analysis is effective. Indeed, these may be some of the strongest results in the entire psychotherapy outcome literature, and they indicate that psychoanalysis is a potent instrument. The fact that graduates seek further analysis does not mean that the first analysis was a failure, although this is the case in a minority of instances. For most people, the training analysis was helpful, and the second analysis was also helpful, albeit probably in a different way. The fact that many analysts seek more than one personal analysis may speak to the nature of psychoanalytic process, or to the nature of emotional demands that are placed on practicing professionals. In terms of the nature of psychoanalytic process, the first analysis may have focused on oedipal issues, the second on pre-oedipal issues: The first may have been with a male, the second with a female (as Jungians recommend), or the first may have focused on the past, the second on the present, and so on, and the complementarity between the two treatments may facilitate greater self-knowledge that one treatment alone. Given that the person of the analyst strongly affects the transference-countertransference configuration and the ensuing analytic material, it may in fact be therapeutically advantageous to experience more than one analyst and more than one analytic style, and to work out material now with one approach, now with another.

As an analogy, a violin student may study or many years with one teacher, and then with a second teacher. The fact that the student studies with a second teacher does not mean that the first teacher was a failure. The first teacher would likely be more helpful than not, and so to the second teacher. The violinist, for example, may have learned fundamentals from one teacher and musical expression from the other. A professional violinist would be one who would more likely study with more than one teacher.

In this light, it is of interest to discuss Kohut's two analyses of Mr. Z. Since the second analysis was more helpful than the first, it is common for Kohutians to view this case history as a dramatic example of the revolutionary power of the psychology of the self, while classical analysts have dryly commented that in the second analysis Kohut did what he should have done in the first place. In my reading, both treatments seem plausible, since certain analytic events transpired in the first analysis and other analytic events in the second. The technique and thinking of any analyst likely develops with time, and patient issues may similarly change as life calls forth particular dynamisms, so I would suggest that any reanalysis would be different from the first analysis, and that the experience of the first analysis would contribute in diverse ways to the success of the later experience.

I would like to draw the following conclusions:

1. Everyone favors the idea of the analyst experiencing a personal analysis.
2. The training analysis seems to be about as successful as any other analysis. Unsuccessful training analyses appear to be most likely the result of severe countertransference problems.
3. Psychoanalysts more often than not pursue more than one analytic experience, and frequently pursue nonanalytic experiences as well.
4. The reporting function of the analyst is not the apparent cause of unsuccessful first analyses, and does not seem to impact on the success of the treatment. Concern about the importance of the reporting function seems to be a function of the analyst's predominating countertransference, which derives from the analyst's value system about psychoanalysis.
5. As many have stated, the special features of the training analysis provide material for analytic understanding. Given a mature, nonpathological analyst and a reasonably developed analysand, these issues would be ironed out analytically.

REFERENCES

Cooper, A. (1986). *The training analysis: From an interpersonal (Sullivanian) perspective.* Paper presented to American Psychological Association, Washington, August 23.

Dulchin, J., & Segal, A. J. (1982a). The ambiguity of confidentiality in a psychoanalytic institute. *Psychiatry, 45,* 13–25.

Dulchin, J. & Segal, A. J. (1982b). Third-party confidences: The uses of information in a psychoanalytic institute. *Psychiatry, 45,* 27–37.

Fleming, J. (1973). The training analyst as a educator. *The Annual of Psychoanalysis, 1,* 280–295.

Goldensohn, S. S. (1977). Graduates' evaluation of their psychoanalytic training. *Contemporary Psychoanalysis, 5,* 51–64.

Meisels, M., and O'Dell, J. W. (1980). A preliminary report of the 1980 membership survey of the Division of Psychoanalysis (39) of the American Psychological Association. Mimeo. See also M. Meisels, & J. W. O'Dell, A synopsis of findings of the 1980 membership survey, *Psychologist-Psychoanalyst,* 1980, *1,*(II), 8–10.

Orgel, S. (1982). The selection and functions of the training analyst in North America. *International Review of Psychoanalysis, 9,* 417–434.

Racker, H. (1968). *Transference and countertransference.* London: Butler & Tanner.

Schecter, D. E. (1979). Problems of the training analysis: A critical review of current concepts. *Journal of the American Academy of Psychoanalysis, 7,* 359–373.

Shapiro, D. (1974). The training setting in training analysis: A retrospective view of the evaluative and reporting role and other "hampering" factors. *International Journal of Psychoanalysis, 55,* 297–306.

Shapiro, D. (1976). The analyst's own analysis. *Journal of the American Psychoanalytic Asociation, 24,* 5–42.

Szasz, T. S. (1962). The problem of privacy in the training analysis. *Psychiatry, 25,* 195–207.

Weinshel, E. (1982). The functions of the training analysis and the selection of the training analyst. *International Review of Psychoanalysis, 9,* 434–444.

Winnicott, D. W. (1975). Hate in the countertransference (original, 1947), In D. W. Winnicott (Ed.), *From pediatrics to psychoanalysis.* New York: Basic Books.

Wolf, E. *The training analysis: From a self-psychological (Kohutian) perspective.* Paper presented to American Psychological Association, Washington, August 23.

15

Position Statement on the Training Analysis Question for Worcester Conference of Division 39, American Psychological Association

John E. Gedo

In a previous discussion of the unavoidable difficulties inherent in the education of psychoanalysts (Gedo, 1984, chap. 2), I articulated the view that it is counterproductive to include the personal analysis of candidates in a set of requirements for professional qualification. I would assert that if we make the overall educational program rigorous enough, this stringency will suffice to screen out applicants who might otherwise abuse a system that refrains from concerning itself with the private problems of its students. I assumed then and still believe that individuals possessing the proper qualifications to achieve real adequacy as psychoanalysts will, in fact, strive to master their personal conflicts and to overcome their psychological deficits by seeking psychoanalytic assistance from the best clinicians available to them. It is hardly necessary to provide such candidates with a scorecard about the competence of their senior colleagues, in the form of a list of so-called Training Analysts, in order to protect them from falling into the hands of less than satisfactory clinicians.

The matter can be put even more strongly from the opposite vantage point: It is common knowledge that psychoanalysts have often been disappointed with the outcome of analyses conducted under the official auspices of an institution. We would do well to remember that the business of our educational institutions is to ensure that their graduates have surpassed an agreed-upon standard of adequacy—not to act like oversolicitous parents who would intrude upon their offspring with continual reminders about doing homework, brushing teeth, or performing an "analytic toilette."

I am well aware that my recommendation is utopian, for the Training Analyst system was established not for the benefit of students but for that of psychoanalytic faculties. Not only does it forestall the development of heterodox ideological positions by requiring candidates to choose analysts who conform with the views prevalent at the Institute; it also gives the senior members of the faculty an effective monopoly on a substantial amount of clinical work. Many of you will recall that the American Psychoanalytic Association, in its surveys of the activities of its membership, found that on the average Training Analysts carried two analytic cases more than did practitioners who were not designated to perform the treatment of candidates. By my rough calculations, the average Training Analyst has two candidates in analysis; in other words, this official appointment permits him or her to fill almost a quarter of a full-time practice with analytic work unavailable to his competitors. In the contemporary buyer's market, this is an economic advantage so decisive that we cannot expect anybody to give it up.

In order to minimize the antitherapeutic impact of the quasicompulsory system of treatment they have established, many Institutes now attempt to make as complete a separation as possible between the training analysis and other aspects of the educational experience, although we should not forget that it is still quite common to urge inadequate students to overcome their handicaps by having some more analysis. I shall come back to this irrational procedure in a moment; but first I should like to go on record with the claim that it is essentially fatuous to believe that any analysis conducted under Institute auspices can remain immune from public scrutiny. In any case, the most damaging of "leaks" is the habitual tendency of Training Analysts to communicate, mostly without words but occasionally via "off-the-record" statements, that *their* analysands are doing well and constitute excellent recruits to the psychoanalytic cause. I have been a Site Visitor to half-a-dozen Institutes of American Psychoanalytic Association and have found the phenomenon of such "convoying" to be ubiquitous. Nor is this vicious practice to be laid directly at the door of individual Training Analysts; their friends and admirers will do it on their behalf, whether they expect it or not. The problem was already apparent in Berlin and Vienna; could an analysand of Abraham, Ferenczi, or Freud ever be disqualified?

A personal analysis is invaluable for the would-be psychoanalyst even if he or she does not need treatment to overcome psychoanalogical problems, for there is no substitute for the living experience of an analytic transaction as instruction in every aspect of the procedure. This fact actually formed the basis of making the "training analysis" a required and preliminary part of Institute curricula from the very inception of organized psychoanalytic training. Over the years, however, this rationale has been subordinated to the legitimate therapeutic aims of these analyses. From the vantage point of the candidate, this shifting of priorities is actually desirable, for the therapeutic regression necessary to set the analytic process in motion is unlikely to occur without a personal motivation for change. To state this is quite a different matter, however, from the widespread expectation on the part of Education Committees that the candidate's training analysis should eliminate various obstacles in the way of his or her analytic effectiveness.

Am I trying to say that a personal analysis cannot eliminate any of these obstacles? Not at all. We are all very familiar with dramatic examples to the contrary. To speak only from my own, limited experience as an analyst of younger colleagues, I have witnessed the lifting of characterological impediments to the work—for instance, of largely unconscious but profound, settled convictions that patients are the victims of childhood abuse and are in need of compensatory therapeutic experiences of empathy and love. Many years of analytic work were required before the candidate in question became capable of allowing his patients to re-experience the horrors of their childhood within a transference setting. In another instance, the obstinacy and rebelliousness embedded in an obsessional character structure had to be overcome before the prospective candidate could hope to gain anything from supervised experiences or classroom instruction. And so forth. I have no doubt that the better an analyst has been analyzed, the more capable he or she will be of the broadest range of effectiveness in his or her work.

At the same time, we must face the fact that almost everywhere candidates are permitted to start analyzing patients under faculty supervision before having achieved perfection in their personal analysis. This practical necessity has impelled the American Psychoanalytic Association to recommend to its Institutes that they make the best of a bad situation. Candidates are now *expected* to be in analysis through most of the period of their supervised experience. In these circumstances, as supervisor, I have encountered occasional problems in informing supervisees about gross instances of countertransference or counteridentification difficulties because, in conformity with the constraints of their own analytic progress (or the lack of it?), they were not prepared to accept such judgments from anyone but their idealized analyst. In some cases, candidates discontinue such a contentious supervision to seek out instruction that does not challenge their illusions about the perfection of their analysis.

On the other side of the same coin, as Training Analyst, I have learned about severe problems of the same kind that candidates were unwilling to discuss with seemingly complaisant supervisors—to put the matter differently, the supervisor's positive evaluation of the candidate unsatisfactory clinical performance created well-rationalized obstacles to the illumination of certain primitive enactments on the stage of the candidate's clinical work. In other words, both training analyses and supervision conducted under Institute auspices tend to conform with the lowest common denominator prevalent within that setting, and faculty members who hold out for higher standards are likely to be labeled as hostile, unreasonable, and arrogant.

In my judgment, the only way to mitigate the problem of eroding standards is uncompromising rigor on the part of Education Committees. The burden of proof of satisfactory performance must be on the student. If the problem is remediable through further analysis, the decision to make an effort to remedy it should be the candidate's alone—it is not a matter psychoanalytic educators need to address directly. As far as I can judge, moreover, most of the obstacles encountered by candidates in learning to analyze are *not* remediable through any form of personal treatment. They are the consequences, instead, of the student's cognitive style, or capacity to perceive psychological configurations, or skill in encoding ideas in language meaningful for the person addressed, or other abilities and disabilities in the performance of the manifold tasks of a psychoanalyst. We do not recommend a therapeutic analysis for prospective musicians, athletes, scholars, or mathematicians who are lacking in talent for their chosen endeavor—why do we continue to pretend that our "impossible profession" is accessible to anyone who can obtain a graduate or professional degree?

In actuality, though "many are called, few are chosen." The most frequent disability I have encountered among would-be psychoanalysts is the need to understand every bit of clinical material in terms of some familiar category. To put this differently, many candidates are so bedazzled by the similarities between their observations and the patterns they have been taught to look for that they are essentially unable to note the differences also present. Such rigidities are often rationalized by looking upon psychoanalytic generalizations as universal biological truths. Yet this resort to illusions of possessing some key to the secrets of human nature is merely intended to allay the anxiety of confronting a field of limitless possibilities the candidate is incapable of organizing in a meaningful manner. The most flagrant instance of this problem in my experience was that of an analysand who was literally unable, without the assistance of his wife, to grasp the story line of the movies he attended. Psychoanalytic narratives utterly bewildered him; he had no choice but to accept the judgment of his supervisors about which of our clinical theories might be most applicable and to try to force the patient's communications into that mold. After many years of analysis that yielded enormous benefits in other areas, there was no real change with regard to this cognitive limitation.

Nor did several periods of analysis overcome the crucial handicap of one of my supervisees, a man who was largely unable to put any but the simplest and most concrete of messages into language with consensual meaning. He was quite skilled at reading and conveying affects through gestures, facial expressions, and the paraverbal aspects of speech, so that he was a rather successful psychotherapist, but the task of encoding complex meanings into secondary process continued to elude him. I should perhaps add that both this person and the analysand I spoke about a moment ago were men of superior ability as measured by standard tests of intelligence, and they had done better than well at educational institutions with stringent requirements. Yet neither was any better suited to be a psychoanalyst than to be a ballet dancer.

Instead of trying to give you further examples of individuals' lacunae in talents essential for a psychoanalytic career, let me conclude by reminding you that I have offered these vignettes in order to illustrate that the most important qualifications for our profession, constitutional and acquired, must be freely available to the candidate who matriculates in our Institutes: The training analysis cannot be burdened with the magical expectation of turning a sow's ear into a silk purse.

REFERENCE

Gedo, J. (1984). *Psychoanalysis and its discontents*. New York: Guilford Press.

16 Personal Analysis

Sabert Basescu

Although my topic in this presentation is the role of one's personal analysis in psychoanalytic training, I would like to preface it with some more general commentary on characteristics of psychoanalysis. There is, by no means, universal agreement as to defining characteristics. For example, some claim it is not psychoanalysis unless the frequency of sessions is at least three times per week, or four, or five. It used to be six. On the other hand, there are those of us who feel that while there are advantages to more frequent sessions, psychoanalysis can be conducted on a less than three-times-a-week basis, with at least some people. The relationship between frequency and efficacy is most often assumed, but rarely investigated.

Similarly, there are those who feel that the regressive re-experiencing of early childhood trauma, or the formation of a transference neurosis, is essential for the psychoanalytic enterprise. But, there are those of us who feel that such developments may not only not be necessary, but may even be detrimental to progress. It may be the case that people change not because of a transference neurosis, but in spite of it. This too is an issue about which assumptions are made in the absence of investigation.

The use of the couch is another feature often assumed to be a necessary condition of psychoanalysis. My own opinion is that it is not only not necessary, but even contradictory to basic tenets of interpersonal psychoanalysis. Ah, that may be the rub! Perhaps we are headed toward a recognition that there is more than one kind of psychoanalysis. Or that our conception of psychoanalysis must be broadened.

Some of these issues are cogently discussed in Merton Gill's paper, "Psychoanalysis and Psychotherapy: A Revision," in the *International Review of Psychoanalysis*, (1984, vol. 11, p. 161).

In examining the role of personal analysis in training, I will rely heavily on my own experience as a faculty member at five different analytic Institutes. This experience, while varied, may be biased in that they are all in the New York area.

To begin with my conclusion, the less requiring, the better. The less the training program intrudes on the candidate's personal analysis, the better for the analysis. The proving ground is the candidate's work as an analyst. The supervisors' and instructors' evaluations of that work are the true and final tests of the candidate's readiness.

A distinction is often made between a training, or didactic, analysis and a personal analysis. In my view, it is fallacious to make a distinction between the two. It is either a personal analysis or it is a mechanical, cognitive exercise. The fact that it may be required is irrelevant to the conduct of the analysis itself—or at least it should be. Contrary to the notion that candidates frequently go on to a personal analysis when they finish their training analysis, I've seen very few candidates who have not had rather extensive analyses before they ever applied for analytic training. Most of the people who are interested in training as psychoanalysts are up to their ears in the kind of self-examination that has long since led them into personal analyses.

In most cases, there is no problem getting candidates into analysis. About 90% of the candidates, on their own, are doing the things that any training Institute would require them to do. There is sometimes a question, however, about who the analyst is.

Most of the Institutes I'm familiar with require that the analyst be a graduate of a recognized training program and have at least 5 years of posttraining experience. And most do not require that the candidates' analysts be members of the Institute, although obviously they often are.

The involvement of the analyst in the candidate's training and evaluation is not an issue when the two are not members of the same Institute. When they are, it has been my experience that whenever the discussion of a candidate arose, the analyst would leave the room. That protection for the sanctity of the analytic relationship may be partly obliterated by the ways in which analysts can indirectly communicate their feelings about their candidate/patients. I have not witnessed that to be a major problem. The consensus among the faculties of the Institutes I'm familiar with is essentially that the analyst should remain separate from all other aspects of the candidate's training.

There is a question as to when a relevant personal analysis takes place. Is a prior analysis acceptable? How much prior? Most of the candidates have had prior analyses or prior analytic experiences, if not completed analyses. I'm not sure that the field is in a position at this point to make a determination as to what constitutes a completed analysis. Many people have multiple analyses that go on after their training experiences. Life goes on. Problems arise. People in the field value the experience of analysis as a vehicle for furthering self-understanding.

What has happened with the Institutes I'm familiar with is that they tend to arrive at the judgment that candidates should be in analysis for at least part if not all of their training. As a result of the stresses and strains of analytic work and the kinds of personal and emotional reactions, problems, and experiences that are elicited by working analytically, candidates feel it is quite appropriate that they be involved in their own analytic experience while they are training as analysts. For example, at the Westchester Center for the Study of Psychoanalysis, we do require that candidates be in analysis during at least some part of their training. Here again, the supervisors' evaluations of the work are the proving ground. That is the litmus test of the candidate's readiness, not some appraisal of the candidate's personality independent of the work.

Frequency and duration are probably the issues that have caused most controversy in the field. I find it hard to see how effective analytic experience can be defined by numbers. That is not to say that I don't feel it is often more effective and helpful to work more intensively than less intensively. But the history of our field suggests that the magic number has changed over time, and it has changed for reasons that have nothing to do with the effectiveness of the work. It went down from six and seven times a week in Europe to five times a week in the United States because American analysts liked their weekends. And, as Clara Thompson points out, it went down to four times a week because analysts wanted longer weekends. And during World War II it went down to three times a week because of problems with transportation and expense and so on. I don't think there has ever been an objective study to determine the correlation between effective analysis and frequency of attendance.

What has happened in analytic Institutes that I'm familiar with is, because of the variety of points of view ant theoretical divisions among the faculty, there have been accommodations and compromises. For example, at New York University we formerly required 240 hours, preferably in 2 years but no longer than 3. Now we require 300 hours without any stipulation as to duration. At the Westchester Center, a policy that has evolved over time now stands as follows: Candidates are required to have at least a 1-year experience at three times a week, and it is highly recommended that they have at least a 2-year experience.

Finally, the issue of fees, which is one that I think training programs are going to have to pay more attention to. Are the fees the candidates pay the analysts when their analyses are considered part of the training program privately arranged or set by the program? I think when candidates are required to be in analysis with a member of the Institute, then the Institute should be involved in some stipulation of the fees, for example, requiring each training analyst to be available for at least one candidate at a reduced fee set by the Institute. If candidates are not required to have analysts from the same program, it is much easier to let that be a private arrangement, although the Institute could still make the same stipulations for its faculty.

That sums up my own experiences and opinions. I repeat the conclusion that the less intrusion in a personal analysis on the part of the training Institute, the better for both the candidates and the Institute.

17 Supervision and the Training Analysis: Repetition or Collaboration?

Herbert J. Schlesinger

Formal psychoanalytic training as we know it today has been described as a tripartite arrangement, or more figuratively, as a stool that stands on three legs: the training analysis, supervision, and the didactic curriculum. Anyone who knows the system intimately, however, would observe that unlike a stool, the three legs are not of equal size or importance. Whatever the actual contribution of each "leg" is to the personal and professional growth of the candidate toward becoming a competent psychoanalyst, analytic educators tend to give most weight to the training analysis, next to the supervision, and least to the didactic curriculum. We see these weightings most clearly in the arrangements that Institutes make for the appointment and assignment of training analysts, and the mystique that surrounds the training analysis.

Becoming a training analyst is the pinnacle of professional ambition in psychoanalysis. The individuals who hold this position exert great power and influence in Institutes and our professional associations. The quality of the training analysis, however one might define or measure quality, is held to be the key element in the successful passage of the candidate through the Institute. The question usually asked if difficulties in training arise is, "Is the candidate analyzable?" not, "Is he or she teachable?"

Institutes give relatively low weight to the didactic curriculum, as can be seen in the care (or lack of care) taken to evaluate its effectiveness, the relative lack of standards for the appointment of teachers, the relative casualness with which Institutes conduct the didactic curriculum and the general lack of concern for the integration of the didactic curriculum into the tripartite structure.

I shall consider here mainly the supervision element and in particular its relationship to the training analysis. Only secondarily will I refer to its relationship to the didactic curriculum. While the training analysis is now assigned the greatest responsibility for the success or failure of the training enterprise, it was not always so. Historically, the training analysis became institutionalized fairly late in the development of our field. As colleagues gathered around Freud to study the new science of psychoanalysis, and to learn how to become practitioners, the only educational agency other than this colloquium and reading was individual supervision. The training model was informal and consisted essentially of apprenticeship. Having what one hoped would be a suitable case, one sought the advice and counsel of a more experienced colleague. The idea that it would be useful for the would-be analyst to have some analysis of his or her own came later, and did not become prescribed for psychoanalytic training until the organization of formal Institutes, the first of which was in Berlin in 1925.

It would be interesting to trace the history of this differential attribution of value to the three elements of training, but that would take us too far afield. I will concentrate instead on the effects of exalting the training analysis above the other two elements, and in particular on the fear, which I believe is widespread in Institutes, that unless much care is taken, supervision is likely to impinge unfavorably upon the training analysis, and distort it, and also intrude upon the prerogatives of the training analyst.

When supervision is discussed seriously, as in a seminar for supervising analysts, and such seminars are rare events in Institutes, one frequently hears this concern expressed. Especially if one colleague advocates a more active teaching stance in order to address a supervisory problem, others will fear that the supervisor would then certainly be intruding on the task of the analyst, and remind the group that one must be careful not to try to analyze or therapeutize one's supervisee. One even hears that the supervisee should "not be allowed" to say certain things to the supervisor that "belong to the analysis." The training analysis seems to be viewed as a delicate affair that could easily be disrupted by incautious supervision and possibly other extraneous factors. In contrast, I believe the training analysis, like all analyses, is quite a sturdy affair, and the analyst has ample resources at his disposal to deal with intrusions, real or fancied.

But this turn in my discussion begs the question of what the proper relationship should be between the supervisory process and the training analysis. The assumption underlying my discussion thus far is that the training analysis is indeed the main leg of the stool, and most responsible for the success or failure of the training endeavor. This attribution, as everyone is sadly aware, persists in spite of widespread awareness that many presumably competent analysts are themselves as persons miserable and unfulfilled, while other, presumably well-analyzed persons are at best indifferent analysts.

It would not be difficult to make the case that there may be no relationship at all between the success of one's personal analysis, and one's ability to analyze. One may well be sufficiently analyzed for all practical purposes and yet have no special talent for helping patients to analyze. From this stance, the primary importance given to the training analysis could thus be seen to be both mistaken and possibly harmful.

If this position is cogent, what is the place of the training analysis in psychoanalytic education? I shall make the case that the training analysis is indeed essential to analytic training, if not primary, because it is indispensable to support the supervisory process, which I propose is the most important of the three legs.

It is generally recognized that the training analysis has several functions. It is altogether a good idea for the would-be analyst to have some taste of the analytic process as it involves oneself as patient. It is good also to learn firsthand about what one means to do to or for others. Indeed, this simple familiarizing function was recognized quite early. The term "training analysis" after all derives from the German *Lehranalyse*, which is more literally translated as "teaching analysis." The original point was simply to acquaint the would-be analyst with the nature of the analytic experience. Some months of analysis was considered sufficient for that purpose. It was only later that more ambitious purposes were conceived for the training analysis, such as the possibility of prophylaxis or that the would-be analyst might have therapeutic purposes of his or her own to achieve on the way to becoming an analyst. But, for most would-be analysts, the requirement of a *Lehranalyse* was hardly necessary. They after all became interested in becoming analysts as a result of the therapeutic experiences of the analysis they had originally sought to deal with their own neurotic problems. For many, no doubt, wanting to become an analyst was a derivative of that therapeutic experience and probably reflected unanalyzed transferences to their analysts as well as difficulties in terminating the personal analysis, but that is a story for another occasion.

While conceding that it is important to acquaint the would-be analyst with the nature of the experience, and also to resolve to the extent possible his neurotic problems (which is not essentially a training matter), I propose that the main function of the training analyst is to support the analytic work done by the candidate with several supervisors.

At least some Institutes recognize the centrality of this purpose by requiring that the candidate be in training analysis during the first supervised case. But even under this enlightened policy, the reason usually given is that attempting to do analysis may reawaken neurotic problems of the would-be analyst, and thus indicate that more personal analysis is needed. It is not usually stated explicitly that the training analysis, or more accurately, continuing personal analysis, might be essential in order to support the supervisory process by dealing with the candidate's neurotic inhibitions of the capacity to analyze, or what are usually if not correctly called "blind spots."

The reader will surmise from this inversion of the usual value system that I do not have great respect for the educational value of the training analysis. This point has also been made repeatedly in the literature, usually under some heading that implies the question, "is the training analysis training or analysis." Usually after making trenchant observations that "analysis ought to be analysis" no matter what adjective precedes it, the point is allowed to dissipate with a bland statement such as, of course, "both values are served."

From the vantage point of having done supervision for many years, I believe that the educational value of the training analysis has been vastly overestimated. I do not want to be misunderstood here. I believe a personal analysis, and a very thorough personal analysis, whether it is called training analysis or not, is essential to the total process of becoming an analyst. It is necessary, but not in any way sufficient. Calling it a vital or essential element does not make it an education one in the sense that it imparts specific content or skills needed to become an analyst.[1] Let us consider the function or task of the training analysis. We might discuss first that it helps prepare the ground or a psychoanalytic education. It does so by treating, in the ordinary analytic sense, neurotic or characterological disturbances that could make it difficult to become an analyst. These disturbances might give rise on the one hand to inhibitions, failures to observe, insensitivity or reluctance to draw proper inferences, ("blind spots" or "dumb spots") or on the other hand to tendencies toward impulsive behavior. These training analysis may also have some prophylactic value by alerting the candidate to areas in which he or she may be vulnerable to regression, and the circumstances under which it may be precipitated. It also serves to let the candidate explore at leisure the meaning of the wish to become an analyst. As I observed earlier, however, I believe its main *educational* value only becomes realized when the candidate starts to do supervised work. At that time, the material of the supervised work—the relationship between the candidate and the patient, and also the relationship between the candidate and the supervisor will furnish "material" galore for the training analysis. The major question than becomes, "what will the mill do with this grist?" One would hope that the training analyst will see the opportunity to take up issues that probably were noticed before, but perhaps not in such an urgent context. Paradoxically, the supervisory situation may in fact make the training analysis a better personal analysis by providing a kind of laboratory exercise in which the fruits of the analysis either can be demonstrated or shown to be lacking.

But the main educational tool or procedure for learning to become an analyst

---

[1]Candidates do, nevertheless, learn quite a bit about analyzing in the personal or training analysis. I use "learn" here in the way behaviorist might, behavior is altered as a function of experience; candidates tend to conduct analyses in the way their analysts dealt with them. Usually the adoption of the analyst's style, technique, mannerisms, and even accent is unwitting—a form of Skinnerian behavioral modification; though in this context one might prefer to refer it to unconscious identification. In either event, if the supervisor inquires about why the candidate acts in that way, the candidate is generally at first astonished that there could be another way, and then realizes sheepishly that it's the way his or her own analyst did it!

is supervision. It is here that the "educational diagnosis" must be made. Unlike the training analyst, who has only one function[2]—to analyze—the supervisor has at least two. The supervisor must not only teach, or better allow the candidate to learn, while providing a setting that facilitates learning, but he or she also must evaluate whether in fact the candidate is able to learn, is actually learning, and what the limits on his or her professional growth might be. An essential aspect of evaluation is communicating ones observation effectively (i.e., respecting "dosage" and timing) to the candidates so that they can recognize the problem and, to the extent that it reflects a neurotic problem, work on it also in the training analysis. Evaluating in the supervisory situation takes great skill. Making and refining an "educational diagnosis" is a complicated and subtle process, one in which under the best of circumstances, candidate and supervisor will collaborate. I mean collaborate quite seriously. Evaluation ought not to be an adversarial process. After all it is in the candidate's best interest also to discover what he or she needs to learn, and whether psychoanalysis is the correct field to invest one's lifetime.

By educational diagnosis I mean broadly does the difficulty we are seeing represent a "dumb" spot or a "blind spot." Does it reflect an area of ignorance for which additional information or experience might help, or an area of neurotic inhibition or impulsivity, for which more analysis would be the instrumentality of choice. Usually, of course, the difficulty reflects some of both, since a neurotic inhibition will also interfere with acquiring relevant information, but it is generally more one than the other.

An educational diagnosis may also involve a third issue, difficulties in learning in the supervisory situation. Supervision is no more a panacea than is the training analysis. Supervision can be done well or badly, and the supervisor's knowledge about analysis in general, about the personality and dynamics of the patient he or she hears about only secondhand, and about teaching in a dyadic situation may all be wanting. We should not blame the student for the sins of the teacher. But the candidate may also manifest what are fairly described as resistances to learning. These resistances show up regularly in the supervisory situation. It is, after all, a situation which has some impressive parallels to the analytic situation. There is a candidate and a supervisor, who is not incidentally also an analyst. The subject matter is analysis, and the temptation may be strong for the candidate to put oneself in the place of the patient as the subject matter for supervision. There is the opportunity to compare the approach of the supervisor with that of one's analyst. There is also the clear opportunity to displace transferences, or to develop independent transferences, to the supervisor.

Rather than being seen as inevitable and possibly even useful, the possibility that neurotic expressions may emerge in supervision is regarded by some supervisors as an avoidable evil. I have heard it suggested quite seriously that if the

---

[2]I am assuming a "nonreporting" Institute.

supervisor does *not* pay attention to expressions of the candidate's neuroticism, transferences, or resistances in supervision they will go away. Other supervisors, I should add in the interest of fairness, find the temptation so strong to take over and improve on the analysis of the candidate that if they are not to act on it, they must deal with it by suppression or avoidance. I believe, in contrast, that in failing to take up in supervision the neurotic disturbances that interfere with the candidate's learning, the supervisor shortchanges the candidate, and imposes unnecessary limits on psychoanalytic education.

The question, however, which surely has occurred to you also, is how can the supervisor deal with the candidate's neurotic difficulties, call them resistances or whatever, in the supervisory situation without intruding upon the training analysis and without taking over inappropriate analytic or therapeutic functions.

I leave the question open, with the expectation we will address it further in our panel discussions and workshops.

18

Finding One's Voice in the Analytic Chorus: Some Thoughts About Psychoanalytic Education

Ava L. Siegler

The education of psychoanalysts raises crucial questions about the entire nature of the psychoanalytic enterprise. Do we limit the training of candidates to only the technique and methods of psychoanalytic practice? Do we teach candidates psychoanalytic theory as the basis of a general psychology, (as Freud envisioned it)? Or do we enlarge our cultural scope to include psychoanalysis as "a whole climate of opinion," to make use of Auden's felicitous phrase?

In his 1926 paper, *A Question of Lay Analysis*, Freud directly addressed the issue of a complete psychoanalytic education:

> "If, which may sound fantastic today, one had to found a college of psychoanalysis . . . alongside of depth psychology (which would always remain the principal subject) there would be an introduction to biology, as much as possible of the science of sexual life, and familiarity with the symptomatology of psychiatry. Analytic instruction would also include the history of civilization, mythology, the psychology of religion and the science of literature . . . . Unless he is well at home in these subjects, an analyst can make nothing of a large amount of his material. (p. 246)

It is striking how far short of this ideal course of study most of our psychoanalytic training falls. How are we holding up our end?

Psychoanalytic education has traditionally been supported by three structures which merit inspection: (1) didactic instruction, (2) the training analysis, (3) supervision.

141

DIDACTIC INSTRUCTION

The actual coursework we offer our candidates seldom makes reference to any of the studies Freud suggests in the context of an ideal psychoanalytic education. Rather, we either assume in our candidates prior exposure to myth, religion, literature, biology, and psychiatry, (no matter how brief) or, what is worse, we ignore the contribution of these fields to the professional training of a contemporary psychoanalyst.

This is largely because we have implicitly adopted certain historical models in setting up our training centers. These models have explicit limitations which continue to exert their pressure on our institutions.

1. *The religious or monastic model.* Here questions of faith, dogma, belief, abstinence, and heresy are central to the analytic calling. But what can be gained in consistency and constancy of purpose is often lost in vitality and freedom of thought.

2. *The guild or trade union model.* In this model, psychoanalysis is conceptualized as a technical craft to be mastered through a rigorous apprenticeship, wholly controlled by senior members of the guild. Since the guild holds out the promise of both financial livelihood and membership to its apprentices, its political life is rife with rivalries and restraints.

3. *The art academy model.* Here the emphasis falls on the selection of candidates with special talents, and there is a high level of competition in order to gain acceptance into the academy. Once inside, one learns special skills from master teachers. A professional livelihood is not necessarily the outcome of one's studies, and individuality rather than colleagiality is applauded.

4. *The university model.* Here, only the capacity for intellectual inquiry is necessary to one's ongoing study, and the demonstrated acquisition of a body of knowledge testifies to one's advancement and eventual certification.

Most of us would wish to think of psychoanalytic education in the context of the last two models, that is, an art academy allied with a university—art and science, hand in hand, with their shared enjoyment of rare talent and intellectual mastery. But, more often than not, institutional psychoanalytic training, in both its procedures and its politics, is more vulnerable to the critical limitations of the first two models: taking the vows of a religious order, or undertaking a guild apprenticeship.

Freud concluded that his new discipline could/should be approached from three vantage points:

1. As a general theory of mind,
2. As a scientific method of investigation,
3. As a therapeutic treatment.

Alas, most psychoanalytic training, dominated as it has been by the medical establishment, has almost exclusively focused on psychoanalysis as a therapy. Freud himself worried about this narrow focus. In 1922, he wondered if training in the therapy would eventually ruin his newly established science, (a concern raised more recently by Phillip Holzman).

On the other hand, an exclusive preoccupation with psychoanalysis as a scientific method of inquiry, could similarly constrain our vision. We could wind up, as Leo Stone feared, in a sort of

> Genteel quasi-retirement; a type of practice where patients who are prosperous, intelligent, gifted, articulate, not really very sick, but genuinely curious about themselves, are treated by scholarly and scientifically committed analysts, unimpeded by intrusive therapeutic responsibility. (1975, p. 356)

Meanwhile, the challenges of psychological research over the past decade (infant studies, splitbrain exploration, evoked potential experiments et al.) have clearly precipitated us into a new psychoanalytic era in which the ideas developed by Freud in the last century, may yet take their place in a theory of mind in this century. Yet we seldom present any courses which analyze research to candidates, nor do we place psychoanalysis in the larger framework of general psychology, or of culture.

All of this suggests that in order to be adequate, let alone excellent, a contemporary psychoanalytic education should address all three of the approaches originally outlined by Freud: psychoanalysis as a theory of mind, as a method of investigation, and as a therapeutics.

THE TRAINING ANALYSIS

And what of the second structure upon which psychoanalytic education has rested, the training analysis? Surely, though didactic instruction may be a bit shaky, the training analysis remains sturdy? It has been the traditional means by which an analysand could be transformed into an analyst. Indeed, in the early history of psychoanalysis, it was practically the only means to a professional psychoanalytic end.

The assumption that one's analysis *can* or indeed *should* be at the core of psychoanalytic *learning* rather than psychoanalytic *experience*, derives its justification from the guild model of training with its accompanying ideas of apprenticeship. Thus, the institutional persistence of the term, "training" analysis.

As Stone states, "With regard to the so-called training analysis, any colleague of some experience knows that its distinction from therapy is essentially fictive." (1975, p. 353)

And if it is not? If, in fact, the training analyst attempts to teach the analysand how to conduct an analysis from his or her own treatment, might not the entire analysis be called into question? Would we not be in grave danger of producing generation after generation of young analysts trapped in an unconscious infantile identification with an institutionally approved ego ideal? We are caught in a paradox: If there is *no* difference between a training analysis and any other well-conducted personal analysis, then the vast institutional fabric we have woven about the title seems threadbare. If there *is* a difference, then both the therapeutic and the educational intent of such an analysis is hopelessly contaminated.

This is not to say, of course, that a well-conducted psychoanalysis is not central to the emotional well-being of the candidate and essential to his or her professional life. Rather, I would like to make the point that while both didactic instruction and a personal analysis are *necessary* to a psychoanalytic education, it is only in the unique experience of analytic supervision that a psychoanalytic education can become *sufficient*.

This is because one becomes a psychoanalyst only by beginning to think psychoanalytically, and one can only learn how to think psychoanalytically through consistent and persistent exposure to this point of view. In supervision, all the previous strands of one's education begin to be gathered, and one's fragmented ideas begin to feel as if they are cut out of whole cloth.

SUPERVISION

The supervisory experience has been likened to the psychoanalytic situation itself. It is true, for instance, that the supervisee shares an aspect of the patient's plight: He or she is both the *observer* and the *observed*. It is also true that (as in psychoanalysis) considerable *power* and therefore considerable *peril* accrue to the supervisory experience. Because of this similarity, both psychoanalysis and supervision must take place under conditions of complete emotional safety. But here I wish to limit the analogy, because the differences between psychoanalysis and supervision are more crucial than their similarities, and not to take note of this constitutes a corruption of both experiences.

For one thing, the bargain between supervisor and supervisee is entirely different than the one entered into by an analyst and an analysand. This means that both the data generated within the experience and the uses to which this data are put, must also be entirely different. The psychoanalytic method relies heavily on the interpretation of conflict, particularly in its reappearance in the transference. The shared educative focus of supervision leaves no room for, and no authority for, interpretation; inasmuch as it would be based on insufficient evidence, it would constitute wild analysis. In supervision, patterns of personal limitation may be noted for the supervisee, but they may not be interpreted.

If we stay within its proper boundaries, supervision offers us something splendid, indeed: a way to integrate our scientific, artistic, and therapeutic concerns. Together, both parties will embark on a scientific journey. This journey will require careful observation, exploration of the data, the generating of hypotheses, and finally, a proper search for confirmation. Is this not a way to bring the science back into the therapy?

At the same time, supervision offers us an opportunity to encourage the artistic development of the candidate. As one chooses the timing, shape, and placement of one's intervention, one's own ingenuity is evoked. And it is here that we will make use of his special talents, his or her "natural" abilities for which he or she was so carefully selected.

It is through the supervisory process, too, that one can most fully convey the depth of the fascination with the devotion to the human mind. Whatever is curative in the psychoanalytic encounter will emerge out of this devotion.

Since all learning is always embedded in a developmental framework for both the teacher and the student, at any particular point in the process, one must know what theory is being taught to what candidate, at what time in his training, and by whom? The supervisor, the supervisee, *and* the theory are all undergoing dynamic change from moment to moment. In fact, it is psychoanalytic theory itself, which teaches us that as the mind develops, old information takes on new meanings, and one's understanding broadens and deepens. Because of this, the supervisor must taken into account the capacities and the limitations of his or her student, as well as the level of the student's experience with the matter at hand.

For the supervisor, this will turn out to be a matter of theoretical competence, clinical skill, strategical inventiveness, and personal style. For the supervisee, it is probably a matter of character, maturity, receptivity, and talent. A good supervisor, like a good analyst, has the power to conceptualize and communicate in ways that the supervisee can hear and absorb. While all psychoanalytic teachers who wish to maintain their moral integrity attempt to *practice* what they *preach*, psychoanalytic supervisors must meet another challenge; they must find a way to *preach* what they practice.

All education leaves a filmy residue of unconscious process which clings to the candidate's identity. Because of this, the supervisor must particularly encourage the candidate to define and defend his or her own position. Otherwise, we will be left with psychoanalysts who go by the book, but will never write any new chapters.

In a good supervisory hour, the candidate should be offered an opportunity to discover and to develop. Food for thought must be laid out on the table, but not shoved down the candidates' throat, stifling their own voice. It is crucial that we begin to take notice of the original in psychoanalytic training. If we continue to ask of a colleague, "Who was her analyst? Who was his or her supervisor?" as if hoping to ensure that he or she will be stamped from the same mold, we may find ourselves like Freud, lamenting that "the goody-goodies are loyal but dull, and the naughty ones leave." As this becomes the case, we will produce mediocre psychoanalytic technicians with nothing in particular to say, and no unique voice to be heard.

One last thought. Perhaps there is another model of training which is more suitable to the making of a psychoanalyst that the ones we have previously described. I refer to the training of a concert pianist: One would begin, of course, with a passion for music, (in our case, a passion for the mind), then one must have technical mastery over one's instrument (oneself), third, one must have musical knowledge of the entire standard repertoire (one's theory), and last, one must have interpretive skills which bring something new to the material (one's own voice).

A complete psychoanalytic education should enable candidates to learn a way of *seeing* (the development of acute powers of observation) a way of *hearing*, (listening *for* the unconscious and then listening *to* it) a way of *understanding*, (familiarity with theory and strategy) and finally, a way of *speaking*. Through this sometimes muddled, but, always magnificent learning process, one eventually comes to find one's voice in the analytic chorus.

REFERENCES

Freud, S. (1926). *The question of lay analysis*. Standard Edition of the Complete Psychological Works of Sigmund Freud, Volume 21.

Stone, L. (1975). Some problems and potentialities of present day psychoanalysis. *Psychoanalytic Quarterly*, XLIV # 3, 331–370.

19

Introduction: Becoming a Psychoanalyst of One Persuasion or Another

Ester R. Shapiro

The papers addressing the curriculum component of the tripartite model focused on the process of theoretical learning and integration, rather than on specific recommendations for coursework. With the significant body of classical papers in Freudian psychoanalysis, as well as the recent expansion of relational psychoanalytic literatures such as object relations and self-psychology, a psychoanalyst in training needs to approach his or her reading of the psychoanalytic literature as a career-long process which is only begun during the training years. These papers emphasized that psychoanalytic learning at its best involves a process of communication of diversity, systematic exploration of differences, and unique personal integration. In this process, the tensions inherent in exploring and reconciling opposing views are valued not only for enhancing personal learning, but also as means of advancing the growth of psychoanalytic theory.

Stephen Appelbaum, Ph.D., recommended his paper, ''Is The Impossible Profession Possible?'', as background reading (Appelbaum, 1985). In it, he proposed that psychoanalysis was too often treated as a homogeneous theory and technique based on too narrow a reading of Freud. He argued that the medicalization of psychoanalysis, and the requirement of professional school background for nonmedical analysts, slanted the selection of psychoanalysts in the direction of being intellectual, ambitious, conscientious, and conventional. Appelbaum suggested that Freud, who did not receive a proper training analysis by today's standards, has to be read in the context of his own creative theoretical and technical development, often in self-contradiction, over many years. He concluded that the capacity to tolerate paradox, to extend one's thinking by facing and exploring contradictions, is the hallmark of the first-rate mind required by psychoanalytic theory and technique.

In his conference paper, Appelbaum observed that any theory offers just one subjective way of organizing reality. He proposed that a classical/romantic tension runs through psychoanalytic theory, technique, and politics, as it does through most human affairs. He described the "classical" side as an expression of an obsessive-compulsive orientation which shows itself in elaborate theory, devotion to the basic model and technique, and devotion to ideas more than feelings, a stereotypically male orientation. The romantic side is reflected in an hysterical orientation, as can be seen in less worked-out theories, more comfort with deviations in technique, and more emphasis on feeling and action, a stereotypically female orientation. The classical tradition is carried by the so-called orthodox Freudians, while the romantic tradition is represented by interpersonal, object-relations and self-psychologists. Appelbaum concluded that because human beings are dauntingly complex, a complete psychoanalytic theory needs to explore the tension between these opposing polarities and their integration into a more complete psychoanalytic theory addressing human development and gender differences as part of a general psychoanalytic psychology.

Murray Bilmes, Ph.D., *and* **Nathan Adler,** Ph.D., discussed the founding, purpose, and current problems of the Center for Integrative Psychoanalytic Studies in San Francisco. In their introduction to the philosophy of the Center, Bilmes and Adler described the purpose of the Center as the pursuit of a systematic psychoanalytic psychology committed to creative dialogue, joint teaching, and the furtherance of theoretical and clinical investigations by scholars, practitioners, and students of classical and contemporary Freudian, Jungian, and existential/cultural analytic orientations.

In their paper, Bilmes discussed the benefits of collaboration toward integration, as an alternative to the fragmentation of theoretical schools which has characterized psychoanalysis. At the Center, diverse perspectives remained under the one roof, and students were exposed to collaborative seminar teaching and supervision in which comparative psychoanalysis was actively discussed and practiced. Adler warned, however, that one danger of an integrative attitude is the false consensus and homogenization of theory which eradicates vital differences and prevents their scientific exploration, where some points of view are integrated but others are discarded. He added that psychoanalysis as a science suffered from the idealization of the Cartesian scientific method, as represented by Grunbaum (1984), and has not yet integrated the hermeneutic method, represented by the work of Barratt (1984), more compatible with the development of social science. He concluded that the exploration of these underlying views of scientific method will give students better tools with which to examine the real distinctions underlying different theoretical perspectives.

Esther Menaker, Ph.D., was originally invited to present a paper, but was unable to attend because of her health. Her own best-known work (Menaker & Menaker, 1965) redefined psychoanalytic ego psychology by integrating it with biological evolutionary theory and sociocultural perspectives. In a summary of her thinking on the topic of theoretical diversity and integration, she stated that the best approach to creating appropriate psychoanalytic training programs was to engage in open-minded dialogue rather than insist on rigid ideology at the expense of mutual communication and learning. She proposed that a structured curriculum offering a historical perspective on the development of diverse psychoanalytic ideas will naturally lead to examination of different perspectives and the creative evolution of a student's personal style. She concluded that since the effectiveness of psychoanalysis has been shown to depend on the quality of the relationship between analyst and patient rather than on the therapist's theoretical or technical orientation, training programs should provide students with the richest possible experience of human relatedness rather than with ideologies.

REFERENCES

Appelbaum, S. (1977). *Anatomy of change*. New York: Plenum.

Appelbaum, S. (1985). *Is the impossible profession possible?* Paper presented at the Division of Psychoanalysis, Local Chapters Training Conference, "The Formation of the Identity of the Psychoanalyst," Washington, November. Published in *Psychoanalyst Psychologist*, 4(1), 1987, 81–88.

Barratt, B. (1984). *Psychic reality and psychoanalytic knowing*. Hillsdale, NJ: The Analytic Press.

Eagle, M. (1984). *Recent developments in psychoanalysis*. New York: McGraw–Hill.

Greenberg, J., & Mitchell, S. (1983). *Object relations in psychoanalytic theory*. Cambridge, MA: Harvard University Press.

Grunbaum, A. (1984). *The foundations of psychoanalysis: A philosophical critique*. Berkeley: University of California Press.

Holt, R. (1985). The current status of psychoanalytic theory. *Psychoanalytic Psychology*, 2, 289–315.

Menaker, E., & Menaker, W. (1965). *Ego in evolution*. New York: Grove Press, Reissued, New York: DeCapo Press, 1984.

20

Reflections on the Role of Theory in Psychoanalysis

Stephen A. Appelbaum

A tension between classicism and romanticism runs through all human affairs, showing itself in such polarities as form and substance, agedness and youth, formal and informal. In psychiatry that tension shows itself diagnostically in the dimension of obsessive-compulsive and hysterical personalities. That can be seen in the obsessive-compulsive emphasis on thought before action, the invoking of abstract principles to explain and guide decisions, the emphasis on the cleanliness of precision and accuracy, and the importance of being right, among other traits; and it can be seen in the hysterical emphasis on intuition, concreteness, feeling, the quick if not precipitous taking of action, and comfort with impressionistic thinking. In applying the classic–romantic tension to choices of theory, there are those theories that take as an objective the meticulous accounting for every detail of life, freely use mechanistic models, strive to create abstractions, and are designed to function in a closed, controllable, predictable system; and there are theories that make do with little system, content themselves with imprecise language, are *laissez faire* with respect to data that fail to conform with the theory, and whose theorizing barely contains the nascent belief that feeling and intuition are more important than theory anyway.

As applied to psychotherapy, there are therapists who guide their behavior through close and persistent inner consultation with theory, and therapists who operate intuitively letting their feelings be their guide. Differences in technique have been epitomized within psychoanalysis by the debate between Wilhelm Reich's (1949) character analysis and Theodore Reik's (1948) less-disciplined approach. Reich formulated strategy like a military campaign: first invite the patient's attention to a style or trait or defense, then work with the patient toward recognizing its disadvantages so that it becomes unwanted by the patient, or ego-alien. Then the contents that the behavior symbolizes, defends against, or partly expresses, come to awareness. Reik, on the other hand, while aware of theory, listened with his third ear, confident that what he heard would serve to guide the work without elaborate planning.

The classic–romantic polarity plays itself out dramatically between psycho-analytically informed therapies, and those therapies born to popularity as part of the human potential, consciousness-raising, counterculture movement of the last 25 years. The medical arm of that movement has spawned such therapies and quasitherapies as Gestalt Therapy and Psychosynthesis, Est, Silva Mind Control, and a variety of procedures that combine psychology with manipulation of the body, as in bioenergetics. Such therapies tend toward the romantic in their informality, their emphasis on feeling and the present moment, and in their rosy belief in unlimited possibilities for growth and change. As to theory, most of them show a curious ambivalence. They define themselves in large part as antitheoretical, deprecating the use of theory as intellectualizing. But they are not quite the noble savages that they pretend to be. The time of the atheoretical noble savage as psychotherapist, if it ever much existed, has gone the way of the 1960s firebrands. Such atheoretical therapists would not be different from a friend over the backyard fence, the local pastor, or a newspaper columnist counselor. Indeed, even friends, pastors, and columnists guide themselves according to some theory of what is good for people, however undisciplined and inexplicit or captive of special interests their theories might be. The debate is thus less between theory and no theory than it is between different contents of theory, different criteria for the makings of theoretical statements, and differences in willingness to recognize the role of theory in the understanding of people and in the making of clinical decisions.

The classical-versus-romantic polarity is now a major issue within psycho-analytically informed therapy. The classical tradition is carried by the so-called orthodox Freudians; the romantic tradition by interpersonal, object-relations and self-psychologists. In the present time of ferment, these approaches alternate between splitting from and crashing against one another. The result is in doubt; conceivably, one will win and the other will lose, though not likely—they have too much in common for that, often more than their adherents notice in the heat of partisanship. More likely the two will coexist, at first uncomfortably, then more or less comfortably as they notice their similarities and learn to exploit their differences.

Discussion and debate about choice of theory ordinarily are carried on in the formal terms of science. Frequently, however, formal scientific considerations are less central to the choice of theory than are the personality characteristics of the chooser, with scientific considerations serving largely as rationalizations. The evidence for this is the high correlation between personality characteristics and seemingly disparate opinions. Note, for example, that those who believe in the right to read *Playboy* tend also to be concerned about the natural environment, separation of church and state, the rights of consumers, and the saving of whales. These issues are less decided on their separate, intrinsic merits than because they all arouse the same impulses. So, too, we can consider the opinions that cluster around those obsessive-compulsive and hysterical personalities which adhere to classical and romantic positions.

Take, for example, the dimension of time. Romantic figures mature early, find their place and make their mark in a precocious burst, and then tend to extinguish themselves in shifting interests or early demise. In psychological work such people are more receptive toward short-term therapy, and with techniques that feature action, perhaps marked by impulsivity; they are impatiently experimental and innovative; they find abstinence and silence, indeed all delay of gratification and maintenance of tension, onerous. And they believe in the perfectibility of the human spirit. By contrast, those who adhere to the classical position believe that good things come to those who wait. Thus, they tolerate abstinence and silence well, for in good time what needs to be said will be said. People with classical personalities are comfortable with continued years of unvarying routine as decreed by custom. They look askance at innovation, especially as these imply impatience and impulsiveness which, after all, are expressions of impulse, drive, affect. These should, according to them, be dealt with only after careful preparation, and in good form. To such people formal psychoanalysis is ideal. They find ideal, also, the control that is implicit in conceiving of psychology as intrapsychic, as manageable since there is only one person to manage, and that person is held in a circumscribed field. The interpersonal is experienced as threateningly likely to get out of hand; it involves other people outside the consulting room, and therefore is less subject to control. Even the dyad of therapist and patient may seem uncomfortably unmanageable to the classicist. The classical personality finds lonely rumination to be more compatible than the busy interaction with others which is more compatible with the romantic personality.

Clinicians will have noted that the obsessive-compulsive person, corresponding to the classical position, tends to be found more often in males than in females, and hysterical persons tend to be found in females more than males. Thus, it should be no surprise that the classical psychoanalytic position carries forward Freud's phallocentric orientation, his confessed confusion about women (Freud, 1933) and his emphasis on the oedipal conflict, a developmental period when the male emerges forcefully into the psychological field. In sociopolitical terms, entrenched members of the classical orthodoxy comprise the "haves" in a "have–have not" tension. Those who espouse the romantic approach, the "have-nots," seeking to gain ascendancy against a power structure, emphasize the primacy of the female. They push backward in time for earlier determining influences on the child, thus emphasizing the influence of early mothering. Comfortable with young children, they opt for direct observation more than, or adjunct to, removed reconstructions of childhood by way of the consulting room's less immediate surrounds. True to their nurturing ways, the feminine side focuses on growth and mastery, is sensitive to normal developmental processes as against an overabsorption with pathology. Such people tend toward a nursing conception of care more than an intrusive doctoring one. Thus, there is a male–female split as one shifts from the abstractions of metapsychology to phenomenological appreciation of the self and object; in short from theories emphasizing ideas to theories emphasizing experience.

Differing emphasis in theories of psychoanalytic technique provide further examples of the classical-versus-romantic tension. Classicists adhere to the so-called basic model, an austere way of being and working that requires strict attention to structural and procedural rules laid down, though evidently not scrupulously practiced, by Freud, and holds as ideal intervening only interpretively. The romantic position is to deviate from such an ideal freely on the basis of clinical judgment, and minimize and learn from any harmful effects of such deviations by analyzing their meaning to the patient; in other words "anything goes" so long as it is analyzed, and sometimes even if it isn't. In the latter instance, the patient is said to benefit from the interpersonal experience, from a second chance to be mothered in a 'holding environment' (Winnicott, 1958).

When Goethe said that whatever was in fact was already a theory, he meant, I think, that facts are found by way of selection and interpretation as guided by theory. With theory we anticipate certain facts; the theory foreshadows them. With different theories we look in different places to find different things. Evenly hovering attention or free-floating awareness is not arbitrary. It is theoretically informed attention that surveys the associative landscape from above ready to descend when a psychic act cogwheels with a theoretically prepared opening.

Theories can be thought of as lenses: We see the same phenomena in different ways with different theory-lenses. Thus Freudians "see" Freudian dreams and associations while Jungians "see" the same material in Jungian images. Most of us have noticed that what is discussed in supervision tends to appear immediately in sessions with the patient discussed. Or we study a particular theory and straightaway find our patients bringing material that corresponds to the theory now fresh in our minds. Rather than coincidence or telepathy being responsible, it is likely that we have brought new lenses to the clinical encounter.

The more one uses the lenses and the greater their magnification, the more psychotherapeutic material there is, both in quantity and depth. Therefore, all other things being equal, the richer the theory, the longer the treatment. (Paradoxically, skilled therapists who know a lot of theory can sometimes accomplish a great deal in short treatments.) Treatments conducted with minimal theory perforce become short-term; after a while there is nothing more to say. Such treatments may go on for a long time, but they are short-term with respect to what is discovered, worked through, and resolved. They go around and around either becoming intellectualized, or degenerating into chit-chat. Expatients of nonanalytical, alternative and poorly trained therapists report that they became tired of slogans, of urging that they use willpower, at being taught clever ways of sizing up and maneuvering interpersonal relations the outcome of which makes little long-term difference in their lives.

The lens is, obviously, not the thing, the object, the reality; it should be equally obvious that the same goes for a theory. But the power of the word is such that arguments about theories sometimes sound as if actual realities were being debated rather than words, symbols, representations of reality. Where tentativeness and hypotheses should reign, we tend to get dogmatism, pronouncements, and competitions. It is as if the protagonists forget that theories are here today and gone tomorrow, and are imperfectly or not at all substantiated by formal research.

Often, differing and apparently conflicting psychoanalytic theories are merely overlapping restatements of shared ideas in different languages. "The narcissism of small differences" is indulged as reputations are made, and sometimes schools established, on the basis of a few perhaps novel ideas, which are cleverly embroidered and freshly emphasized. Not infrequently the apparent differences come about through the use of different levels of discourse rather than reflecting inherent clashes. For example, much of the controversy positing object-seeking satisfaction as alternative to drive satisfaction could be leavened through recognizing that the object becomes attractive in large part because of its promise of drive satisfaction, and through considering that there may be drives other than sex and aggression. Harlow's (1971) monkeys were willing to pass up oral drive satisfaction, as measured by intake of food, in exchange for terrycloth mothering, meaning, in the eyes of some, object satisfaction. Yet how difficult it is to separate object satisfaction, in this instance, from satisfaction of a drive to experience touch. When we say we care or are passionate about another are we not saying we are driven or are acting upon drive, impulse, or instinct? And when we achieve the object and relax our quest is there not a reduction of tension? Relaxation itself under some circumstance is an oral experience: The measurement of food intake is but one of many measures of the oral drive. The problem may be more in conceptualization, or in a too narrow or literal reading of Freud, or in differing levels of discourse than in clashes inherent in the phenomena.

Apparent differences in theory also often stem from differences in technique that have been adopted by open-minded clinicians responding to differing requirements of patients. Unfortunately their discoveries, based upon how best to work with one or another kind of patient, may become transmuted into theoretical propositions which are set against those appropriate to and derived from work with other patients rather than being understood as extensions of the earlier formulations. I wonder whether Kernberg and Kohut, functioning as clinicians with the same patient might not do exactly the same thing. Or, whether, if they failed to be guided by the patient's needs, they might see, or even create, patient behavior with which to support their theories.

For all these reasons, to focus and isolate current controversies in theory one must be somewhat arbitrary, sidestep straw men, and be alert to the danger of substituting semantics for substance. With that disclaimer here are some, to me, interesting and important current controversial issues in theory.

A tension has always existed between viewing people as potentially good, only made bad by evil society and its harsh prohibitions; or seeing people as fundamentally savage, and in that sense bad, as their behavior runs afoul of moral codes established to contend with their savagery in order to make society possible. Fenichel, consistent with his socialist politics, espoused the former (1954). Freud, consistent with what is variously called his pessimism or flinty realism espoused the latter. Kohut and Kernberg carry on this tension though in different terms. Kohut seems to say that if only mother would properly mirror the child, the child would learn to love itself and behave lovingly to others, a version of the frustration-aggression hypothesis of academia and, later, pop psychology. To Kernberg, at least with borderline patients, that rosy scenario is spoiled by basic, relentless oral aggression.

Allied to that biological-versus-cultural issue is the dichotomy posed between people being driven to reduce the tension of drive as contrasted to people's being driven to seek objects. Other forms of that controversy are intrapsychic emphasis versus interpsychic emphasis, universal urges versus urges specific to cultures and familial influences, and a closed, hydraulic system versus an open, humanistic system.

The biology-versus-culture controversy is expressed perhaps most heatedly with regard to the theory of female psychology. Do women struggle with feelings of inferiority because of their anatomy, which they perceive as being inferior under the inexorable influence of the castration complex, or do such feelings stem from the teachings of a male-centered, male-dominated culture?

While it is a psychoanalytic truism that the past influences the present, *when* that influence most significantly takes place is increasingly controversial. Freud's emphasis on the oedipal conflict gave primacy to the fourth and fifth years of life. However, his psychosexual sequence, which tends to be under-emphasized in discussions of temporal influences, highlighted influences at each of the first 5 years of infantile sexuality. Melanie Klein took oedipal and superego issues back to the first year of life, based on supposed clinical reconstructions. Mahler mapped that first year, and subsequent years of infantile development, through direct observation, somewhat linked by her, and linkable, to clinical reconstruction.

The early implicit view of the mind as a blank screen at birth, to be written on by environmental influences, is contradicted by the increasing recognition not only of individual differences at birth but of more differentiated receptivity and functioning at birth than was first thought. It seems that ego and its functions do not simply develop out of frustration of the id. And anyway there is the problem of how to account for change, learning, and development out of a timeless and unchanging id. Hartman's solution to that dilemma was to posit an undifferentiated matrix, independent of conflict, from which developed basic ego functions such as perception, memory, execution, and judgment (1958). Recent research suggests that such functions are present at birth, observations that weigh against the positing of an autistic phase, whether that of Mahler or of Freud's primary narcissism (Stern, 1977). For what it may prove to be worth, I have come to believe in the long-range determining effects on personality of experiences just before, during, and immediately after birth, and before that perinatal period, while the child is *in utero*. I have been persuaded along these lines by consistencies of apparent recall in thousand of cases studied in the course of LSD research by others (Grof, 1976), and through my applying these ideas clinically (Appelbaum, 1985). These ideas have direct precursors in underemphasized statements of Melanie Klein (1964) and Winnicott (1958). These ideas are inferentially supported by the needs felt by Jung (1939) and Freud (1913) to assert that personality propensities, and even knowledge, exist from the beginnings of life, though they did so more on the basis of phylogenetic inheritance than birth and prebirth experience.

The multiplicity of theories, perspectives, clusters of data, and ways of viewing them in psychoanalysis is daunting. Except for those hot-blooded partisans who are unwilling to look and consider any ideas other than their own, psychoanalysts resonate to the rightness of every theorist from time to time. One might ask, how can everyone be right? The answer lies in the immense complexity of people for which so far no one theory has been able fully to account. If one searches any person long and capably enough, any theory can find its empirical expression. Some people are best understood by one theory or another, and a theory may be more or less relevant as the person changes over time. By and large, I have Freudian patients, Kernbergian patients, and Kohutian patients, and at different times all these approaches in one patient. Rather than having to choose among theories absolutely, we should school ourselves in all of them, the better to use them when they are apposite. The chief means of discriminating psychoanalysis from the panoply of other therapies and its great power lies in its many theories, but we must use theory without being encumbered by it.

However diverse the personal identities of psychoanalytic psychotherapists a well-functioning clinician should be facile with at least three of the psychoanalytic theories—a developmental theory, a theory of the differing psychologies of men and women, and a theory explaining how the mind works; that is, a general psychoanalytic psychology.

The need for a developmental theory stems simply from the fundamental belief that the early past influences the present, that people are different at different chronological ages, and they struggle with typical developmental challenges at every age. To understand how an event repeated from the present stems from the past, one has to know what the typical psychological environment was at the time of the event. For example, under the sway of an oral fixation, a burnt birthday cake might typically mean that security, even survival, cannot be taken for granted, that proffered nurturance may be a seductive sham, and deprivation and disappointment lie in wait. At the phallic-oedipal stage the same cake might be experienced as having been subjected to an unfortunate accident, but with candles upright and intact it nevertheless carries the reassuring message that one is getting older and bigger and that one can glow in the light of admiration.

With regard to a theory of sexual differences there are crucial differences in the developmental vicissitudes undergone by each sex, whether or to what degree these differences are rooted in biology, or learning, or some combination of the two. The political activist is concerned that such differences not lead to political, economic, and legal favoritism. The libertine delights in the differences. The psychoanalyst recognizes that the differences in developmental paths of the sexes need to be understood if the person is to be understood.

With regard to general psychology an understanding of how the mind works is necessary so long as one believes in defense and adaptation, in how people interpretively perceive, in the roles of fantasy and affect, in the conscious and the unconscious. In addition to answering the question of what the mind works on, and why it does so, there is always the question of how the mind works. That question taps individual differences whose analysis can yield genetic and motivational information as does the analysis of all psychic acts.

Apart from what theories one chooses or emphasizes, individual differences in how a theory is used is part of the greater question of how analysts analyze. Paradoxically, that question is rather slighted. For a variety of reasons analysts gloss over such personal and idiosyncratic matters, at least compared with the harsh light that they throw on theoretical differences. Many psychoanalysts seem implicitly to assume that there is such a thing as *a* psychoanalysis or *a* psychoanalyst even though they intellectually recognize that no two psychoanalyses are alike, and no two matches between psychoanalyst and patient are alike. To know how a theory is used by any one analyst would involve knowing the subtle interplay of how he or she uses induction and deduction, affect and ideation, intuition and ratiocination. Analysts vary in their degree of use and attention to each of these, when to employ what, how much to weigh them, how comfortable and capable they are with one or another of them. To know fully the role of theory in psychoanalysis one must know fully one's self.

SUMMARY

The tension between classicism and romanticism runs through human affairs, including that between obsessive-compulsive and hysterical thought styles, and results in compatibility with one or another kind of theory. This tension underlies many putatively scientific controversies, such as emphasis on long-term and short-term treatments, reflectiveness and action in technique, oedipal or pre-oedipal importance, stereotypically male or female orientations, preference for the basic model or parameters of it and other variations in technique. Powered by classical and romantic dynamics, controversies are polarized and politicized, thus obscuring their similarities. Such current controversies include views of people as fundamentally bad or good, being impelled by drives or pursuing objects, intrapsychic or interpsychic conceptualizing, biology versus culture, and how early psychic life can be assumed to be in existence and influential on later life. Rather than one or another theory being universally right, one should recognize that different people, and the same person at different times, may be best understood with one theory or another.

REFERENCES

Appelbaum, S. A. (1985). The state of the art in psychotherapy. *Psychotherapy, 22,* 696–701.

Fenichel, O. (1954). *The collected papers of Otto Fenichel.* Second Series. New York: Norton.

Freud, S. (1913). *Totem and Taboo. Standard Edition of The complete psychological works of Sigmund Freud* (Vol. 13). London: Hogarth Press.

Freud, S. (1933). *New introductory lectures. Standard edition of The complete psychological works of Sigmund Freud* (Vol. 22). London: Hogarth Press.

Grof, S. (1976). *Realms of the human unconscious.* New York: Dutton.

Harlow, H. (1971). *Learning to love.* New York: Albion.

Hartman, H. (1958). *Ego psychology and the problem of adaptation.* New York: International Universities Press.

Jung, C. J. (1939). *The integration of the personality.* New York: Farrar & Rinehart.

Klein, M. (1964). *Contributions to psychoanalysis.* New York: McGraw–Hill.

Reich, W. (1949). *Character analysis.* New York: Orgone Institute Press.

Reik, T. (1948). *Listening with the third ear.* New York: Farrar Straus.

Stern, D. (1977). *The first relationship.* Cambridge, MA: Harvard University Press.

Winnicott (1958). *Through pediatrics to psycho-analysis.* London: Hogarth Press.

21

Becoming a Psychoanalyst: An Example From an Integrative Program

Murray Bilmes and Nathan Adler

MURRAY BILMES

What I will talk with you about could be called the erosion of an idea exposed to the weather. That idea, something Nathan and I will elaborate on, was in general, born from the desire to start a fresh psychoanalytic program in the San Francisco Bay area.

By the way of background, I should tell you that the Bay area, at the time we began in the late 1970s, was not very receptive to psychoanalytic thinking. True, there was the San Francisco Psychoanalytic Institute, but that was merely an enclave, like the Vatican. Psychologists in particular, as well as other mental health professionals, showed comparatively little interest in the things that people do to get psychoanalytic training, things that are taken for granted in New York or Chicago. Secondly, important to my background, was that before going into psychology, and then psychoanalysis, I had studied to become a physicist. On reversing careers I went to graduate school in psychology then took my analytic training at the New York Postgraduate Center; I became aware of the fact, that whereas in physics, there were at least as many sharp theoretical divisions as I later found there to be in psychology, they were handled differently. In physics, at the time I was studying, there existed intense controversy among different theorists about the nature of the universe, about Euclidean and non-Euclidean geometry, about the particle theory and wave theory, and so on. Such differences continue to this day. What was interesting to me is that in physics, there seemed to be something like a family for theories. When a new child was born, even if the child turned out difficult or to require special attention, was perhaps not even as impressive as the other children, the child

161

remained part of the family. Everyone in physics remains a physicist. In physics, it is not dictated that if you go to a school on one side of the street you learn Newtonian physics but if you go to the school on the other side of the street, you learn Einsteinian physics. This is done because of the conviction that several theories are essential, plausible and useful for explaining phenomena. Perhaps some day a comprehensive theory will come along but this day was not that day. So you learned the different theories. This doesn't mean they are all considered equally valuable: It doesn't mean you create a smorgasbord. It means you don't prematurely eliminate reasonable alternatives in order to create pseudo-order. The extraordinary contemporary achievements of physics are, in part, I believe, the result of this attitude applied to training and practice.

What I found in psychoanalysis was just the opposite. In effect, if you went to the school on one side of the street, you learned Jungian analysis and if you went to the school on the other side of the street, you learned Freudian analysis. The model in psychoanalysis seemed more like a beehive. It periodically became very agitated and then, at some critical point, a swarming mass flew out with a new queen to start a new hive somewhere else. Members of either hive never swarmed together again.

So, in 1980, I organized a group of 10 to see if we could develop (what we eventually came to call) a Center for Integrative Psychoanalytic Studies. We had in that group Jungians, Sullivanians, Freudians, and Existentialists. We did *not* want to blend these theories (which ultimately only gives you a fifth theory) but to teach these theories. This is what we had in mind. Disputed techniques or explanations would be brought back to the issues they originated from. We would try to see how different theoretical persuasions understood a given problem and had then gone about trying to solve it. We hoped to create a place where advocates of the different schools could come together, discuss these ideas, its literature, and from this create a center for teaching and research.

The group met for 3 years before the program actually began. Through much of that time, we were meeting twice a month. Once each month we met to discuss general administrative issues—all the things that need to be done to start a new program, recruitment, curriculum, evaluation, and so on and then at another time each month we would meet and each of us in rotation, present a paper, or discuss a pet notion to the group. The idea was to seek an atmosphere among ourselves congenial to the ways we thought. Essentially it was an experiment to do with ourselves the very thing the program was going to attempt to do with our students. The kind of program we were looking for vacillated in our thinking between a full psychoanalytic program or, something short of that, a psychoanalytic psychotherapy program. There were many, many debates around this issue. In addition our program was under the general umbrella and auspices of the California School of Professional Psychology. There were administrative issues within that larger system that interacted with our own. Some of these were theoretical; some of these dealt with the institution's perceived mission and its own preferences about how its money should be spent. We decided after much debate to start a psychoanalytic Institute as the training arm of the center. This failed because we did not draw enough qualified applicants. We then decided to modify our approach and offer a 2-year psychoanalytic psychotherapy program. This is what we have now. The fourth class just entered a few months ago.[1]

You might be interested in some of the problems we have encountered. We ran into difficulties with the Freudian analytic community. Several of our faculty and supervisors were members of the San Francisco Psychoanalytic Institute, one of them a psychiatrist (who was also part of our original group). At a certain point after we began, considerable pressure was placed on him by high-ranking Institute members. Two had been presidents of the San Francisco Psychoanalytic Institute. They reprimanded him for aiding our enterprise. To his shame and our regret he withdrew from our program. (This again illustrates problems in developing training that our lawsuit is addressing.) I heard that during one Institute meeting, there was even discussion from the floor about suing us. We were very surprised when we heard that some felt we were "teaching psychoanalysis without a license." Nothing, however, came of the idea for a lawsuit. Eventually, the then-current president of the Institute became one of our supervisors!

We ran into difficulties with members of our wider faculty at the California School of Professional Psychology. Not all psychologists,, of course, are of psychoanalytic persuasion, even of an integrative kind, and some of these non-analytic psychologists were upset that the school was backing a psychoanalytic program. In their view the school was subverting itself and moving into fields not its proper purveyor. Comments were not nasty or unpleasant, but splits developed comparable to the classical academic division between experimental and clinical psychologists.

Finally, I want to say something about our effort to develop a curriculum appropriate to an integrative analytic program. I'm not yet sure how well it is working. Let me describe it to you. What we evolved, aside from the obvious (i.e., reading courses in the Freudian, Jungian, etc., literature), were special courses in which two instructors would be present. For example, in the Clinical Use of Dreams course and in Case Seminars, we did not merely insist on coteaching, but insisted that faculty members must represent different theoretical persuasions. Again, the idea was to study issues from different perspectives. Antonovsky was talking yesterday about psychoanalysis as a certain mind quality, a certain way of thinking. And at its best this is what we were trying to develop. A certain way of thinking that would transcend the parochialism of being bound constantly to a particular figure, or view, a kind of Oedipal stickiness where either you defended the father or attacked the father. Our

---

[1]Since this presentation was made the center has temporarily ceased to admit new classes.

allegiance would, we hoped, be more for knowledge. Again the model I advocated was the one from physics. We also tried and have followed a principle in which supervision would encompass different theoretical orientations. This is how it works: In the first year a student has one supervisor. In the second year, they are assigned a new supervisor who must have a different theoretical orientation from the first-year supervisor. When the candidates graduate from the program, they must make a case presentation to two faculty members. We insist that the two faculty members represent different theoretical perspectives.

Sometimes this confuses the students, for like all of us they seek "truth," and "the answers." One impish student even suggested I rename the program the Center for Disintegrative Psychoanalytic Studies. However, by graduation most have come to enjoy this approach and to feel it is a good educative method.

There has been considerable satisfaction for me personally in undertaking this endeavor. There has also been disappointment and unexpected hurt. You gain some empathy for those who prefer just to go along but also consolation from and even deeper respect for those who dared to attempt the new. If you wonder whether our program can really work, and perhaps fear the worst, in the spirit of our school it will be useful for you to hear a differing voice, presented by Nathan Adler.

NATHAN ADLER

One indication of the culture that we have tried to establish in the Berkeley group is that we can disagree. The case I wish to make and the values I wish to emphasize diverge from the perspective Bilmes presents. We need to clarify the differences between dialogue and eclecticism. A scientific enterprise differs from the civility of a pluralist society. One is concerned with the elaboration and validation of a systematic position, the other with the appreciation and tolerance that celebrates a pluralistic society. The overriding theme of these meetings it seems to me, has been to let a thousand flowers bloom. Within the American ethos of psychology we emphasize individual differences; we affirm a commitment to the democratic ethos and perhaps in reaction to the American Psychoanalytic Association seek to create the basis for new Institutes which will be less dogmatic and authoritarian. No one can fault the commitment to a democratic ethos as a civic and social policy. But I am troubled when one seeks to carry such an ethos into a scientific enterprise. A supermarket of ideas where all brand names are equally acceptable may do for commodities but a supermarket of brand names is not appropriate when scientific theories need to be developed, evaluated, extended, or ultimately rejected. Such a pluralistic ethos culminates in the kind of Rotary Club ecumenicism which holds that Jews, Catholics, and Protestants are said not to differ really since they all affirm fellowship. That is the ethos of homogenization, which may be acceptable for the melting pot tradition. I'm not sure what it accomplishes to create a democracy of denied distinctions, a democracy huddling around consensus and the rejection of necessary discriminations in knowledge.

I was particularly impressed when Sandler, in her address, contrasted training methods in British, Italian, and French institutions, and suggested that these involved different styles, and different personality modes. Those differences seemed to me to be closely related to issues of ethnic psychology and national character structure. She described a British Institute very much like the British capacity to cue up and behave, to debate, to defer to authority, and her description of the procedures in the Italian Institute reminded me of trying to get on a train in Naples at midnight where the devil takes the hindmost. The following day we were presented with an American model; sons are supposed to overtake and surpass father, who, after all, is 50 years old and doesn't count as much as he used to. In the 1950s Martha Wolfenstein's book, *Movies* (1950), examined national character structure and noted the ways in which British, French, and American films differed in construing the role of the hero. Alternative models presented by Sandler and others demonstrate and are consistent with the Wolfenstein formulations about national character. Is the ethos of Division 39, and are some of the models projected here, about theories, and how everybody is as good as everybody else, and how a thousand flowers ought to bloom, within that Wolfenstein formulation of the American hero as adolescent overtaking his father?

In speaking of integration at the Center for Integrative Psychoanalytic Studies, I maintain that integration must not mean homogenization, integration does not celebrate the eclectic. To provide for a number of supervisors presenting alternative persuasions in the same place, we need not maintain that one position is as good as another. We must not confuse authority with authoritarianism. Integration for us does mean the insistence on examining points of view in a scholarly discourse, to see what can be made part of a richer theory, and what is alien to the theory and has to be excluded.

Contemporary psychoanalytic theory in the United States, like American academic psychology, has been minimally responsive to current developments in structuralism and hermeneutics. While these developments have influenced scholars in anthropology, history, belles lettres, and the humanities, psychology has remained a cultural laggard, locked into the empirical and positivistic tradition, and unable to move beyond a monadic reductionism. The psychoanalytic movement responded to Grunbaum's book (1984) deferentially and with a sense of culpability, apologizing for lapses from the positivistic paradigm. Writers within psychoanalytic institutions responded to Grunbaum by trying to justify their position within the scientific establishment and eagerly seek his sanction to legitimize psychoanalysis as a positive science. They are not prepared in rejoinder to maintain that psychoanalysis can more appropriately be classified as a historical field, a science of traces, a *Spurrenwissenschaft*, as Siegfried Bernfeld (personal communication) used to say, more concerned with meanings, rather than with manifest events and communications. Unconscious complexes need to be approached exegetically rather than as empirical "facts." The positivists remain lost in the stimulus error, confusing events and significations. At the same time, little attention had been paid to Barnaby Barratt's book, *Psychic Reality and Psychoanalytic Knowing*, (1984), which represents an alternative within the hermeneutic perspective. Barratt recognizes that psychoanalysis and its clinical practice is to be understood not within a biological model, but rather as a historical study, a study that belongs more appropriately within the social sciences. The case that Grunbaum makes leaves unquestioned the Cartesian mythology that has kept us in a lockstep for the last two or three hundred years and has created psychology's hundred years of solitude.

How does one find the alternative models around which to ground psychology? The issues that arise when Appelbaum speaks of classic versus romantic, the formulations in terms of object relations, still operate within a framework which assumes the distinction between the object and the subject. Such assumptions are precisely what we must examine. In some of the group meetings at this conference, we heard discussions about how to get at the truth and overcome illusion. We struggle with "truth" or "illusion" instead of examining the constituted, explore and locate theoretically the distinctions between schools, see that schools are not merely matters of reductionism, predilection, of taste, but that schools represent what Vico (1984) long ago and Foucault (1981) more recently meant when they spoke of knowledge in relation to power. Schools are hegemonic. Schools formulate a system, representing an establishment, a critique. If we can get past the notion, as good Americans, letting all of us "do our thing, yours as good as mine and mine as good as yours," we could begin to examine some of the hegemonic implications of the schools and clarify the contextual relevances in which they operate. It has become clear to us in our Berkeley program that in trying to offer a dialogue about integration, our students are often frustrated. They don't welcome the dialogue. They prefer advocacy. They want testimonials. They operate within the framework of their resistances, in which nothing is more threatening than to explore the differences between a neognostic psychology and an Aristotelian paradigm that may be the underlying distinction between different schools. What might be the differences between a Cartesian psychology and a hermeneutic psychology? When such issues are examined, the educational process begins to disclose the social or ideological distinctions which students bring into a program, or that instructors advocate. Then we can begin to explicate the underlying issues which differentiate the various schools we promote in our supermarkets.

REFERENCES

Barratt, B. (1984). Psychic reality and psychoanalytic knowing. Hillsdale, NJ: Analytic Press.

Foucault, M. (1981). Power and knowledge: Selective interviews 1972–77, and other writings. New York: Pantheon Press.

Grunbaum, A. (1984). The foundation of psychoanalysis: A philosophical critique. Berkeley: University of California Press.

Vico, G. (1984). The new science of Giambattista Vico, Edited by T. Bergin & M. Fisch. Ithaca, NY: Cornell University Press.

Wolfenstein, M. (1950). Movies: A psychological study. New York: Atheneum.

22

Introduction: The Psychoanalyst's Identity Vis-à-vis Other Therapies and the Discipline of Psychology

Ester R. Shapiro

The psychoanalytically oriented psychologist has grown accustomed to being an outsider, in relationship to both psychoanalysis and to psychology. Until the recent settlement (September, 1988) of the antitrust lawsuit against the American Psychoanalytic Association, psychoanalysis in the United States has been designated a medical specialty, and psychologists have had limited access to full psychoanalytic training. Psychology has tended to see clinical psychology in general, and psychoanalysis in particular, as unscientific and theoretically arbitrary. Both the medicalization of psychoanalysis, and the alienation of psychoanalytically oriented psychologists from mainstream psychology, have detracted from the full contribution clinical psychologists can make as psychoanalytic theorists, researchers, and practitioners.

In fact, psychoanalytic psychologists bring a unique perspective to psychoanalysis as well as to psychology. The medicalization of psychoanalysis has encouraged an attitude toward learning emerging from the medical model, where the student is an apprentice, learning by memorization, imitation and example, working toward internalizing a distinct body of knowledge. The teaching of psychology is based in the university, where a critical, scholarly attitude is encouraged, and the goal of an education is to create the next generation of new ideas. Medical psychoanalysis is based on metaphors of illness, with physician as healer and expert guide. Psychology approaches psychoanalysis with more access to the diverse, overlapping models required to understand human learning or development over the life course.

Within psychology, where the requirements of experimental methodology too often take priority over the substance of the research questions, clinical psychologists are constantly challenged to face the tension between the simplicity of research models and the complexity of human situations. Psychologists drawn to psychoanalysis and the comparative case study method implicit within it find that an analytically informed clinical practice offers an opportunity for systematically exploring the emotional realities that seem to matter most in people's lives. A definition of a scientific attitude in the broadest sense, which borrows from anthropology and history as well as from the physical sciences, offers the most expansive directions for new learning in psychoanalytic theory and therapy. In those instances where the interviewer is the research instrument, the psychoanalytically trained therapist has the advantage of being thoughtfully educated in a process of self-exploration, which offers the best hope for a rigorous, questioning attitude toward one's own subjective responses.

The two papers in this section are based on innovative technical applications of psychoanalytic theory to clinical work, sharing several important commonalities: an integration of psychoanalysis with other therapeutic modalities; a commitment to scientific research through both experimental studies and through systematic study of effective interventions in the clinical situation; and an interrelationship between theory building, hypothesis testing, and development of technique.

In his paper, **Paul Wachtel,** Ph.D. observed that psychoanalytic training has perpetuated Freud's confusion of the psychoanalytic situation as at the same time offering a method of treatment and a method of research. He argued that this confusion has interfered both with the expansion of psychoanalytic research beyond the use of the clinical situation, and with the expansion of clinical technique beyond the classical analytic method. He concluded that Freud as an original thinker offered an intellectual orientation and modeled a process of self-examination, which can best be honored through its scientific development and technical expansion rather than through imitation which restricts the development of both theory and technique.

George Silberschatz, in collaboration with the Mount Zion Psychotherapy Research group, has participated in the development and testing of a model for short-term psychoanalytically oriented therapy. Their approach proposes that psychopathology stems from unconscious pathogenic ideas or false beliefs, typically based on traumatic childhood experiences, and that the patient enters therapy with an unconscious but deliberate plan for his or her own improvement. These researchers have tested hypotheses confirming that therapist interventions are more effective when they are compatible with the patient's plan, and especially when the therapist does not confirm the patient's pathogenic beliefs in the therapeutic relationship (Weiss & Sampson, 1986).

Silberschatz, in his paper, emphasized that psychologists can contribute to the development of psychoanalysis by expanding the traditional clinical methodology and thereby providing scientific research which tests psychoanalytic propositions. He gave examples of findings from the Mount Zion research projects, in which hypotheses derived from the clinical situation, using session transcripts from psychoanalysis and psychoanalytic psychotherapy sessions, were rigorously experimentally tested (Silberschatz & Curtis, 1986). He concluded that objective research in psychoanalysis does not need to sacrifice clinical relevance for scientific rigor.

Ester Shapiro, Ph.D. included a background paper which described a study of parental development at transition to parenthood as an example of family research on the interpersonal nature of early family development (Shapiro, 1986). This family developmental perspective offers a model for exploring the nature of relational development, thereby providing a foundation for understanding the impact of the therapy relationship in affecting personality change (Shapiro, 1988). The family developmental approach can also be applied to the study of intergenerational relationships in psychoanalytic training, a theme which will be expanded in the concluding chapter.

REFERENCES

Curtis, J., & Silberschatz, G. (1986). Clinical implications of research on brief dynamic psychotherapy I. Formulating the patient's problems and goals. *Psychoanalytic Psychology*, *3*(1), 13–26.

Shapiro, E. (1988). Individual change and family development: Individuation as a family process. In C. Falicov (Ed.), *Family transitions*. New York: Guilford Press.

Shapiro, E. (1986). *Individuation as a family process: Identity development at transition to parenthood*. Paper presented at the Massachusetts Association for Psychoanalytic Psychology, Boston, January.

Silberschatz, G., & Curtis, J. (1986). Clinical implications of research on brief dynamic psychotherapy II. How the therapist helps or hinders therapeutic progress. *Psychoanalytic Psychology*, *3*(1), 27–38.

Wachtel, P. (1977). *Psychoanalysis and behavior therapy: Toward an integration*. New York: Basic Books.

Wachtel, E., & Wachtel, P. (1985). *Family dynamics in individual psychotherapy: A guide to clinical strategies*. New York: Guilford Press.

Weiss, J., & Sampson, H. and the Mount Zion Psychotherapy Research Group. (1986). *The psychoanalytic process: Theory, clinical observation, and empirical research*. New York: Guilford Press.

23 Should Psychoanalytic Training Be Training to Be a Psychoanalyst?

Paul L. Wachtel

The question I am raising may strike some of you as peculiar. Psychoanalytic training and training to be a psychoanalyst have been so closely associated historically that it is easy to equate the two unreflectively. But they are not necessarily the same thing, and our efforts to devise the most effective and forward-looking training model require us to be clear about the differences and their implications.

The distinction I am alluding to is between, on the one hand, training in a particular point of view and a particular set of empirical discoveries and, on the other, training in a particular technique. The conflating of the two is rooted both in the history and the language of psychoanalysis. As we are frequently reminded in the literature, the term psychoanalysis has three different meanings: a theory of the mind, a method of treatment, and a method of research. A usual assumption that accompanies this tripartite description is that the three dovetail very nicely and enhance each other. Our theory guides our practice, which in turn (because our very method of therapy is "exploratory") provides us with new data that help us to modify and improve our theory; the new discoveries then help us to increase still further the effectiveness of our therapeutic efforts. It is a pretty picture, but I am not at all sure it is an accurate one.

This picture came closest to being accurate—indeed had a considerable degree of truth—in Freud's own work and, to some degree, in the work of some of the other early analysts. Freud was engaged in a bootstrap operation. He had to invent both his theory and his therapeutic method and—for both substantive and economic reasons—he had to rely on his practice as the chief source of his research. It is one of the marks of his genius that he could pull this off. He did indeed modify his techniques as he made new discoveries. As he gained greater understanding of the role of resistance and defenses, for example, he placed greater emphasis on their analysis as essential to effective treatment. This in turn, by directing more of his attention *to* resistance and defense phenomena— remember that the treatment technique was also the "laboratory" for his research—led to greater theoretical understanding of these phenomena, which in turn further modified the treatment technique.

But relying on his treatment method as his almost exclusive research tool had a high cost, both for therapy and for research. As Freud would be the first to point out, no gains are achieved in human affairs without some price; nothing is achieved without something else being given up. As brilliant and important as Freud's solution was, it had its limitations and introduced its own distortions. We in the psychoanalytic community, who are most of all students of conflict, must not fall into the bland and rose-colored view that the needs of research and the needs of therapy never clashed. Doing his research via the practice of his therapy was a brilliant tactic, and probably an essential one at that stage, but it had its consequences both for research and for therapy.

The consequences for research are probably more obvious. To begin with, any science that relies so exclusively on one method for gathering its data—even if the method is relatively sound—is highly vulnerable. The danger is increased very substantially when in addition the method is one that relies very heavily on subjective considerations and on data whose implications require elaborate inter- pretive efforts and are in addition not usually reported in their raw form but as filtered through the interpretive assumptions of the reporter.[1] The danger is further compounded when the method is one in which the controls typical of scientific investigation are very largely lacking. A good proportion of the more sophisticated analysts and students of psychoanalysis (e.g., Eagle, 1984; Grun- baum, 1984; Holt, 1985) are aware of these difficulties. Indeed, analysts with a research bent are increasingly trying to do something about them, engaging in such activities as systematic observation of infants and children, experimental investigations of psychoanalytic propositions, or innovative attempts to use computers, tape recorders, and other technological aids to use therapeutic situa- tion for research that is truly research in the modern sense. (Dahl, 1972; Gill & Hoffman, 1982; Luborsky, 1977; Masling, 1982).

Much of the impetus for these research efforts derives from concerns (of the sort just noted) regarding the status of psychoanalytic data as evidence for psychoanalytic propositions. But, perhaps even more important in the present context, it almost certainly derives as well from a recognition that there are very substantial limits to how much we can continue to rely on the practice of the therapeutic method we call psychoanalysis as the primary source of *new* discov-

---

[1]Increasingly scientists and philosophers of science are recognizing that *all* scientific data are subject to selective and interpretive sets that bias what is reported. But the degree to which this is a problem in psychoanalysis is orders of magnitude greater.

eries in our field. Freud was able to do wonders with this method, both because he was an individual of unusual genius and—we should not forget—because he was essentially starting from scratch. The method he used was a marvelous initial exploratory procedure. But there is good reason to think that we have discovered most of what this method as a research tool (unaided by modern technological and methodological innovations) is capable of yielding. After almost a hundred years of using this method for our research, the vein has been rather thoroughly mined. This is important for us to come to terms with, not only because it leads us to look for other strategies of gaining further knowledge about unconscious motives, defenses, the consequences of various developmental experiences, and the relative role of biological and experiential factors in behavior—topics of fundamental concern to the psychoanalytic point of view, but not necessarily best investigated via the clinical practice of psychoanalysis—but also because one key reason why the practice of psychoanalysis proper (in contrast to other therapeutic applications of the psychoanalytic point of view) is still regarded as the centerpiece of psychoanalytic training is the notion that it is through the practice of this method that the continuing course of discovery in our field can best be approached.

I have spoken thus far about the limitations introduced by attempting to use the clinical practice of psychoanalysis as a research tool, and have noted that a number of leading psychoanalytic thinkers have been aware of the problematic implications of this for psychoanalytic research. In contrast, the task of considering how psychoanalysis as a *therapeutic* method may have been limited by its simultaneous role as the discipline's chief method of research has scarcely begun. One might wonder, for example, whether we have assumed too readily that the exploration and uncovering that are essential to the research task of psychoanalysis also happen to be exactly what is most important in bringing about therapeutic change. That would certainly be a convenient gift for Nature to bestow on us, but Freud has taught us to be wary of Nature's ironic sense of humor. We might also wonder, in this context, whether detailed exploration of the patient's past is as essential to the therapeutic aim of helping the patient change the patterns of living which distress him or her—patterns which, whatever their origins, have by now been built into the warp and woof of his relationships with others and have become self-perpetuating—as it is to the research aim of understanding the etiology of the disorder.

In any event, we are left with a situation in which the aims of both research and therapy have rested upon the same method, thus giving that method a weight and centrality that is probably unparalleled in any discipline. That would not necessarily be problematic if there were clear evidence that in fact the psychoanalytic method did produce results that were special. It has been an essentially unquestioned assumption in the psychoanalytic community that this is the case—that a classical analysis (or any of the variations of it that are still called psychoanalysis in distinction to psychotherapy) can produce the greatest amount of change of any of the psychotherapies (at least if the patient is "analyzable"). But in fact evidence is lacking—at least evidence conforming with any reasonable canons; evidence that does not require being convinced of the truth of the proposition to begin with in order to be persuaded. It is difficult to argue the case for a special effectiveness of psychoanalysis proper without resorting to notions such as "structural change"—a concept that sounds impressive but is terminally vague and serves as a virtually untestable notion behind which claims can be asserted in a way that rejects any reasonable empirical criterion as superficial or beside the point. (Wachtel, 1987).

What evidence there is regarding the comparative effectiveness of psychoanalysis proper and psychoanalytic therapy does not point to such a unique role for psychoanalysis. Wallerstein (1983), reporting on the results of the Menninger study, notes that his own expectations were considerably challenged by that study, in which full-scale analyses did not accomplish any greater discernible change than did psychotherapies which were expected to have substantially less effectiveness. As in any study, questions can be raised and I am not characterizing these finding as definitive. But clearly a report by a former president of the American Psychoanalytic Association on a study conducted at one of the foremost psychoanalytic training and treatment centers in the country cannot be dismissed as an antipsychoanalytic diatribe.

The implications of studies such as this should not be misinterpreted. The reasonable conclusion to draw from the research conducted thus far is not the nihilistic one of implacably antipsychoanalytic critics such as Eysenck. The Menninger study, like much other research, does show that therapies guided by psychoanalytic assumptions have a demonstrable therapeutic effect. Rather, the issue is that these effects, while reliable and important, are still far too limited for us to be very complacent or content; and that that is as true for psychoanalysis as for psychoanalytically oriented psychotherapy.

In no other field is the original research tool and/or the original treatment method still used with anything like the fidelity to the original that we find in psychoanalysis. To put it kindly, our ideas and methods seem to be more enduring than those of other disciplines; their rate of obsolescence is rather slow.

It is possible, of course, to question how close the methods in use by analysts today really are to the original method. Clearly there have been changes over the years, from the increasing sophistication over time by Freud and other early analysts regarding the analysis of transference and of resistance, to the more recent changes introduced by the British School, by Kohut and his followers, and by others. But it is easy for us, immersed in the field as we are, and hence acutely aware of subtle differences, to overestimate the extent of these changes. To the outside observer it is likely to appear that the apples have not really fallen very far from the tree. The continuities in practice over the years are extremely impressive. The fact that we can still use a term such as "classical analysis" with little sense of irony or embarrassment attests to that. Consider how bizarre (and terrifying) it would be if you were questioning an individual who was about to perform surgery on you and were told that he or she practiced "classical surgery."

One of the central factors constraining change in our practice is the tendency in the psychoanalytic community to draw a sharp distinction between psychoanalysis and psychotherapy. This sharp distinction—in the face of what it takes considerable effort not to see as a continuum—has a constraining effect on the practice both of what is called psychoanalysis and of what is called psychoanalytically oriented psychotherapy. With regard to analysis, if one introduces too much innovation, however therapeutically useful it turns out to be, one is open to the charge that what one is doing is not really analysis, it is only psychotherapy.

One effect of this is that innovations are more readily introduced in the context of psychotherapy than in analysis. But there is also a considerable constraint in the latter realm by virtue of the way in which the distinction is used in the psychoanalytic community. For one of the chief purposes of the dichotomy is an honorific rather than descriptive one. If we look between the lines at how the distinction is used—if we look with the hard, honest gaze Freud modeled for us—we can see that there is, not far below the surface, a clear implication that being a psychoanalyst is *better* than being a psychotherapist. Consider, for example, how different to our ears are the following two sentences: "That was not analysis, that was just psychotherapy." And: "That was not psychotherapy, it was just psychoanalysis." The first sounds unexceptionable. It is familiar and seems to make sense. We have all heard and read sentences like it many times. The second sentence, I would venture to say, might, if you read it, first strike you as a typo. It seems to make no sense. No one ever says such a thing. Nor does anyone ever refer in our literature in any context to "merely psychoanalysis" in the way that "merely psychotherapy" is a part of the language our ears are attuned to hear.

Given this state of affairs, it is not surprising that those who practice psychoanalytically oriented psychotherapy tend to try to model it as closely as possible after psychoanalysis itself. The differences one finds tend to be differences viewed as necessary due to exigencies of time, money, or patient characteristics; they are not differences derived from an effort to *improve* upon psychoanalysis.

Such a strategy for the development of a psychoanalytic approach to therapy makes sense only if we assume that the *procedure* or *technique* we call psychoanalysis is the best that the *intellectual tradition* of psychoanalysis can do. It is the latter, I believe, that is our real source of strength, and it is being seriously constrained by a reverence for a method which served its purpose well at the time it was developed, but which should by now be viewed as outmoded and in need of being replaced.

Now to some of you these comments—particularly the suggestion that the clinical method we call classical analysis may be outmoded—are likely to sound dismissive or even antipsychoanalytic. My intent is quite the contrary. I take psychoanalysis very seriously—seriously enough not only to have devoted much of my professional life to studying and writing about it but, even more importantly, seriously enough to think that its enormous potential has only begun to be fulfilled, and to be interested in what might be holding it back. I ask you to consider: Does it seem similarly disrespectful toward another of the great geniuses in the history of Western thought, Galileo, to notice how the power of his telescope pales before the great reflector at Mount Palomar or the various electronic devices currently in use to explore the secrets of the stars and galaxies? Placed in its historical context, Galileo's remains an epoch-making achievement; and not the least of the marks of its greatness is the transcendent modifications it has spawned. Do we really honor Freud by attributing to his discoveries less of a capacity to spur new inventions—new inventions of the sort that, in any truly fruitful science, necessarily render obsolete those methods with which it began? By holding on so to the particular therapeutic *method* called psychoanalysis as an ideal we betray what should be our ideal—the continually evolving insights into the human condition that Freud set us on the path to attaining.

These considerations lead me to a conclusion that may seem paradoxical at first but which I believe on closer examination is perfectly straightforward: The best way to be true to the psychoanalytic tradition—to the tradition bequeathed to us by that great questioner of homilies and verities—is to question our commitment to the method which has also gone under the name of psychoanalysis. This does not mean abandoning that method. That would certainly be premature. But it does mean a rather substantial shift in the *centrality* we have given that method both in our training Institutes and in our literature.

One likely implication of this position would be that the curriculum of any training program following this philosophy would give considerably greater weight to the various efforts which have been made in the areas of brief psychoanalytic therapy and of psychoanalytically oriented psychotherapy in general. The innovative efforts of analysts such as Alexander, Malan, Sifneos, Weiss and Sampson, and others would not only receive greater attention than is now common in psychoanalytic training programs; they would also receive a different *kind* of attention. They would be studied without a presumption that they were necessarily compromises, alloys of the "pure gold" of the classical method with various baser elements. The (heretofore heretical) notion that they might incorporate—or at least point us toward—*improvements* on the classical method would be seriously explored.

A clear commitment to the psychoanalytic intellectual tradition, rather than to the practice of the particular technique we call psychoanalysis—and a clear recognition that the two commitments are not nearly as compatible as we have assumed in the past—would likely also lead to a greater interest in the relation between psychoanalytic ideas and methods and those which have been important in other therapeutic orientations. The exploration of the interface between psychoanalytic ideas and those of other approaches has been at the heart of my own work for many years, and because I have written extensively on the topic in other contexts I do not intend to address it very focally here. I do wish, however, to note that in recent years such integrative efforts have greatly accelerated, and a host of creative efforts have appeared which hold great promise. Indeed, just a few years ago an international organization, the Society for the Exploration of Psychotherapy Integration, was founded; included among its members are a number of prominent psychoanalysts. A growing number of serious studies have appeared examining the relation between psychoanalysis and Piagetian theory (e.g., Greenspan, 1982; Tenzer, 1983, 1984; Wachtel, 1980), behavior therapy (Arkowitz & Messer, 1984; Birk & Brinkley–Birk, 1974; Feather & Rhoads, 1972; Goldfried, 1982; Marmor & Woods, 1980; Wachtel, 1977) and family therapy (e.g., Sander, 1979; Gurman, 1978; Stierlin, 1977; Wachtel & Wachtel, 1986) as well as a variety of other fascinating explorations of border territories (e.g., Appelbaum, 1979; Bowers & Meichenbaum, 1984; Erdelyi, 1984).[2] I think that many members of Division 39 would be surprised at the extent and the richness of this literature. It seems to me that this body of work has reached the point where anyone well trained in psychoanalytic psychology should be familiar with it, not just because of the specific contributions it contains, though they are clearly important, but also because of the spirit it implies about the way to approach the psychoanalytic enterprise and psychoanalytic discoveries.

The potential of psychoanalytic psychology will not be fully realized if we follow the tired and conservative path of the psychoanalytic Institutes that presently exist. As psychologists we are in a position to inject new vitality into psychoanalysis, rooting our training in the theory and the evidence rather than in the authority of those who for one reason or another have attained the status of training analysts. Our tradition is strong and vital enough to face frankly the strengths *and* the weaknesses of present versions of psychoanalytic thought and practice. We must approach the task of training new psychoanalytic psychologists with the sense that our mandate is not only to pass along what we know but to convey clearly what we don't know—or are not sure if we know—and to imbue in our trainees a commitment to further investigation. That commitment, and not the time-bound vehicle through which he expressed it, is Freud's lasting legacy.

---

[2]See M. R. Goldfried and P. L. Wachtel (Eds.), *Newsletter of the Society for the Exploration of Psychotherapy Integration*, May 1984, (Vol. 2, No. 1) for a fairly comprehensive bibliography of the literature bearing on integration to that date.

REFERENCES

Appelbaum, S. (1979). *Out in inner space: A psychoanalyst explores the new therapies.* New York: Doubleday.

Arkowitz, H., & Messer, S. (Eds.). (1984). *Psychoanalytic therapy and behavior therapy: Is integration possible?* New York: Plenum.

Birk, L., & Brinkley-Birk, A. (1974). Psychoanalysis and behavior therapy. *American Journal of Psychiatry, 131,* 499–510.

Bowers, K., & Meichenbaum, D. (Eds.). (1984). *The unconscious reconsidered.* New York: Wiley.

Eagle, M. (1984). *Recent developments in psychoanalysis.* New York: McGraw-Hill.

Erdelyi, M. (1984). *Freud's cognitive theory.* New York: Wiley.

Feather, B., & Rhoads, J. (1972a). Psychodynamic behavior therapy: I. Theory and rationale. *Archives of General Psychiatry, 25,* 496–502.

Feather, B., & Rhoads, J. (1972b). Psychodynamic behavior therapy: Clinical aspects. *Archives of General Psychiatry, 26,* 503–511.

Goldfried, M. (1982). *Converging themes in psychotherapy.* New York: Springer.

Greenspan, S. (1982). *Intelligence and adaptation: An integration of psychoanalytic and Piagetian developmental psychology.* New York: International Universities Press.

Grunbaum, A. (1984). *The Foundations of psychoanalysis.* Berkeley: University of California Press.

Gurman, A. (1978). Contemporary marital therapies: A critique and comparative analysis of psychoanalytic, behavioral, and systems theory approaches. In T. Paolino & B. McCrady (Eds.), *Marriage and marital therapy.* New York: Brunner/Mazel.

Holt, R. (1985). The current status of psychoanalytic theory. *Psychoanalytic Psychology, 4,* 289–316.

Luborsky, L. (1977). Measuring a pervasive psychic structure in psychotherapy: The core conflictual relationship theme. In N. Freedman & S. Grand (Eds.), *Communicative structures and psychic structures.* New York: Plenum.

Marmor, J., & Woods, S. (1980). *The interface between the psychodynamic and behavioral therapies.* New York: Plenum.

Masling, J. (Ed.) (1982). *Empirical studies of psychoanalytic theory.* Hillsdale, NJ: Lawrence Erlbaum Associates.

Sander, F. (1979). *Individual and family therapy.* New York: Jason Aronson.

Stierlin, H. (1977). *Psychoanalysis and family therapy.* New York: Jason Aronson.

Tenzer, A. (1984). Piaget and psychoanalysis, II: The problem of working through. *Contemporary Psychoanalysis, 20,* 421–436.

Tenzer, A. (1983). Piaget and psychoanalysis. *Contemporary Psychoanalysis, 19,* 319–339.

Wachtel, E. F., & Wachtel, P. L. (1986). *Family dynamics in individual psychotherapy.* New York: Guilford.

Wachtel, P. L. (1987). *Action and insight.* New York: Guilford.

Wachtel, P. L. (1980). Transference, schema, and assimilation: The relevance of Piaget to the psychoanalytic theory of transference. *The Annual of Psychoanalysis* (Vol. 8, pp. 59–76). New York: International Universities Press.

Wachtel, P. L. (1977). *Psychoanalysis and behavior therapy.* New York: Basic Books.

Wallerstein, R. S. (1983). Psychoanalysis and psychotherapy: Relative roles reconsidered. Paper presented at Symposium on "Psychoanalysis Today: The Integration of Theory and Practice," Boston Psychoanalytic Society and Institute, October 29, 1983.

24 Psychology's Contribution to the Future of Psychoanalysis: A Scientific Attitude

George Silberschatz

We are living in a very exciting period in the history of psychoanalysis, not only in terms of expanding training opportunities for psychologists but also in terms of developments in psychoanalytic theory, research, and practice. In this chapter I shall discuss the role that psychology can and should play in helping to shape the future of psychoanalysis: fostering a scientific attitude. I use the term "scientific" in the broadest sense of the word—that is, using accessible data that can be examined by independent observers employing rules of logic and evidence. I shall argue that psychoanalysis needs to go beyond the traditional case-study method and must rely more on scientific data as evidence for its basic postulates. A number of studies of the psychoanalytic process will be reviewed to show how scientific methods can be profitably applied to psychoanalysis.

Psychoanalysis has been extremely ambivalent regarding its status as a science. On the one hand, psychoanalysis represents an effort to explain all of the various complexities of human behavior and seeks to develop lawful relationships regarding conscious as well as unconscious motives, thoughts, feelings, and behaviors. At the same time, however, Freud and many other analysts since him have said that psychoanalysis does not require scientific tests in the usual sense, for every analysis represents a scientific experiment and provides validation of basic psychoanalytic premises:

> It may turn out that every analyst who merely follows the method he was taught to follow will discover that he has been doing *research*, just as Monsieur Jourdain, of Moliere's *Le Bourgeois Gentilhomme*, suddenly discovered that he has been speaking prose for forty years without knowing it. (Ramzy, 1963, p. 74)

Much of the teaching and dissemination of psychoanalytic theory has followed this antiscientific point of view. Psychoanalytic training, as others at this conference have noted, has been much too dogmatic and authoritarian; elaborate jargon is often employed to intimidate and mystify students. In an article which reviews several COPER reports (the American Psychoanalytic Association's Conference on Psychoanalytic Education and Research), Holzman (1976) noted that the spirit in psychoanalytic Institutes is "far removed from the scientific community in that challenges to basic theoretical assumptions are felt to be obstructions to the teaching of what is considered to be already well established" (p. 260). Although Holzman doesn't state it this strongly, he implies that many Institutes follow the monastery or religious order approach that Dr. Ava Siegler described in her chapter. Unfortunately, in psychoanalysis—like in religious orders much of what has become "well established" has become so through *ex cathedra* pronouncements. A particular point of view or proposition becomes fact largely because an expert said so (see Eagle, 1984, for many well-documented examples).

If psychoanalysis is to survive, this kind of dogmatic, religious approach will have to change. Indeed, the COPER report concluded that it is essential "to have an educational atmosphere that encourages open-mindedness, scientific curiosity, and an interchange with scientists in related fields" (Holzman, 1976, p. 261). In his recent review of "The current status of psychoanalytic theory," Holt (1985) put it more strongly:

> We have been living in a fool's paradise, believing that our clinical theory was soundly established when in fact very little of it has been, and virtually all of that thanks to the efforts of nonpsychoanalysts. It is not enough merely to reassure ourselves that psychoanalytic theory has great clinical value. It is, indeed indispensable, but to affirm that does not release us from the obligation to test, purge, and improve it. (p. 297)

For psychoanalysis to thrive and to draw outstanding students, a scientific attitude must be incorporated into the teaching and practice of psychoanalysis. Brenner (1968), in his presidential address to the American Psychoanalytic Association, eloquently stated the essence of what I have in mind by such an attitude:

> Science has to be defined, not as a noun, but in an adjectival sense. It implies a critical, inquiring, skeptical, self-critical attitude; an attitude which attempts to make sense of what is available as evidence; an attitude which takes into account logic and some idea of causality, however one may wish to define that term; an attitude which adapts methods to problems, rather than being dogmatic about the necessity of using a particular method, like mathematical analysis or experiments; an attitude which recognizes . . . that the best of our guesses are provisional ones, without minimizing the value and importance of the hypotheses we do have. (p. 683)

In recent years, there have been a number of contributions reviewing psychoanalytic theory which reflect the kind of broad scientific, critical attitude to which Brenner refers. Many of these (e.g., Eagle, 1984; Gill, 1976; Holt, 1976, 1985; Klein, 1976; Rubinstein, 1976) have raised serious questions about central aspects of psychoanalytic theory and have suggested that some of the cornerstones of psychoanalytic theory, such as metapsychology, drive theory, and the structural model, are untenable.

Perhaps the most neglected aspect of scientific investigation in psychoanalysis is the raw data of psychoanalysis or psychoanalytic therapies, and it is to this area that I shall devote the remainder of my remarks. Criticism regarding the scientific status of psychoanalysis has a long history (e.g., Grunbaum, 1984; Hook, 1959). The essence of this criticism is that psychoanalytic propositions are not scientifically testable or "falsifiable" (Popper, 1963). Popper felt that psychoanalysis was little more than a pseudoscience; he argued that the theory is so pliable it could explain any human behavior and therefore it could not be falsified. These critiques have been cogently refuted; for instance, Wallerstein and Sampson (1971) showed that psychoanalytic propositions could be stated as formal predictions which could be empirically tested and falsified. Rubinstein (1976) has explicated the logic of testing psychoanalytic predictions, noting that predictions can be tested either experimentally or nonexperimentally:

> Although not all scientific predictions can be tested by experiment they can all be tested. . . . The important point is that experimentally and nonexperimentally testable predictions have the same logical form, namely, the form of the statement "If A happens, then B will also happen." Expressed in general terms, the only difference is that in the case of experimental testing a person makes A happen while in nonexperimental testing nature, so to speak, does it. (p. 400)

Most research on psychoanalytic sessions will inevitably be nonexperimental in nature, but as Rubinstein shows, that does not make it any less scientific. Careful, systematic studies of psychoanalysis and psychoanalytic therapies have a rather short history. Nonetheless, there are some interesting findings from these studies which should influence the teaching and practice of psychoanalysis. For instance, methods have been developed to enhance the reliability of psychodynamic case formulations (Caston, 1986; Curtis, Silberschatz, Sampson, Weiss, & Rosenberg, 1988; Luborsky, 1977, 1984; Luborsky, Crits–Christoph, & Mellon, 1986). Using dynamic case formulations, therapist interpretations can be reliably classified in terms of their degree of accuracy or suitability for a particular patient; moreover, significant correlations have been found between the suitability of interventions and patients' therapeutic progress (Bush & Gassner, 1986; Crits–Christoph, Cooper, & Luborsky, 1988; Fretter, 1984; Silberschatz, Fretter, & Curtis, 1986). Space does not permit me to review these and several other contributions to psychoanalytic research. Many of the investigators who have studied psychoanalysis describe their work in a forthcoming book, *Psychoanalytic Process Research Strategies* (Dahl, Kachele & Thomae, in press), and the final report of one of the earliest research efforts in psychoanalytic therapy—The Menninger Psychotherapy Research Project—was recently published by Wallerstein (1986b). I shall review several studies carried out by the Mount Zion Psychotherapy Research Group in order to illustrate three key points: (1) The raw data of psychoanalytic therapy (i.e., the tapes or transcripts of therapy sessions) can be studied in a scientifically rigorous and clinically meaningful way; (2) Psychoanalytic hypotheses about how psychoanalysis or psychotherapy works can be evaluated; and (3) It is possible to identify competing psychoanalytic hypotheses which can be empirically tested to determine which is more predictive of what transpires in therapy—in other words, psychoanalytic hypotheses are falsifiable. In order to give the reader a sense of how the raw data of psychoanalytic sessions can be rigorously studied and how competing hypotheses can be tested, I shall describe one study in some detail. Two other studies carried out by the Mount Zion Psychotherapy Research Group will be described more briefly to highlight certain research findings which do not corroborate widely held psychoanalytic views.

TESTING ALTERNATIVE HYPOTHESES OF THE PSYCHOANALYTIC PROCESS

Weiss (1986) has identified two distinct models within psychoanalytic theory which make different predictions about how a patient is likely to respond to the analyst. These different predictions were tested in an empirical study of a psychoanalytic case (Silberschatz, 1978; Silberschatz, Sampson, & Weiss, 1986). This study focused on patient–analyst interactions frequently observed in psychoanalytic treatment: the patient's transference demands, by which I mean those instances in which the patient, either overtly or covertly, makes a demand on the analyst to respond in some particular way. The patient may, for example, demand affection, special attention, advice, criticism, punishment, rejection, or humiliation. A central aspect of the psychoanalytic theory of therapy is that the analyst should maintain an analytic or neutral stance and should not accede to the patient's demands. There are, however, two fundamentally different theories regarding the nature of the patient's transference demands. These theories contain different explanations for the therapeutic value of the analyst's not acceding to the patient's demand and make different (opposite) predictions about how the patient is likely to behave if the analyst does or does not accede to the demands.

The first explanation is based on what Weiss (1986) has termed an Automatic Functioning (AF) model. According to this model, the patient makes a transference demand in order to gratify an unconscious wish. When the analyst does not accede to the patient's demand, the patient's unconscious wish (transference longing) is frustrated. As a result, the wish is intensified and is eventually pushed into consciousness. The other explanation is referred to by Weiss (1986) as a Higher Mental Functioning (HMF) model. According to this model, when a patient makes a demand of the analyst he or she does so primarily to test a pathogenic belief and to establish a sense of safety. For example, the patient may demand advice from the therapist to test the distressing pathogenic belief that the therapist, like a parent in childhood, wishes to run his or her life. If the therapist does not accede to this demand, the patient will fell reassured, more relaxed, and more productive in the therapy.

Both the AF and HMF models agree that the analyst should generally maintain a neutral stance in response to the patient's demands. However, they differ sharply in explaining how the analyst's neutrality is helpful to the patient. In fact, these two models make opposite predictions about the patient's affective response. According to the AF model, a patient would be likely to feel unhappy, distressed, upset (frustrated) by the analyst's neutrality. This hypothesis was explicitly stated as one of the formal predictions made in the Menninger Psychotherapy Research Project: "patients whose neurotic needs are not gratified within the transference respond to this frustration with regressive and/or resistive reactions, and/or painful affects . . . " (Sargent, Horwitz, Wallerstein, & Appelbaum, 1968, p. 85). By contrast, the HMF model predicts that the patient is generally reassured by the analyst's not acceding to the demand (because doing so disconfirms a pathogenic belief), and that the patient's satisfaction is often demonstrated by becoming more relaxed and productive in the session.

Because the two models differ in their predictions about the patient's response to the analyst's neutral stance, it was possible to test empirically which model better fits observation. Is the patient frustrated and distressed as the AF model predicts, or is the patient generally satisfied and relaxed as the HMF model predicts?

In order to compare the AF and HMF hypotheses, it was necessary to identify instances of the patient's making transference demands which fit the criteria of both models—that is, instances which psychoanalysts who use AF concepts would identify as the patient seeking to gratify a key unconscious wish, and which psychoanalysts applying HMF concepts would identify as the patient posing a key test of the analyst. The analyst's responses to the patient's transference demands were rated by AF psychoanalyst judges for the degree to which they were neutral in the sense of frustrating the patient's wish, and by HMF psychoanalyst judges for the degree to which they "passed or failed" the patient's tests. A passed test is one in which the analyst's response is likely to disconfirm the pathogenic belief which the patient is testing; a failed test is one in which the analyst's response is likely to confirm the pathogenic belief. Finally, the patient's behavior immediately before and after each response was compared (using several different patient measures) in order to test the predictions of each model.

The verbatim transcripts of the first 100 hours of a tape-recorded psychoanalysis were the primary data for this study. The patient, a 28-year-old professional woman with an obsessive-compulsive personality structure, sought treatment because of her inability to enjoy sexual relations with her husband. The treatment was a five-time-a-week psychoanalysis carried out by an experienced (Freudian) psychoanalyst. The analysis went on for some 1,100 hours and was successfully terminated long before this study was planned. Nine clinical raters read through the transcripts of the first 100 sessions and identified all instances of the patient's transference demands. Eighty-seven transference demands were identified (these included attempts by the patient to elicit approval, affection, guidance, punishment, etc.). Typescripts of each of the segments were prepared; they included the patient's transference demand and the analyst's response, which in some instances was silence.

Five psychoanalyst judges accustomed to applying the AF model in their clinical work and four judges accustomed to applying the HMF model independently rated the analyst's interventions. The AF judges rated each analyst's intervention (on a seven-point scale) for its degree of neutrality from the AF perspective—that is, the degree to which the analyst frustrated the patient's wish. Similarly, the HMF judges rated the extent to which the analyst passed or failed the patient's test. Interrater reliabilities were satisfactory for both ratings.

The next step in this study entailed identifying those transference demands which were pertinent to both the AF and HMF models. Three AF judges identified those instances in which the patient was attempting to gratify a key unconscious wish, and three HMF judges identified all instances of key tests. Each judge made a selection on the basis of a case formulation written from his or her perspective (i.e., AF or HMF). A total of 34 transference demands were identified by both groups of judges as key transference events to which their theories applied. Data analyses were based only on the 34 overlapping instances that were identified as both key wishes and key tests.

To test the predictions of the AF and HMF models, the patient's behavior before and after each of the 34 key incidents was rated on several process scales. Segments of patient speech (averaging about 6 minutes in length) immediately before (presegment) and immediately after (postsegment) the transference demand were rated independently by different teams of judges on the Experiencing Scale (a measure of patient productivity, involvement, lack of resistance), the Boldness Scale (the patient's capacity to confront new material boldly), the Relaxation Scale (a measure of associative freedom and relaxation), and Dahl's (1979; Dahl & Stengel, 1978) affect classification system, which measured the patient's level of fear, anxiety, love, and satisfaction. All of these ratings were made with satisfactory levels of interjudge reliability.

Correlations between ratings of the analyst's behaviors and changes (from pre- to postsegments) in each of the seven patient process measures were computed. Predictions derived from the HMF model were supported while predictions of the AF model were not. All seven correlations were in the direction predicted by the HMF model and were opposite to the direction predicted by the AF model. These findings indicate that when the analyst did not accede to the patient's key transference demands the patient did not feel frustrated or upset; rather, the patient became more relaxed and spontaneous, more bold in tackling issues, and more positive in his or her attitude toward others. These results support the view that when the patient expressed a transference demand, he or she was testing a pathogenic belief. By not acceding to these demands, the analyst's behavior provided reassurance against the danger associated with the patient's pathogenic belief.

FURTHER STUDIES OF ALTERNATIVE
PSYCHOANALYTIC HYPOTHESES

How does previously repressed material emerge into consciousness? I shall now review another study of this same analytic case which was designed to shed light on how a patient becomes conscious of mental contents (i.e., wishes, attitudes, memories) which had previously been warded off by defenses (Gassner, Sampson, Brumer, & Weiss, 1986). Two alternative psychoanalytic hypotheses were empirically tested: the first suggests that previously warded off (PWO) contents emerge because they become increasingly powerful (due to analytic neutrality, abstinence, frustration) until they finally either break through the patient's repressive barrier ("breakthrough" hypothesis) or emerge as a compromise formation. The second hypothesis emphasizes the sense of safety that the analyst's attitude provides the patient and suggests that the patient is able to regulate the emergence of PWO contents and will comfortably bring forth PWO contents when he or she feels safe to do so ("unconscious regulation" hypothesis). These two hypotheses make very different and testable predictions about how the patient will feel when PWO contents (that had not been interpreted by the analyst) become conscious. The breakthrough hypothesis predicts that the patient will be tense, anxious, or highly defensive (e.g., isolation of affect). The unconscious regulation hypothesis assumes that the patient will not bring forth PWO contents until the anxiety connected with the contents has been overcome; it is therefore predicted that the patient will not feel anxious as PWO contents emerge and will not defend against them.

The investigators identified all new themes that emerged between hours 41 to 100. Then a group of psychoanalytic clinicians rated which of the new themes had been previously warded off by the patient. Thirteen PWO themes were identified by the judges. The treating analyst independently rated the same items as the clinician judges and rated as highly warded off 11 of the 13 items which the judges had selected. There was thus converging, reliable evidence that the method did identify PWO mental contents. To assess whether the patient was anxious or conflicted as these contents emerged, three anxiety measures were employed: Mahl's speech disturbance ratio, the Gottschalk–Gleser Anxiety Scale, and clinical ratings of anxiety. Another measure, the Experiencing Scale, was used to determine how vividly (i.e., nondefensively) the patient was able to experience the PWO contents.

The results showed that the patient felt more relaxed and showed significantly higher levels of Experiencing following PWO contents than she felt following randomly selected, non-PWO contents. There was clear empirical support for the "unconscious regulation" hypothesis and no support for the "breakthrough" hypothesis.

The Emergence of the Transference Neurosis.

It could be argued that powerfully warded-off contents (i.e., those that are strongly repressed) typically do not develop until later phases of analysis such as the transference neurosis. In a study of a second analytic case (Silberschatz & Young, in preparation), we sought to determine how the transference neurosis develops; does it emerge through increasing mobilization of conflicts and a breakthrough of the patient's defenses (breakthrough hypothesis) or does it emerge under the patient's unconscious control regulated by the patient's sense of safety (unconscious regulation hypothesis)? The transference neurosis phase of the analysis was identified by independent clinical judges and was then corroborated by the treating analyst. Separate judges rated the patient's level of relaxation during the first 110 hours of the analysis and during the transference neurosis phase (some 300 hours later). The patient's level of relaxation during these two periods was compared. Results showed that there were no differences in the patient's level of tension; at no point during the transference neurosis was the patient's level of tension higher than during the first phase of treatment. These results are inconsistent with the breakthrough hypothesis and support the view that the patient unconsciously regulates the emergence of the transference neurosis.

CONCLUSION

If psychoanalysis is to continue to thrive there will have to be fundamental changes in how the theory is taught and developed. Propositions cannot be accepted or presumed to be true simply because a highly regarded psychoanalyst claims them to be true and cites case material as evidence.

> We are approaching a postapostolic era in psychoanalytic history. In a few years, we will no longer have with us colleagues who had direct or indirect contact with the Founding Fathers. Our confidence in our work will have to rely not on the memories of bygone heroes, but on solid observational data, meticulously gathered in the analytic situation and objectively evaluated, for it is upon this set of procedures that the claim of psychoanalysis to a place among the empirical sciences is based. (Arlow, cited in Wallerstein, 1986a, p. 447)

Sherwood (1969) noted that " . . . in perhaps no other field has so great a body of theory been built upon such a small public record of raw data" (p. 70). A few psychoanalysts find this situation intolerable (see, for example, Holt, 1985; Wallerstein, 1986) and have pointed to the need for more public records (i.e., tapes or transcripts) of psychoanalytic sessions. Public records of completed therapies can serve multiple purposes. They can be used to test psychoanalytic hypotheses rigorously—as exemplified in the research described—and they can also be used to develop new ideas which can then be examined, modified, or expanded by *independent observers*, a process referred to by Mahrer (1988) as "discovery-oriented" research.

I am not advocating that psychoanalytic training Institutes adopt a Boulder Model of training scientist-practitioners. The primary mission of training Institutes is to train competent psychoanalytic practitioners. However, I believe that systematic studies of what actually happens during psychoanalysis brings a crucial—though neglected—component into psychoanalytic training: an insistence that ideas be stated clearly and logically, a critical assessment of evidence for various propositions, an openness to the variety of ways by which hypotheses can be tested, and finally a receptivity to new findings and new ideas. Historically, analyst's case reports and recollections of therapy sessions have been the primary source of psychoanalytic data. Such reports have been very useful for generating new hypotheses. However, they can not be relied upon to confirm hypotheses since our preconceptions inevitably shape how we process and report clinical data. Thus, for the scientist and practitioner alike, there is much to be learned from systematically reviewing records of psychotherapy sessions.

A broad scientific outlook is the foundation of training in psychology. In developing our psychoanalytic training centers we should not lose sight of our distinctive origins as psychologists. We must avoid the pitfalls that have been evident in many medically dominated Institutes where challenges to basic theoretical propositions are often experienced as obstacles to learning "well-established facts." Psychologists can play a leading role in placing psychoanalytic theory on a more solid base of observational and empirical data and can thus foster a scientific attitude in the practice and teaching of psychoanalysis.

REFERENCES

Brenner, C. (1968). Psychoanalysis and science. *Journal of the American Psychoanalytic Association, 16*, 675–696.

Bush, M., & Gassner, S. (1986). The immediate effect of the analyst's termination interventions on the patient's resistance to termination. In J. Weiss, H. Sampson, & the Mount Zion Psychotherapy Research Group (Eds.), *The psychoanalytic process: Theory, clinical observation, and empirical research* (pp. 299–322). New York: Guilford Press.

Caston, J. (1986). The reliability of the diagnosis of the patient's unconscious plan. In J. Weiss, H. Sampson, & the Mount Zion Psychotherapy Research Group (Eds.), *The psychoanalytic process: Theory, clinical observation, and empirical research* (pp. 241–255). New York: Guilford Press.

Crits–Christoph, P., Cooper, A., & Luborsky, L. (1988). The accuracy of therapists' interpretations and the outcome of dynamic psychotherapy. *Journal of Consulting and Clinical Psychology, 56,* 490–495.

Curtis, J. T., Silberschatz, G., Sampson, H., Weiss, J., & Rosenberg, S. E. (1988). Developing reliable psychodynamic case formulations: An illustration of the plan diagnosis method. *Psychotherapy, 25,* 256–265.

Dahl, H. (1979). The appetite hypothesis of emotions: A new psychoanalytic model of motivation. In C. E. Izard (Ed.), *Emotions in personality and psychopathology* (pp. 201–225). New York: Plenum.

Dahl, H., Kachele, H., & Thomae, H. (Eds.), (in press). *Psychoanalytic process research strategies.* Berlin: Springer.

Dahl, H., & Stengel, B. (1978). A classification of emotion words: A modification and partial test of de Rivera's decision theory of emotions. *Psychoanalysis and Contemporary Science, 1,* 269–312.

Eagle, M. (1984). Recent developments in psychoanalysis: A critical evaluation. New York: McGraw Hill.

Fretter, P. B. (1984). The immediate effects of transference interpretations on patients' progress in brief, psychodynamic psychotherapy. *Dissertation Abstracts International, 46,* 1415-A. (University Microfilms No. 85–12,112).

Gassner, S., Sampson, H., Brumer, S., & Weiss, J. (1986). The emergence of warded-off contents. In J. Weiss, H. Sampson, & and the Mount Zion Psychotherapy Research Group (Eds.), *The psychoanalytic process: Theory, clinical observation, and empirical research* (pp. 171–186). New York: Guilford Press.

Gill, M. M. (1976). Metapsychology is not psychology. In M. M. Gill & P. S. Holzman (Eds.), *Psychology versus metapsychology: Psychoanalytic essays in memory of George S. Klein* (pp. 71–105). New York: International Universities Press.

Grunbaum, A. (1984). *The foundations of psychoanalysis: A philosophical critique.* Berkeley: University of California Press.

Holt, R. R. (1976). Drive or wish? A reconsideration of the psychoanalytic theory of motivation. In M. M. Gill & P. S. Holzman (Eds.), *Psychology vs metapsychology: Essays in memory of George S. Klein* (pp. 158–197). New York: International Universities Press.

Holt, R. R. (1985). The current status of psychoanalytic theory. *Psychoanalytic Psychology, 2,* 289–315.

Holzman, P. S. (1976). The future of psychoanalysis and its institutes. *Psychoanalytic Quarterly, 45,* 250–273.

Hook, S. (1959). *Psychoanalysis, scientific method, and philosophy.* New York: New York University Press.

Klein, G. S. (1976). *Psychoanalytic theory: An exploration of essentials.* New York: International Universities Press.

Luborsky, L. (1977). Measuring a pervasive psychic structure in psychotherapy: The core conflictual relationship theme. In N. Freedman & S. Grand (Eds.), *Communicative structures and psychic structures* (pp. 367–395). New York: Plenum.

Luborsky, L. (1984). *Principles of psychoanalytic psychotherapy.* New York: Basic Books.

Luborsky, L., Crits–Christoph, P., & Mellon, J. (1986). Advent of objective measures of the transference concept. *Journal of Consulting and Clinical Psychology, 54,* 39–47.

Mahrer, A. R. (1988). Discovery-oriented psychotherapy research. *American Psychologist, 43,* 694–702.

Popper, K. R. (1963). *Conjectures and refutations: The growth of scientific knowledge.* New York: Basic Books.

Ramzy, I. (1963). Research aspects of psychoanalysis. *Psychoanalytic Quarterly, 32,* 58–76.

Rubinstein, B. B. (1976). On the possibility of a strictly clinical psychoanalytic theory: An essay in the philosophy of psychoanalysis. In M. M. Gill & P. S. Holzman (Eds.), *Psychology versus metapsychology: Psychoanalytic essays in honor of George S. Klein* (pp. 229–264). New York: International Universities Press.

Sargent, H. D., Horwitz, L., Wallestein, R., & Appelbaum, A. (1968). Prediction in psychotherapy research: A method for the transformation of clinical judgments into testable hypotheses. *Psychological Issues, 4*(1, Monograph 21).

Sherwood, M. (1969). *The logic of explanation in psychoanalysis.* New York: Academic Press.

Silberschatz, G. (1978). Effects of the analyst's neutrality on the patient's feelings and behavior in the psychoanalytic situation. *Dissertation Abstracts International, 39,* 3007–B. (University Microfilms No. 78–24,277).

Silberschatz, G., Fretter, P. B., & Curtis, J. T. (1986). How do interpretations influence the process of psychotherapy? *Journal of Consulting and Clinical Psychology, 54,* 646–652.

Silberschatz, G., Sampson, H., & Weiss, J. (1986). Testing pathogenic beliefs versus seeking transference gratifications. In J. Weiss, H. Sampson, & the Mount Zion Psychotherapy Research Group (Eds.), *The psychoanalytic process: Theory, clinical observation, and empirical research* (pp. 267–276). New York: Guilford Press.

Silberschatz, G., & Young, N. Empirical study of the transference neurosis. Manuscript in preparation.

Wallerstein, R. S. (1986a). Psychoanalysis as a science: A response to the new challenges. *Psychoanalytic Quarterly, 55,* 414–451.

Wallerstein, R. S. (1986b). *42 lives in treatment: A study of psychoanalysis and psychotherapy.* New York: Guilford Press.

Wallerstein, R. S., & Sampson, H. (1971). Issues in research in the psychoanalytic process. *International Journal of Psychoanalysis, 52,* 11–50.

Weiss, J. (1986). Introduction. In J. Weiss, H. Sampson, & the Mount Zion Psychotherapy Research Group (Eds.), *The psychoanalytic process: Theory, clinical observation, and empirical research* (pp. 3–21). New York: Guilford Press.

25 Introduction: The Relationship Between The Division of Psychoanalysis and Local Chapter Training Programs

Ester R. Shapiro

The panel discussion was organized to continue the Division's dialogue on training: How can the Division of Psychoanalysis support local training efforts, without constraining the flexible creation of training programs suited to local needs? In his introductory chapter, Meisels identified the development of local chapters, and the antitrust lawsuit against the American Psychoanalytic Association, as major developments supporting psychoanalytic training for psychologists. Because the conditions and needs of different communities were too diverse to implement a uniform national training program, the Division supported the development of local training efforts appropriate to each community. In 1985, after preliminary meetings on training, the local chapters petitioned the board to become a Section, thereby becoming a political power base within the division to support their goals, especially their training goals.

In 1984, Bryant Welch, Ph.D., and three plaintiffs, Tony Bernay, Ph.D., Helen Desmond, Psy.D., and Marvin Schneider, Ph.D., obtained the Division's support to file an antitrust suit against the American Psychoanalytic Association for unfair restriction of trade in failing to admit psychologists to their Institutes. In the process of developing psychoanalytic training programs for psychologists, the lawsuit served two vital functions. First, the American Psychoanalytic Association began releasing its faculty to teach in interdisciplinary programs, so that as local chapters developed their training programs it became more possible to involve medical faculty which was especially important in those areas with few or no psychoanalytically trained psychologists. More importantly, we psychologists gained a sense of empowerment and personal authority, since the lawsuit was a statement of our right to determine by our own actions the nature of our participation in the psychoanalytic enterprise.

In addressing the issues of the best relationship between the Division and local chapters on questions of training, **Fred Pine**, Ph.D., then president of the Division, stated that in his experience as the director of an internship program reviewed by the American Psychological Association, or as a member of the New York Psychoanalytic Society and Institute whose training is reviewed by the American Psychoanalytic Association, he could understand the importance of the wish for personal autonomy and control over one's own vision of training. On the other hand, he felt that these reviews often brought forward important questions whose discussion benefited the training programs, as long as there was no attempt to control or create a stamp of uniformity, which in his experience neither APA imposed. He concluded his remarks with the statement that issues of personal creativity, and the capacity to think independently, are essentially intrapsychic problems, always present in organizations large or small, because they are a fundamental aspect of human relations.

Jonathan Slavin, Ph.D., focused on the difficulties psychologists experience in believing they have the authority to define their own identities as psychoanalysts, because the medical control of psychoanalytic training has created a political condition similar to apartheid, with intrapsychic consequences. He suggested that when psychologists emphasize the definition of a special psychoanalytic identity in response to the narcissistic injury of medical exclusion, they foster obeisance to external authority at the expense of the substance of psychoanalytic knowledge. The capacity to create new training programs which neither repeat the old nor reject the new depends on the exploration of these inner responses.

Rochelle Kainer, Ph.D., suggested that superego and ego-ideal formation phenomenon enter into the development of training programs. Training programs can develop out of identification with harsh superego introjects which represent moralistic or punitive authority, or out of identification with the "loving and beloved superego" or ego ideal. She proposed that ego-ideal phenomena come more into play with those who wish to create something new, while still needing and maintaining a connection to the existing psychoanalytic culture. She suggested that the Division can offer a national training committee not as a superego model but as a transitional object, linking the newly emerging identity with the existing community on the basis of shared ideals and mutual respect.

In conclusion, the creation of the Division of Psychoanalysis has given psychoanalytic psychologists an organization which can support their greater participation in psychoanalysis and psychoanalytic education. While the Division began with a plan for a national training program, it was acknowledged that individual communities needed to develop locally responsive training programs, with the Division's support but without the imposition of uniform requirements or standards for training. Both the impact of the lawsuit, and the formation of a local chapters section supporting local training efforts within the Division, show the importance of active organizational and political change in freeing psychologists to create their own psychoanalytic identities. The definition of an independent psychoanalytic identity for psychologists was also facilitated by a political acknowledgment within our own group that the American medical monopoly unfairly defined psychologists as unable to practice psychoanalysis. These processes within the Division illustrate the importance of a flexible capacity for active institutional change in promoting the most expansive development of individual identities.

26 The Division and Local Chapters

Fred Pine

Pine discussed the issues regarding a central review and evaluation process for training programs that evolve in various local areas. He discussed his experiences with reviews of the psychology internship at the Albert Einstein College of Medicine (by the American Psychological Association) and of the New York Psychoanalytic Institute (by the American Psychoanalytic Association). In both instances, he felt that the reviewers cast a constructive critical eye on programs. Outside review was, overall, a valuable experience. While recognizing that the idea of outside review arouses anxieties regarding control over or standardization of programs, he emphasized that his experiences gave no support for such anxieties; reviewers were oriented toward evaluation and constructive criticism, not toward imposition of their own ideas.

Pine suggested that the danger of homogenization of thinking proceeds less from institutional review and more from more intimate sources. He suggested that the freedom to think independently, or its opposite, thought slavery,

Are essentially intrapsychic issues and are as much present in small organizations as in national ones—probably more so. Thought slavery is something many people rush into in this field, in the face of the field's uncertainties and the supportive function of belief-sharing. More cynically, but not unrealistically, referrals too, follow from shared beliefs. For a field such as psychoanalysis, restrictions on thought are ultimately more a problem of human relations and intrapsychic functioning than of organization control.

---

[1]Dr. Fred Pine was unable to prepare a formal version of his remarks on this panel. The following is a brief abstract of those remarks.

27 Authority and Identity in the Establishment of Psychoanalytic Training: Questions Regarding Training Models

Jonathan H. Slavin

Even a brief journey into discussions of psychoanalytic training makes it clear that they can be very charged and can stir very powerful emotions. Somehow, a lot seems at stake, and concrete questions about this or that facet or detail of a training model can arouse a level of controversy and personal investment in the discussants that appears to go well beyond the real importance of the issue in question. Thus, although discussion of the issues are generally couched in educational terms, educational questions per se seem rarely to be solely or even centrally at stake.

As local chapters organize and begin to consider undertaking some form of psychoanalytic training, it behooves us as psychoanalytic psychologists to try to understand some of the meaning and sources of the emotionality that underlies much of the discussions about training—to try to understand what is really at stake—so that we can more reasonably assess the relevance of the underlying emotional issues to the concrete educational decisions we will be called upon to make.

The core of the emotional issue at stake in this discussion has to do, I believe, with our own views and uncertainties of our identity as independent professionals able to provide *and* validate our own training. Thus, questions of curriculum, supervision, standards for teachers, the role and type of personal analysis, admission criteria, and the like, are all influenced, not simply by the specific organizational and educational questions they raise but also by our own sense of our capacity as professionals to undertake psychoanalytic training by ourselves, for ourselves, and by our ability or lack of it to view what we do as substantial and rigorous.

Unfortunately, our professional identity, which plays such a major role in how we view our work, has not been, historically, completely under our own control. Indeed, I believe we would be foolish not to ask ourselves whether decades of systematic exclusion by the medical Institutes (except for the second-class inclusion of a selected few) has left a problematical legacy upon our professional self-concept and, if so, how that legacy will affect our view of the psychoanalytic training programs we may choose to create. Have these decades of exclusion placed us in the position of having to prove somehow beyond doubt that any program we may create is not second rate? Is there a legacy of professional apartheid within us that suggests to us, at least secretly (and even among New Yorkers with their own long-established Institutes) that, in truth, only the medical analysts possess the real thing, the *real* analysis, the *real* analysts and the *real* training? Has the general exclusion and close rationing of a few coveted slots established the medical analysts and medical Institutes within our professional psyche as the *real* sources of authority and validation of our professional endeavors. And, if so, how shall we relate to that embedded inner authority?

More specifically, how much does a training program we establish borrow from the model of established medical Institutes because we think that such borrowing makes good educational sense, and how much will we feel compelled to replicate those models slavishly because we fear that to do otherwise would not be seen as valid by the internalized representation of their authority. Given the legacy of exclusion I have suggested, can we have a model of training that takes the best of established, traditional models while making appropriate changes to fit the real needs and interests of an independent and mature professional group? Or shall we view any change or modification in substance or ritual as a deviation or dilution of what *really* should be. And if we make changes can we then view such a model as equally rigorous and as providing equally high-quality psychoanalytic training.

It is my view that the establishment of a training model that we can consider to be substantial and will truly be substantial can only come if we have—through a process of examination of the psychological effects of exclusion—managed to free ourselves from an ingrained sense of established authority that internally mirrors our professional exclusion. I want to make clear, however, that to free ourselves, however, does not mean simply to rebel. It does not mean to reject, for the sake of rejection, the best of what the other group has to offer us in terms of a model, as well as in terms of individual teachers and supervisors. If we rebel and if we go our own way only for the sake of going our own way we will not have genuinely freed ourselves from that authority but will be simply reacting to it in a different and equally impoverished manner.

How do these general questions relate to the specific issues of developing a training model on a local level? These questions apply to how we see such a model from its outset. Do we see it as beginning in a fixed and final form, beyond imperfection and beyond question, in order to appease an inner voice which will otherwise not validate our efforts, or can we see it as a practical educational system which will necessarily change with time and experience? With regard to the specifics of what model we may elect to pursue I think some questions, in my view at least, are more easily answered and others are much more difficult. The one that, in my opinion, is most easily answered has to do with curriculum. Anyone who has had the opportunity to examine the curricula of a broad variety of psychoanalytic institutes, both medical and nonmedical, will find that despite significant ideological differences among these Institutes it's clear that most share a common, core, generic curriculum. This core is fairly easy to articulate: It consists of a knowledge of the evolution of psychoanalytic technique in its classical form and in the alternative perspectives that have been offered; it consists also of an understanding of psychoanalytic developmental theory—classical, interpersonal, and self-psychological. And it consists of an understanding of the history and development of psychoanalytic theory. I think that whatever kind of program we establish in local areas, we will in the end offer some version of that kind of generic curriculum. And to the extent that we cannot expose our students to the broad range of psychoanalytic thinking—while permitting them the freedom to make their own theoretical commitments—we will have failed in freeing ourselves internally.

More difficult questions have to do with who and how we screen and admit to a training program, the role of the personal analysis and supervision. As I see it, these questions also very much relate to how we see ourselves as subscribers to a training program and as mature professionals.

It is important to keep in mind that the subscribers to a training program we may establish would be many of us and our own members. How we deal with admission, graduation and certification, personal analysis and supervision depends on how we see ourselves and what we want a program to provide us. Do we see ourselves as trying to acquire something of a new professional identity— the identity of the psychoanalyst—which will provide us with a kind of validation not available in our current roles or that will compensate for the narcissistic injury of exclusion from a particular identity and set of coveted object relationships? Or, do we wish to acquire a particular perspective, mode of inquiry and understanding as well as a particular skill and craftsmanship in a specialized area of clinical practice?

Clearly, I have framed this question in a dichotomous fashion with an evident bias in mind. There is no question that in acquiring new professional expertise we will also change and solidify something in our professional identity. And the wish to acquire that identity, for example, to aspire to be part of a group of expert and experienced psychotherapists, is not inherently a destructive motivation. It can be an important component in providing the energy to pursue a difficult, arduous journey. However, to the extent that our effort in providing training is too much in the direction of creating a special identity, a narcissistic compensation, rather than in transmitting perspective, knowledge, and professional expertise, and to the extent that we encourage a belief in the power of that identity, I believe we will foster, as Alan Wheelis has noted, an obeisance to authority, a stifling of creativity, a focus on ritual and rites of passage and a scrutiny of the character of the performer of the work rather than on the work and the work product itself. This is inimical, I think, to the development of an empirically based profession and to our own development as mature professionals.

From this vantage point, then, shall we offer training broadly to the professional community or shall we establish severe restraints on who may undertake training? Do we see it as a good thing to offer psychoanalytic experience to as many psychologists as possible or should it be offered to just a few? If identity is too much at stake, rather than perspective, skill, and professional craft, will too much inclusion threaten to dilute the identity we seek to acquire and will we need see ourselves as among a select, "elect" few? Shall we too enact the ritual of exclusion upon our own peers or some other group such as social workers? Shall the individuals in training be selected on the basis of a few screening interviews which predict whether that person can acquire analytic expertise? Or shall we, as Freud recommended with patients, permit individuals a certain trial period in which their actual work in courses and supervision may be examined before reaching conclusions about their suitability. How we view those who may join us, will speak eloquently to the question of how we view ourselves as professionals.

How, too, from the vantage point of psychoanalytic training as the acquisition of a validating identity versus the acquisition of skill and expertise, shall we view the personal analysis? Shall analyses provided by individuals from some approved list be acceptable? Shall individuals in training be asked to switch analysts in midstream or begin a second or third analysis after having completed, to their satisfaction, a first one? Or shall we, beyond requiring a substantial personal analysis by a recognized psychoanalytic practitioner, look first at the quality of the clinical work the individual is doing before concluding that further analysis or a different analysis is indicated? How much we need to depend on the identity of the providing analyst to reassure us somehow of the quality of our candidates versus how much we examine in a careful and coherent way the quality of work actually done by our candidates will be a function, I believe, of how much we have freed ourselves form an authoritarian view of analytic training that has misplaced emphasis on identity acquisition to a view of analytic training as being much like training in any other ordinary mortal craft or profession.

All of these questions, and others, including how much flexibility to meet individual needs our training model can have and how much responsibility each individual professional can take in organizing their own training within certain broad boundaries, will depend for their answers, in part, on how we deal with the issues of authority, identity, and professional craftsmanship. I hope, as these issues are debated, that we will have the ability to deal with these questions wisely and maturely.

28

Superego, Ego Ideal, and Transitional Object Phenomena in Issues of Regional Training

Rochelle Kainer

In those regions which spawned the local chapter movement and supported the momentum for this national symposium, I have observed that efforts to be trained and/or to provide training seem to reflect ideal formation phenomena. These ideal formations play a large part in our thinking about such issues as "who" is a psychoanalyst and "how" one is to become one. For the moment however, I wish to distinguish between the guild issue of becoming a psychoanalyst with that of obtaining or providing a psychoanalytic education. Although they overlap to some degree, the issue of obtaining or providing a psychoanalytic education is not completely subsumed by that of being a psychoanalyst. However, ideal formation phenomena are equally at work in both.

Ideal formations are most clearly seen in the case of those who wish to "become a psychoanalyst of one persuasion or another." Here, superego phenomena—in the sense of Roy Schafer's "loving and beloved superego"— certainly get called into play. In the push of attempting to assume a psychoanalytic identity, there is a strong need to form a bond with existing, recognized, and admired senior colleagues. Many thus wish to replicate their own analysis and to obtain or reproduce existing models of training and form their identity through the well-known phenomena of superego introjects. In this case, we take in the good and wish to identify with this sense of goodness. In the not-so-good aspects of our experience, should they exist, we still may incorporate superego phenomena in the more dubious act of identifying with the agressor.

As we know, most superego phenomena are largely unconscious but form a powerful impetus to our strivings and behavior. They can give us an unquestioned certainty of right and wrong, and for better or worse, become the bedrock of our moral judgments and our belief systems. We know too, that superego phenomena are inexorably linked to our relationship with those in whom we have invested authority. For the developing child, it can be no other way. We are dependent on the minds, hearts, and to a large extent, the superego content of those we admire. Thus, love and the fear of its loss or of disapproval, is the strongest adhesive yet invented. We not only derive comfort for the child part still within us, but there is also a natural mature comfort in knowing that we carry on that which is handed down to us. This formation is important not only in establishing our own identity but in enabling us to contribute to an ongoing culture with whom we can identify.

We have seen this operating so strongly within the culture of psychoanalysis. Both those whom we have idealized and those with whom we wish to be identified become crucial introjects affecting our beliefs about the nature and practice of psychoanalysis—the right and the wrong, the good and the bad. It is this aura of moral certainty that lets us know that we are in the realm of superego constructs. It is this moral certainty that greatly determines our psychoanalytic perspective and posture. It is in the realm of one's psychoanalytic identity that these superego phenomena are most vital.

Yet, in listening to colleagues throughout the country, this is certainly not the only preoccupation and for some, it is of secondary importance, although its importance to others is acknowledged. For a number of people, obtaining and/or providing a psychoanalytic education is of vital concern. Along with, or even in place of the concern of becoming a psychoanalyst is that of deepening one's psychoanalytic knowledge as well as making informed contributions to the body of knowledge that we already have. It is in this latter case in particular that I should like to join those colleagues who have separated ego-ideal from superego phenomena. This will enable me to distinguish, for the purpose of this chapter, what I believe comes more into play for those who strive to create something new within the existing order.

In this latter case, there may be less emphasis on the superego precipitates: the "musts, shoulds and should-nots" of others and more emphasis on the exploration and formation of something beyond that which already exists. By more consciously borrowing *only* the most useful and clinically sound parts of their previous training and experience and by reworking those aspects that seem counterproductive, one exchanges approval and certainly for a possibly stronger and more creative science. Just as Joyce McDougal has made a "plea for a measure of abnormality," I am going to make a plea for a measure of uncertainty. As comforting as it is to be the good and beloved child who faithfully carries out the parental givens, and as painful as it is to stand alone at times, I believe that the cause of advancing our science often requires the latter stance.

In observing and participating in the work and formation of various regional groups, I have not been compelled to focus on the issue of the paucity of resources, though that may indeed be the case for some. I have instead been impressed with regional vitality and resourcefulness. In some areas, guild issues and the failure to respond creatively to developments in the body of psychoanalytic knowledge have demoralized the members of some traditional Institutes and have nearly killed off psychoanalysis as a clinical phenomenon as well as a profound way of thinking. However, there are those who stubbornly refuse to believe in its demise. Psychologists bring something quite special to psychoanalysis. It is a verve, a thirst for knowledge, and a spirit of inquiry perhaps based on our exposure to original research wedded to our love of the psychoanalytic mystery. It is this ideal of questioning that any program of psychoanalytic education must uphold.

However, for those who wish to create the new in greater obedience to self-selected ego ideals, there is still a longing to connect with the existing culture of psychoanalysis both to receive from it and to contribute to it. It has crossed my mind that in regions in which there is a desire to receive and/or provide education and training, that the larger body of the Division ideally serves as a kind of "transitional object." This then is my response to the question I was asked to discuss regarding the relation of the regional groups to the Division in relation to issues of training. As we well know, the transitional object does not function as a superego construct. Its function is to support both the ego development and the creative strivings of the developing psyche. It can come into being only as the child wills it into being and invests it with life and meaning. Without the will of the child, it remains an inanimate object.

There is a great body of knowledge to be handed down in our field. No one person has it all, as no one theory can account for the complexity of the human psyche. For my own part, the ideal is to maintain the unique domain of psychoanalysis without becoming stuck ideologically. That means that we have to understand thoroughly the work of our forefathers and precursors. I believe that is also means we remain open to the dialectic—the theses and antitheses—that have informed psychoanalysis as well as remain open to domains outside of our boundaries whose findings can enrich our knowledge. It means that we have to write and think and question the clinical validity of our findings. That is the foundation of psychoanalysis and although it has not always lived up to its ideal of linking metapsychology with clinical practice, the ideal, to paraphrase Peter Blos, has not died. I believe that we are closer to having a valid clinical metapsychology in psychoanalysis than at any time in its history except perhaps for its earliest beginnings. I believe that it is the shared ego ideal of every one of us not to let that ideal die. I believe too that through the shared diversity of both the leaders and the seekers in the field, that ideal can realized, provided that the ideals of openness, imagination, and excellence underlie the diversity.

29 Summary of Audience Discussion: Division and Local Chapters

Ester R. Shapiro

Marvin Hyman began by reminding the audience that in addition to considering the educational needs of people who have chosen to pursue psychoanalytic training, the discussion should keep in mind two additional constituencies interested in studying psychoanalysis within the local chapters: those who are at an initial stage of exploration, but who seek to expand an already deep and rich psychoanalytic interest, and those who are well established in psychoanalytic careers and wish to use the local chapter's educational program toward their continuing education.

Helen Block Lewis followed, with a call for outcome research in psychoanalysis as the best means of evaluating the quality of psychoanalytic training programs. She pointed out that programs are evaluated, as Fred Pine described, because someone's superego is concerned with the welfare of the students, and underlying that, with the welfare of the patients the student is treating. Evaluating groups are concerned that the program is providing the best patient care possible. She suggested that this purpose of evaluation is so obvious it is often overlooked. Lewis proposed that new local chapter Institutes should develop from the beginning an ongoing research arm designed to evaluate the clinical outcome of their psychoanalytic treatments. Although we can encourage clinicians to do this kind of research in their own practice, most practicing clinicians do not have the time or inclination to conduct outcome research. With an outcome research project in place, the training institution's progress can be monitored not by some outside authorities but by the living evidence of what is happening to the patients being treated.

Murray Meisels began by asking the question, why did the Division find it such a struggle to develop training programs, even to the point of having been

207

reluctant to form an official Division within the American Psychological Association? While there had been talk of a division of psychoanalysis as early as 1946, the Division of Psychotherapy was founded in 1969, and the Division of Psychoanalysis not until 1979. Meisels proposed that the problematical issue is one of separating from the fathers, and Marty Mayman from the University of Michigan agreed that psychoanalysts have problems with the father that take years longer to work out than for other psychotherapists. At some deep level, the issue seems to take the form of psychological parricide, something Meisels has seen more often in the divisional politics than in his own patients. It seemed to him, based on his observations of discussions over the course of the Division's history, that psychologist psychoanalysts could not create their own training programs because they were waiting to be recognized and acknowledged by the paternal authority of the medical psychoanalytic world. In order to move forward from dead center, an act of psychological parricide seemed to be required.

> We have to say to the superego, to the internalized superego, to the father figures in the community, to the analysts who trained us, who analyzed us, who supervised us, we have to say goodbye. We have to walk away from them and not feel that we have betrayed them. We have to appreciate and thank them for what they have done for us, and then move on and develop our own organization. This is a very hard thing to do, and is done with a great deal of guilt.

He observed this same process repeated when the Michigan local chapter began to form its continuing education program, and echoed in the others, such as Boston, which were starting up their own psychoanalytic training programs. It seemed that the anxiety of psychological parricide needed to be faced and worked through again and again.

Meisels also heard these themes of separation as parricide echoed in the papers presented by the panelists. He observed that Pine, who had trained at a medical Institute, and who had in a metaphorical sense "the blessings of the fathers," seemed comfortable with the idea that the Division could support the development of psychoanalytic training for psychologists. Slavin and Kainer, members of local chapters struggling to develop programs, were, in contrast, writing about their struggles with the superego. They suggest a shift from a primitive, punitive superego to a different kind of ideal, as Kainer suggests the Division can act as a transitional object in the process of separation, or as Slavin and Lewis suggest, the ego ideal can be shifted away from the personified father, toward evaluating the quality of the work itself.

He concluded that the Division had to work through a great deal of internal struggle and conflict to allow local chapters to develop, and to support the Clark Conference. In the next developmental phase, where the Division is moving forward toward assuming the role of the father, will the Division be willing to spend money to help local chapters develop training programs? Can the Division adopt and take over that parental, supportive function, or do we believe this authority belongs somewhere else because we haven't yet internalized it? At the last board meeting (August, 1986) the Division seemed reluctant to allocate funds to support local chapter training, at least wishing to wait until after the Clark Conference. Yet the most important function the Division can next serve is to become the new parent supporting the development of local chapter training programs, in the full meaning of the transitional object's developmental role, bridging both external reality in offering financial support, and the internalization of parental functions and parental authority.

Rochelle Kainer asked if we need to make a distinction between parricide and regicide, since some of us may be willing to commit regicide but not parricide, although perhaps we need do neither. (At least, as long as we don't commit suicide.)

Jonathan Slavin responded to Meisels's comments, describing his own observation of Division Board meetings when the formation of local chapters and the Clark Conference were being discussed. He found it extraordinary to think back on the battles that formed around these issues, when the Clark Conference is in fact hardly a communist revolution. The anticipated anxiety at the thought of having this kind of conference was enormous, as though some horrendous and perverse thing were going to happen. As participants in the conference it could be easy to forget how anxiously we all anticipated what has turned out to be simply a fine conference in which reasonable people are trying to talk to each other.

Slavin added that he relates the issue of parricide back to the question of the source and role of authority in our own lives and in psychoanalysis. He was reminded of a wonderful passage in Freud's last essay in the *Three Essays on Sexuality*, describing the adolescent passage into adulthood. In that phase of development through which all individuals ought by rights to pass, from adolescence to adulthood, a certain number are held back, for reasons of neurotic conflict; hopefully, we will not be among those held back. In order to move forward successfully, adolescents have to go through the opposition that naturally occurs between one generation and the next, a tension upon which all human progress is founded. It is a revolutionary view that casts our whole view of authority in a different perspective, and it is striking how much of that developmental or intergenerational perspective has seemed to have gotten bleached out of psychoanalysis.

Fred Pine, while acknowledging the problems in the organization of medical psychoanalytic training, again stressed his belief that the most fundamental aspects of rigidity, freedom of thought, or creativity stem from lifelong personal issues—involving conscience, cognitive style, and identification. Psychologists often share a reassuring view that medical analysts represent a clear outside enemy, while viewing themselves (i.e., psychologists) as more democratic, tolerant of diversity, and freer in their thinking. While reassuring, perhaps, such views are caricatures and do not represent the whole story.

At the center of the story, rather, is the fact that psychoanalysis is an extraordinarily difficult process to learn and to do well. He disagrees with Slavin's implication that analytic training can be viewed like training in any other craft. Some people have intrinsic talent as artists, some as psychoanalysts, and the training builds on that intrinsic talent. Learning to do psychoanalysis involves difficult internal processes, constant self-questioning coupled with constant concern for and attunement to another human being. This process is not for everyone.

Although he, like Lewis and other conference participants, has conducted psychoanalytic research, he suggested that research will always lag behind psychoanalytic practice, and our responsibility as clinicians is to deal with patients here and now. To idealize the research process is to bypass the problems intrinsic to teaching and learning this difficult activity. Also, though it is comforting, and good for group formation, to criticize the medical analytic organization (as has been done throughout the conference), that is not going to resolve the intrinsic problems in this work.

With these remarks, Pine attempted to recenter the discussion at least in part on individual intrapsychic functioning as it operates within the realities of organizational issues in psychoanalysis.

Helen Block Lewis responded to Pine's comments, agreeing that psychoanalysis is a very difficult process to learn. However, she asserts that part of the difficulty is not just intrinsic to the task, but also because she and other colleagues are not comfortable with the outcome results obtained through practicing this difficult art that we have all spent so much energy in learning. It is that uncertainty about therapeutic effectiveness which has been brought into question, and which cannot really be answered by current outcome studies. If we have more certainty that what we are doing is good for patients, it will make learning the art of psychoanalysis a little bit easier.

Gerald Stechler offered a metaphor that might help free the discussion from feeling stuck to moving ahead toward the goals of creating Institutes in the business of doing the work people want to do. He suggests to the psychoanalytic candidates when he trains that they view psychoanalysis as a basketball, that is, something they can learn to toss around, to roll across the floor, to bounce, to pass to each other and throw through the hoop. That is, it is a tool to use, that is external to you, although you have to interact with it and become proficient in its use. What he hears, instead, as a metaphor is the idea of psychoanalysis as an envelope in which one lives, or a belief system one becomes a disciple of or an apostle for. To the extent that psychoanalysis becomes an envelope around one's professional life, if not one's personal life, one will be fraught with all kinds of inhibitions that will make it impossible to move on to the next step. He proposes that reducing the magnitude of the project, seeing psychoanalysis less as the pinnacle of science or of approach to all kinds of treatment, but instead as one very valuable and powerful approach, in parallel with many other valuable models or treatment, then learning psychoanalysis becomes a less awesome proposition. He agrees with Pine that psychoanalysis is very difficult, very engrossing, very complicated, but it should not be awesome, and to the extent it remains awesome, everybody is going to be very intimidated.

Sam Gerson began by agreeing that one goal of the conference is to avoid repeating the mistakes of the past by learning from them, and he appreciated the discussion of ego formation and processes of identification as a means of conceptualizing training. He suggests that some of the authority issues are embedded in the language of the profession, borrowed from psychiatry and our psychiatric colleagues. He referred to the work of Harry Levenson, an organizational psychologist who spoke at Cambridge Hospital and commented that even in a collaborative, interdisciplinary hospital all the departments borrow their organization from psychiatry. Gerson proposes that the influence of psychiatry shows up in our discussion, especially in the language of psychopathology used to describe training, rather than a more task-oriented language. We talk about parricide, transitional objects, concepts that help us understand our experience, but don't talk about using consultants, or mentorship, or generativity, concepts that reflect a task orientation rather than psychopathology. He suggests that we can usefully look to the national divisional organization as a consultant, and the Division can take a generative role in supporting the development of local chapter's training.

Susannah Gourevitch commented that she was in agreement with the last two speakers, who are urging a shift to different language and metaphors reflecting a task orientation. From the beginning of the discussion, though, she felt she had missed a step somewhere, because she was not aware that the Division was considering having a review authority over local chapter training programs. She wished to make a strong statement against such national review, especially in light of Marvin Hyman's paper proposing alternative models for training programs, which need to develop responsive to local communities and their local conditions. With such a model in mind, it seems impossible to have uniform national standards and still encourage the development of a wide range of training options.

Jonathan Slavin made the final comment, stating that he wished to shift the discussion from patricide to fratricide. He observed that it was an enormous relief to the Division that the American Psychological Association could not permit its Divisions to certify training programs, because it stopped us from killing each other over the question of training. It interrupted a destructive process, as anyone attending board meetings could observe, and this interruption was beneficial. Unfortunately, it also stopped discussion of the flow of resources from the

Division to developing training efforts, and the Division is rich not only in its financial resources but also in terms of the caliber of people with training and experience, expertise which could be available to the local chapters. Hopefully, each local chapter will not be left to struggle with these issues alone. Even within the constraints of the APA restrictions on certification, Slavin believed it was still possible for the Division to support the development of training programs in local areas.

30

Introduction: Implications of New Information for Psychoanalytic Training

Ester R. Shapiro

In the initial planning of the Clark Conference, the committee agreed that the broad range of theoretical and technical revisions or innovations within psycho-analysis could not reasonable be addressed in the short time allotted for the conference, which would focus on issues of training in psychoanalysis. Yet a critique of current training, and an exploration of alternatives, could not be undertaken without acknowledging that the structure of current training typically excluded new perspectives both within psychoanalysis and in related fields. Helen Block Lewis was especially committed to the idea that new information in fields outside psychoanalysis could provide an avenue for reassessing and ex-panding psychoanalytic concepts. Lewis felt that new information in the study of human development, especially on the relational attachments of early childhood within the family, and the special perspective of women on family experience could provide a valuable expansion of the psychoanalytic perspective.

There was, as has been discussed, a fair amount of controversy about the Clark Conference from its inception. One of the arguments concerned whether the focus should be on a critique of the existing tripartite model, or on broader formulations such as the impact of new research, or the developmental nature of a psychoanalytic identity. It was no coincidence that the panel on new informa-tion from child development and the psychology of women was held on the last day of the conference, when a substantial number of conference participants had already left. At the same time, this conference panel attracted the largest number of outside registrants who attended only for that one session. Several of the speakers suggested that this process in itself reflected the difficulty in psycho-analysis of learning from the perspectives of child development, psychology of women, and family systems theory.

Gerald Stechler, Ph.D., is a psychoanalytically trained developmental researcher who has participated in a 20-year longitudinal study examining the continuity of personality in family relational terms. In a background paper, "The Study of Infants Engenders Systemic Thinking," he argued that normal assertion in infancy often becomes contaminated with aggression, because parents often define the baby's execution of personal plans, and active engagement with the world, as an act of aggression, and respond to it as such. In his paper, he proposed that psychoanalysis and systems theory are compatible when the clinical aspects of psychoanalysis, such as conflict theory, theory of affect, adaptation or attachment are emphasized rather than the metapsychology. He stated that thermodynamics has held back psychoanalytic developmental theory for 150 years, because entropy is an antidevelopmental theory. Biological systems theory emphasizes that a living system is defined by its context, and the coherence of a system can be discerned at many vantage points, depending on the level of detail of the observation. Traditional metaphsychology argues that psychic structure changes slowly, while systems theory proposes that psychic structure is a web-like structure of cyclical loops, maintained by the context of relationships, reorganized with changes in context.

The papers on the psychology of women emphasized a number of common points. First, the traditionally masculine psychoanalytic perspective has emphasized autonomy and separation rather than attachment and relationships in the construction of the self. Psychoanalytic understanding of human development can best take place with an acknowledgment of the relational nature of development for both women and men. Second, psychoanalysis has tended to ignore the role of reality in the experience of the individual, whether the reality be a sociocultural one or an interpersonal and familial one. Analysis of intrapsychic structure, or the understanding of emotional life, can best take place when the realities of life, including the injustices of cultural and family life, are addressed. Within a male-dominated society, and a male-dominated mental health profession, the defensive attitudes of men toward women and children are supported rather than examined, at the expense of the emotional life of men, women, and children.

Jean Baker Miller, M.D., began with a reminder that psychoanalysis, at its own time in history, was a profoundly revolutionary approach to the emotional life of the individual, which emphasized the personal costs of cultural repression, especially the repression of emotions and sexuality. Among radical psychoanalytic innovations were the technique of free association, where social prohibitions aside, anything could be stated freely; the importance of the patient leading the way for the doctor to follow, rather than the patient being acted upon; the emphasis on discovering the personal truth as freeing or healing; and the realization that masculinity and femininity are not there originally, but that the psychological structures of masculinity and femininity are constructed by the individual child. Once a revolution is institutionalized, it establishes its own pressures toward conformity, with accompanying rigidity and constriction of creativity. Miller concluded that the emotional and relational life which psychoanalysis uncovered is that part of life which the society does not provide well for but rather represses, in both women and men. In a male-dominated society, masculine development is oriented toward educating boys to become members of the dominant sex, at the expense of their "womanly" emotional life or their sense of connectedness to others. She believes that the study of women's experience will not only lead to a better understanding of women, but of the total human experience.

Lenore Walker, Ph.D., stated that psychoanalytic thinking, beginning with Freud's views of women, has contributed to the stereotyping of women as inferior or more disturbed than men; has encouraged women to adapt to their social role rather than to change social conditions; and by analyzing the individual woman's problems has added to a process of blaming the victim of violence for her own predicament. Although the contributions of feminist theorists, including psychoanalysts, to new perspectives on women's mental health have been well documented, she finds that psychoanalysis tends to invalidate theoretical differences rather than integrate new ideas. The real incidence of family violence and sexual abuse has been denied by psychoanalysis, in spite of a growing realization about the prevalence and destructive developmental impact of such experiences. She recommended reducing the hierarchy or distance between patient and therapist, acknowledging the importance of real events, and supporting women's social empowerment. She concluded by stating that psychoanalysis can respond to feminist scholarship as a challenge promoting expansion and growth, rather than as an attack.

Dale Mendell, Ph.D., argued that in order for the psychology of women to be fully integrated into psychoanalytic programs, and not just segregated into an isolated course attended largely by women candidates, its relevance to every aspect of training needs to be discussed. As one example, she reviewed the educational issues involved in educating male candidates on the nature of their work with a female patient. Such an educational process would address normative gender development in men and women, the consequences of developmental differences in identification processes with mothers and fathers, and the implications of these differences for adult relationships and interactions between men and women, as they manifest themselves in a male therapist/female patient dyad. She concluded by stating that scholarship, feminist or otherwise, should lead toward integration of theoretical perspectives rather than their polarization.

REFERENCES

Dilling, C., and Claster, B. *Female Psychology: A Partially Annotated Bibliography.* Project sponsored by the New York City Coalition for Women's Mental Health, 1985, 326 pages (available through the Coalition).

Mendell, D. (Ed.) *Early Female Development: Current Psychoanalytic Views*. New York: Springer Medical and Scientific Books, 1982.

Mendell, D. Cross-gender supervision of cross-gender therapy: female supervisor, male candidate, female patient. *Amer. J. Psychoanal.*, 46, 2, 1986.

Miller, J. B. *Toward A New Psychology Of Women*. Boston: Beacon Press; first edition, 1976; second edition, 1986.

Miller, J. B. *Psychoanalysis And Women*. New York: Bruner/Mazel, 1973.

Stechler, G. The study of infants engenders systemic thinking. *Psychoanalytic Inquiry*, 5:4, 531–541, 1985.

Stechler, G., and Halton, A. The emergence of assertion and aggression during infancy. *J. Amer. Psychoanal. Assoc.*, 1987.

Walker, L. *Women and Mental Health Policy*. Beverly Hills: Sage, 1984.

Walker, L. *The Battered Woman Syndrome*. New York: Springer, 1984.

31

The Integration of Psychoanalysis and Family Systems

Gerald Stechler

INTRODUCTION

The aim of this chapter is to present some bridging concepts between psycho-analytic and family systems approaches. Each offers powerful models for the understanding of the human condition, and despite the apparent incompatibilities and animosities between the two, the parallel dynamic underpinnings fosters the idea of connectability. We are faced with a task similar to the botanist who wants to graft two trees. For the two to be able to grow together, one must get under the bark, or to pursue another metaphor, a successful organ transplant often requires a suppression of the immune rejection system. We must therefore do two things. First, look into the core of the theory so that we are not put off by surface differences, and secondly, hold our distastes in abeyance long enough to give thoughtful consideration to the propositions.

Integration of the two systems of thinking is advantageous for advocates of each school, and for seasoned practitioners as well as students. There are many clinicians who already use both approaches, but who may feel that at any given moment they must choose between the two. A true integration is not attempted because these therapists believe that they are operating across two incompatible theoretical realms. This must be troublesome to the clinician and deprives the patients of the combined strength of the two models.

For confirmed advocates of either of the schools who deal with the other side by rejecting and even condemning it, a word of caution is in order. All of us are so far away from having adequate answers to the complex psychological prob-lems presented by our patients that we should have the humility to be searching always for related scientific models that could increase our understanding and effectiveness.

There are several steps I propose to take in order to facilitate this process. The first involves an inquiry into the extent to which psychoanalysis can be viewed as a general systems theory. If we can designate the aspects of psychoanalysis which conform with the assumptions of general systems theory we shall have a strong base from which to build the bridges to other general systems theories, such as family systems theory.

The second step is to look more specifically at certain central psychoanalytic propositions which not only can be transposed into family systems interventions, but also provide the psychodynamic foundations for those interventions. This constitutes a major contribution of psychoanalysis to family systems thinking.

The final step explores an aspect of family systems thinking that makes an important contribution to psychoanalysis. With that process completed we will have treated both sides equitably and left everyone feeling that they have benefited from crossing the bridge. Who knows what could follow from that?

Psychoanalysis as a General Systems Theory

As George Klein (1976), and others have pointed out, psychoanalysis is not one but two theories. Klein differentiated the clinical from the metapsychological theory, and defended the thesis that the important contributions are in the clinical theory, with metapsychology not only failing to enrich the overall model, but in fact obscuring and distracting from the central insights.

Our differentiation is similar to, although not identical with, Klein's. Our categories are not clinical and metapsychological, but rather systemic and nonsystemic. However, the overlap of the two modes of classification is almost perfect. The clinical theory of psychoanalysis contains many of the attributes of a general systems theory.

1. Psychoanalysis is very broad and comprehensive. It is a general psychology asking the fundamental questions about the nature of human existence. A general systems approach is one in which the understanding of events is based on the broad context within which those events take place. In a network of many interconnected nodes, the functioning of any particular node is understood within the context of the network, no matter how detailed a study one may undertake of the node itself.

2. Psychoanalysis taps many levels of scientific inquiry in order to derive its explanatory propositions. Freud drew from disciplines ranging from anthropology to neurophysiology in the development of his psychology. In Paul Weiss's (1949) view of general systems theory, all levels of inquiry from micro to macro are valid, providing one is able to uncover some coherence at each level. Furthermore, the best general systems models are ones in which there are bridging statements that can integrate across the vertical levels from micro to

macro. By explaining the visible conscious behaviors, thoughts, and feelings of people via an understanding of the invisible unconscious processes, and by bringing coherence and rules to the functioning of the unconscious, Freud greatly increased the general system property of psychology. Transforming a layer such as the unconscious, whose existence had long been suspected, but for which there had been no coherent model of operation, into a coherent layer, fulfills an important mandate of general systems theory. Furthermore, by establishing the rules for the interchanges across the vertical levels of conscious and unconscious, he created the first general systems psychology. Details of the way in which the unconscious works are essential to any application of general systemic principles. An example of this will follow.

3. Psychoanalysis is organismic rather than atomistic. No matter how analytic and detailed it may get, its basic questions concern the integration of elements into a functional unity. The rich admixture of "why" questions as the basis for the "how" questions is another example of the organismic approach. One might almost say that psychosynthesis would be a more appropriate name for the discipline than is psychoanalysis. Any general systems theory must be synthetic and ask questions about how all of the nodes in a network interact as a functional unity.

4. Psychoanalysis is multicausal rather than unicausal. In some respects this is the same as (3), but it carries a somewhat different emphasis. Linear, non-systemic models tend to search for single causes. Freud was certainly embedded in a scientific ethos of linear models, but nevertheless proclaimed the doctrine of overdetermination virtually from the outset (1900). The principle of overdetermination focuses our attention on the multiple and interlocking roots of any symptom, dream, pattern of relationships, and so on. Thus instead of trying to peel away elements so as to find the single essential causal factor, we try to add elements to our network of explanation so as to find the fullest understanding. Few if any important aspects of our psyche are thought to come from single causes. The principle of overdetermination states that the more tributaries there are feeding the stream, the stronger will be the commitment to that channel. We therefore find ourselves searching for networks rather than points.

5. Psychoanalysis is rich in feedback loops. Homeostatic functions are emphasized. Self-regulation in the face of dramatically shifting internal and external circumstances is the subject matter of much of the inquiry within psychoanalysis. The conflict model or dynamic point of view concerns itself with the interplay of forces and the adaptational and developmental consequences of successful or unsuccessful resolutions of the conflicts.

These examples are far from exhaustive, but they have been presented not so much to define fully the field, as to introduce this general mode of thinking about psychoanalysis, and to show that the bridge to other systemic models may not be all that difficult.

PSYCHOANALYTIC CONTRIBUTIONS
TO FAMILY SYSTEMS

One of the rarely mentioned, but fundamental, contributions of Freud to psychology was the transformation from a linear logic to a much more systemic logic. For example, let us take the polar affects of love and hate. In a linear model, since these are opposite affects, they cannot coexist. They are coexclusionary. The presence of one implies the absence of the other. In a linear model that is what opposite means.

Clearly, we know that Freud proposed a very different view. In psychoanalysis not only can love and hate coexist, they must coexist. Through the understanding of the unconscious and of primary process thinking Freud took us out of the age of linear psychology. The mechanisms he elucidated in *The Interpretation of Dreams* (1900) are distinctly nonlinear. Reversal, condensation, denial, and the other dream mechanisms indicate not only the ambivalent roots of all of our powerful wishes, feelings, images, and fantasies, but also the manner in which we manage to blind ourselves to the conscious awareness of the rejected side of the ambivalence. The possibility of virtually instantaneous transformation from one pole to the other lies at the heart of nonlinear systems. In nonlinear systems, qualitatively different states can be separated from each other by infinitesimal boundaries, so that transformations from one state to another do not necessarily involve gradual transitions, the extend of which would be proportional to some metric describing the differences between the two states. Rather, as with electron orbits, the forces at play either keep the electron in a given orbit or cause it instantaneously to jump to a new orbit, with no possibility of remaining in a transitional state. So too with certain psychological states. For example, affective states in infants can shift from euphoric to dysphoric as excitement mounts. When the level of excitement crosses some threshold value, the qualitative shift from joy to distress can be virtually instantaneous. There is no gradual subsiding of one, or a passage through some observable neutral state on the way to a mounting intensity of the opposite affect.

Over the past 25 years, spanning the development of the family systems approach, there has been a tendency to use psychoanalysis as the whipping boy, or more cogently, as the rejected parent. For me this has been an unfortunate aspect of the creation of the new models. Many important family therapists began their training within the folds of psychoanalysis, and it is understandable that in trying to differentiate oneself from one's progenitors the rejection of the past may be a crucial step. In the course of studying family systems during the early childhood period, it has become clear to me that while negation may be a crucial mechanism in the service of differentiation, excessive or exclusive reliance on this mechanism does not occur in the healthiest families, nor does it produce the most satisfactory developmental pattern. A family system that can integrate itself with its own past is in a much better position to move forward than one which has rejected its past. This does not mean that there has to be a slavish loyalty to former belief systems. Rather an appreciation of continuity, and a willingness to give some credit to one's forebears makes sense, whether the treatment is psychoanalytic or systemic.

Let us therefore jump to some of the central technical contributions of the family systems approach and ask what if any may be the connections to psychoanalysis. As a further step we may then ask how an elucidation of those connections can embed the techniques in an appropriate theoretical network and thereby increase their effectiveness.

Joining, reframing, and paradoxical intervention make up a key triad in the technical armamentarium of family systems therapy (Selvim-Palazzolli, 1978). Joining is the method of forming a therapeutic alliance with all of the family members, reframing is recasting the problem so that it can be seen as solvable rather than insolvable, and paradoxical intervention facilitates a rapid change in the face of great resistance.

Joining is a multistep process in the context of family therapy. The ultimate aim is to join and form an empathic connection to each member of the family and with the family system as a whole. Some of the difficulties that stand in the way of that aim are related to countertransference issues that the therapist may encounter with respect to each member of the family, to the conflict and uncertainty the therapist feels when quickly caught up in the entanglements among the family members as each member struggles to enlist the therapist on his or her behalf, and to the countertransferences to the family system as a whole.

Experience in an adolescent inpatient service in which we have tried to integrate family systems and psychoanalytic approaches has taught us that joining with an abusive, addicted, or highly narcissistic parent is often very difficult. Our natural tendency is to feel some strong negative affect toward, and an inability to join with, a parent who is undermining their own child through a process known as destructive entitlement (Boszormenyi-Nagy, 1986). But treatment progress is critically dependent on that joining because if there is a villain–victim split in the therapist's mind, all sorts of problems ensue. The adolescent may feel gratified momentarily by the therapist's allying with his or her expressed negative view of the parent, but that will always backfire in the long run. The youngster's own ambivalence and loyalty toward the parent, no matter how abusive, will always defeat the therapist's misalliance. The parent, of course, sensing an enemy, will destroy the treatment. Technically, the family systems approach informs us of the crucial importance of not falling into this trap. Psychoanalysis via the understanding of the unconscious and its associated ambivalences can inform us about what is going on in each family member as well as in ourselves. We gain the flexibility to shift among opposing affects and images. That greatly enhances our capacity to reframe our own internal perceptions, and to now see that same parent as representing parts of ourselves and our families. At that point joining becomes not only possible, but is a natural, sincere act of true empathy. The worst danger of a purely technical approach to this complex problem is the likelihood of artificiality in the move to join, with all of the incumbent evocations of the false self in the therapist and in the patients.

The second technique, reframing, is related to joining. As just noted, the process of joining may be facilitated by an internal reframing of the therapist's own perception of one or more of the family members. As a therapeutic technique, the same process is used to alter a fundamental perception or construction for one or more persons in the family, or for the family as a whole. That process starts with the therapist's thorough understanding of the nature of the patient's ambivalence. It is not only an understanding of the general principles of ambivalence, but most importantly a sense of the central metaphor by which the patient expresses one or another pole of that ambivalence. If the reframe is to achieve its aim of transforming a central image or construction in the patient's mind, it must capture the personal nuance by which the patient recognizes his or her own meaning. Psychoanalysis can thus give us both the general theoretical model for bringing out the other side of an ambivalent polarity, and also direct us toward the unique personal metaphor that captures the essence of the patient's conflict.

A paradoxical intervention carries the technique of reframing one step further. It speaks simultaneously to both sides of an ambivalence so that if its meaning is taken directly or as its inverse it remains true either way. Typically the paradoxical intervention addresses the unspoken side of the ambivalence. Thus if a patient protests how hard he or she has been working to be supportive of a given relationship the therapist may suggest that the patient has been working too hard to maintain the relationship. At the conscious level the patient may believe he or she has been doing all one can, while the more defended side of the ambivalence is that one feels oppressed in the relationship and wants a way out. The way out is blocked by guilt and loyalty, as well as by the ambivalence of wanting and not wanting the relationship at the same time. The paradoxical statement validates the conscious statement of good faith effort, but also subtly acknowledges the wish to get out, thereby creating an empathic connection with both sides of the ambivalence. At the same time that the patient experiences the positive effect of feeling more totally understood, the terms of the conflict are shifted so that he or she can no longer deal with it by protesting how hard one is trying. Now there is a distinct possibility that the patient can acknowledge and even accept both sides of the ambivalence. Once the ambivalence is out in the open, the resolution of the conflict can be based on integrated rather than split functions. By using the indicated paradoxical statement, the therapist has not aligned oneself as the negative parent. That would have been the case if the therapist had questioned the amount of effort that had been exerted by the patient.

The well-tuned, analytically oriented therapist operating without systemic concepts would still recognize that the patient's claim of great effort in the relationship represented only one side of the ambivalence, but would more likely intervene by asking him or her to look at the other side, namely the wish to leave. In doing so, however, there is a strong possibility of evoking a defensive reaction, perpetuating the split ambivalence. The combination of analytic sensitivity to the ambivalence combined with a better technical appreciation of how to address it, maintains the empathic connection and challenges the patient to integrate rather than split the two sides of the ambivalence.

There is a tendency to view paradox as a specific, powerful, if somewhat gimmicky, technique employed by a systemic therapist at those times when a straight intervention has not worked. This is a misunderstanding of the nature of the psychology of the unconscious and of ambivalence. To the extent that ambivalence is universal, then so too is paradox. It is everywhere around us and is an aspect of every important interpersonal interaction, whether we like it or not. It is there whether or not there has been a conscious decision to employ it as a therapeutic technique.

Any communication from a therapist to a patient must carry multiple meanings. As analytically oriented therapists we are usually aware of the multiple developmental levels, and/or different structural elements, that may be addressed by a single remark. What may be a little less obvious is the inevitable paradoxical component that is implicit in each intervention. Thus, if we accept the idea that all important beliefs, feelings, fantasies, and perceptions are ambivalently held, then we should also accept the idea that it is impossible for any significant message not to be addressing both sides simultaneously. Deliberately, or inadvertently, we are talking to both sides. If the intervention is not carefully planned somehow to validate both sides of the ambivalence, then we may be challenging unnecessarily the defensive functions connected to the side we have not validated. In that way the interpretation could conceivably produce exactly the opposite effect from what was intended. Without any such intention on our part, we have undesirably placed the patient in a paradox, and puzzled ourselves. We have also acted detrimentally on the therapeutic alliance. Validating one side of the ambivalence while invalidating the other leaves the patient feeling only half understood. It is confusingly or subliminally experienced as an empathic break, with a concomitant diminution of the integration of the self, and a loss of connectedness to the therapist.

Shafer (1970), addresses the universality of paradox as embodied in the ironic view of reality. "The ironic vision I shall characterize chiefly as a readiness to seek out internal contradictions, ambiguities, and paradoxes" (p. 50). In combination with the tragic view of life, irony portrays the twisting, convoluted experience of our existence. The aphorism, "No good deed goes unpunished," encapsulates a world view in which we feel stymied that our benign intents do not bear benevolent fruit. At issue, of course, is the fact that our benign intents have a shadow side, the unspoken other side of our ambivalence. If our wishes are ambivalent, then so too are our messages. Added to that are the inevitable ambivalences of the person who is receiving our messages. Thus it is no great wonder that a paradoxical outcome of our initiatives may seem to be more the rule than the exception.

Yet another factor in this equation is the way in which each of us, in part, maintains our sense of autonomy and integrity by resisting directions from the outside. It may be negativism, or it may be something subtler and more complex than that. The outcome, however, is reverse psychology, to use pop terminology. If you want a child to do something, request the opposite. The famous episode when Tom Sawyer wishes to get help from his friends in the onerous task of painting Aunt Polly's fence, he presents it to them as a privilege rather than a favor, thereby placing them in a paradoxical situation.

Given these perspectives, paradox is anything but a gimmick. Rather it represents a natural interpersonal playing out of the universal internal ambivalence. Our task is to know how to use this principle in the service of the therapy, rather than having it operate unwittingly to the detriment of the treatment.

The principle is so fundamental that it extends far beyond the realm of psychology. Hofstadter (1979) weaves the complex, nonlinear tapestry of the natural, aesthetic, and mathematical world to show us that at the heart of every system there lies a fundamental ambiguity that defies determination. Simplistic views of a deterministic world, bounded by concrete reality, are now seen to be more an expression of our own ignorance or infantile wish structure, rather than a statement of scientific principles.

More recently, the new physics of chaos (Gleick, 1987), and of self-organizing systems (Prigogine, 1980), leads us to appreciate the very term paradox as a reflection of our own naïvete. Something is called paradoxical because it is unexpectedly opposite from our anticipations. In time, as our anticipations become more truly systemic, the affect of surprise will perhaps diminish, and the word paradox will become commonplace, or even outmoded.

FAMILY SYSTEM CONTRIBUTIONS
TO PSYCHOANALYSIS

While family systems thinking has, from the outset, been intensely preoccupied with the question of change and how it takes place, psychoanalysis has placed this question much more at the periphery of its concerns. It is precisely around this issue of change that family systems can be helpful to psychoanalysis.

I have reflected with a number of analysts about how change occurs in analysis. There seems to be a consensus that when change does occur, it is likely to be discontinuous in nature. That is, for long stretches the hours are taken up with the continuing exploration of fantasies, of transferences, and of resistances. This is seen as essential to the creation of functional or structural change, but it is not seen as change itself. The actual change, which may occur only very infrequently, can be occasioned by an interpretation or by a spontaneous insight, which then acts suddenly to reorganize some area of the patient's feelings, perceptions, and perhaps actions. This is a rather different picture from one which would explain the long, slow aspect of psychoanalysis as being based upon the minute gradualness with which the changes take place. This reported view is much more in line with that of nonlinear thinking, and is similar to the formulations found in family systems.

One of the major impediments to the development of an effective model of change within psychoanalysis has to do with the concept of structure as defined psychoanalytically. Rapaport (1959), in proposing his five viewpoints of psychoanalysis, defines the structural point of view as addressing those aspects of the psyche which change slowly. There is something circular about that definition because it begs the question of what does or does not produce change. It confuses the terms stability and immutability. Simply because something has been around for a very long time with little or no perceptible change does not necessarily imply that it is immutable. True, if one envisions something like the Egyptian pyramids when one thinks of structure, then any effort to alter them, or remove them to a new site is going to be slow and laborious. But this may not be the only way to conceptualize structure. In a more modern conceptualization, a stable field of forces can also be seen as a structure. The stability and durability may arise from the fact that the multiple loops which comprise the structure are self-sustaining. They act in such a way as to be self-perpetuating. Some of these loops may be entirely internal within a single individual, while others exist in the interpersonal space of family relationships and rules.

This new concept of structure satisfies the criteria of stability and durability, but it need not at all imply the criterion of immutability. The appropriate application of a new set of forces could instantly transform it into some new organizational configuration, and depending on the circumstances, that new organization could be as stable as the old. We need to dissociate stability from immutability. We should be able to imagine that entrenched patterns of internal or external functions can be susceptible to sudden transformation. They way that the analysts described how change did occur in treatment does in fact fit that model.

Once we accept the idea that, at least in principle, psychic structure is open to sudden transformation, a whole new set of questions emerge. They have to do with examining the circumstances that would foster or impede such change, and developing technical models that would facilitate the changes which the patients profess to desire. Clinicians know, however, just how ephemeral that desire can be. Again, based on the understanding of ambivalence, we know that the forces for no change are equal to or greater than the forces for change. With respect to the therapy itself, those homeostatic forces are commonly classified under the heading of resistance.

While the same term may be used within different theoretical approaches, resistance can have varying meanings. In the drive model, resistance may be triggered when the associations approach a forbidden area. Thus resistance is defined as an endogenous process, residing within the patient, and serving to preserve the existing repressions. In the object relations school, in self-psychology, and in family systems, resistance is seen much more as an aspect of the patient–therapist relationship. When resistance is encountered, therapists from those schools are much more likely to ask what has just transpired in themselves or in their relationship with the patient. Has there been an empathic failure?, they might ask themselves.

Within this latter framework one is led to explore many more avenues that could lead to a reduction of resistance and a regenerating of the patient's openness to change, than would be the case in the endogenous model. Further-more, recognizing the ambivalent nature of the change–resistance axis itself allows one to employ all of the technical moves that have been noted in order to play with that ambivalence in a much more creative way. With this model one can be more creative than always having to rely on slowness of the pace and the maintenance of the therapeutic alliance as the only ways to keep the resistance within workable limits. This greater flexibility achieved by integrating the technical developments from family systems approaches into the theoretical framework of psychoanalysis leads to a much more systematic approach to structure and to change within psychoanalysis.

Speaking of resistance, it is worth noting that there is a resistance within psychoanalytic thinking to any change in the patient that seems to happen too quickly. Concepts such as flight into health, symptom suppression, or trans-ference cure are invoked as a means of minimizing the value of any change that does occur very early in the treatment. Psychoanalysts believe that such changes are ephemeral, and therefore it is understandable that not much credence is given to them. There may be something of a self-fulfilling prophecy in this perspective, and it may also be that the transitory nature of those early changes is related to the absence of an adequate technical model of how to make them self-sustaining.

If we accept that nonlinear transformations can occur at any time, but that some transformations are fleeting, then the question for us is not so much to discredit those that seem to be impermanent, but rather to ask whether there is any way for those changes to become more stable. This, of course, gets back to the previous discussion about the concept of structure. Family systems therapists distinguish between first- and second-order change as a way of addressing this issue of transitory gain. A first-order change is unstable in the same way as a flight into health. In general, the change may persist only as long as the therapist is present to give it functional support. At times even that may not suffice and the patterns will revert to the original dysfunctional mode irrespective of interven-tions. Practitioners of all schools struggle to achieve second-order or structural changes that are stable, self-sustaining, and, under optimal conditions, form the nucleus for a chain reaction of beneficial changes.

The issue here is not to try to spell out the complex considerations that make up each school's approach to fostering such changes, but simply to point out that although the language may differ, all thoughtful practitioners have similar therapeutic aims. Again, the antipathies between the parties may be more around style than substance.

Is any school or combination of schools a magic road? Obviously not. These reformulations may help, but the question remains why are so many conditions so recalcitrant. One possible explanation is that the forces that are holding the existing structures in place are not only strong, but also multilayered and heavily entangled. Even if one can get an effective handle on a few of the self-sustaining loops that are holding the system in place, there may be many other unseen or unapproachable loops that operate to undermine the effort to change. That is another important reason to try to get into the patient's and family's metaphorical frame to the greatest extent that is possible. For it is likely that embedded in that central metaphor is the greatest concentration of self-sustaining loops. If that metaphor can be reframed or transformed in some other way, then we probably will have succeeded in changing the greatest number of loops.

Traditionally, stable change has been seen as most difficult when personality disorders or character pathology has been involved. This viewpoint raises the question about the relationship between character and systemic or contextual variables. For me, a reasonably satisfactory approach to this question has been to frame the concept of character in the same terms that I apply to the concept of truth, that is, that they are plural rather than singular terms. There are always "truths" and not "the truth." In the same way, there are, for each of us, character modes rather than a single core character. Any person embodies a range of character types or styles. Functionally, one or another of these types may be ascendant at a particular time, depending on the context, the forces and conflicts that are active at that moment, or even the person with whom we are interacting at that moment. Again, our understanding of ambivalence and the nature of unconscious functioning should alert us to the breadth of modes in which one person can operate. While not claiming to be able to create the proverbial silk purse out of the sow's ear, we may be able to discover, as did one scientist (Arthur D. Little) that the protein strands in a pig's ear, when properly extracted and treated can appear and function just like silk, and can be woven into a very credible looking "silk" purse. For each of us, some of our character modes are developmentally, interpersonally, and adaptively, much more troubling than are others. Moving to the less troubled end of our own spectrum is neither a trivial nor an impossible task. The changes that are both manifested as well as experienced can be durable and can make an enormous difference in one's life and with one's family.

CONCLUSION

Now that gifts have been exchanged both ways, the atmosphere may be sufficiently relaxed to permit us to note some of the other problems without sending the guests scurrying. Whether one person or a whole family is present in the office at any given time obviously affects the mental states of the patient(s) and of the therapist. Making the leap to the multiperson arena clearly can be daunting if one's training and experience has not prepared them. That to me is not nearly as important as whether the therapist has a systemic conceptualization of the disorder, and frames the treatment model in the same terms. Those schools of psychoanalysis that already define resistance in interactive terms are likely to be closer to the proposed integration than are those that are still heavily weighted toward hypotheses of endogenous forces. It seems to me that the struggle may be as much within psychoanalysis itself as it is between psychoanalysis and other schools.

The attempt here has been to demonstrate the possibility of moving toward an integration by picking a few specific concepts and exploring their bridgelike qualities. If commerce between the two schools can increase our understanding and improve our methods of treatment, the patients stand to be the beneficiaries. Needless to say the overall project is very large, and even the discovery of points of true incompatibility, should that occur, will tell us more about the boundaries and limitations of each model.

REFERENCES

Boszormenyi–Nagy, I., & Krasner, B. R. (1986). *Between give and take.* New York,: Brunner/ Mazel.

Freud, S. (1900, 1953). *The interpretation of dreams. The standard edition of the complete psychological works of Sigmund Freud* (Vols, 4, 5). London, Hogarth Press.

Gleick, J. (1987). *Chaos.* New York: Viking.

Hofstadter, D. (1979). *Godel, Escher, Bach.* New York: Vintage Books.

Klein, G. S. (1976). *Psychoanalytic theory.* New York: International Universities Press.

Prigogine, I. (1980). *From being to becoming.* San Francisco: W. H. Freeman.

Rapaport, D. (1959). The points of view and assumptions of metapsychology. In *The collected papers of David Rapaport.* New York: Basic Books, pp. 795–811.

Schafer, R. (1970). *A new language for psychoanalysis.* New Haven, CT: Yale University Press.

Selvin-Palazzoli, M., Boscolo, L., Cecchin, G., and Prata, G. (1978). *Paradox and counterparadox.* New York: Jason Aaronson.

Weiss, P. (1949). The biological basis of adaptation, in J. Romano, (Ed.), *Adaptation.* Ithaca, NY: Cornell University Press.

32 Psychoanalysis and the Psychology of Women

Jean Baker Miller

Eric Erikson once said that psychoanalysis may be at its best when it is dealing with those forces within any society that that society is suppressing at that time. It seems to me that psychoanalysis must exist in any uneasy position within society. If psychoanalysis is truly dealing with what is suppressed, it has to be at least potentially revolutionary. Yet once it becomes institutionalized, pressures toward conformity set in. These pressures lead inevitably to ridigity and the constriction of creativity. Since you are considering the creation of new institutional forms, especially in regard to training, it would be truly valuable to recognize such tendencies and provide processes and procedures to counter them, especially, but not only, as they apply to the understanding and treatment of women.

At its origins, psychoanalysis made innovations which I find compatible with some of the startling new perspectives which modern feminism has created. I won't talk about all of these innovations but will suggest just a few. One was the idea that the patient must lead the way in the process of expressing his or her feelings and thoughts. While this concept certainly has been violated in practice, it represented a major change from the doctor *acting on* the patient as in the medical model before Freud (and enjoying a resurgence today within psychiatry). It follows that psychoanalysis then must be a collaborative task by both patient and therapist. Another major underlying assumption was the idea that the truth will set you free or the truth will "cure." Of course, there has been subsequent debate about what "truth" the patient has to discover.

Psychoanalysis opened as questions huge areas that had been assumed closed or "givens." Probably the most important area was the question of femininity and masculinity. Freud put forward the revolutionary idea that femininity and masculinity are not there originally but have to be constructed over and over again in the mind of each child. In other words, biological sexual characteristics are born but the psychological structures of personhood, or of femininity and masculinity, are made.

Psychoanalysis also created a special arena for its work, free from society's usual rules about what can be expressed and what cannot. Although this arena, the psychoanalytic setting, certainly never was itself free of its own constraints, at least it was different. While the psychoanalytic setting may be in need of re-examination in the light of new understandings today, it did lead to the expression of thoughts and feelings which had not been heard before in the same way.

When we look at the main themes of the content which emerged in the psychoanalytic setting, we can discern certain broad tendencies. Analysts found that men and women talked about, and in terms of, emotions. They were not talking in the form of logical discourse used in society but in the forms of a vivid kaleidoscope of feelings. They talked of childhood and childlike experience. They talked in particular about the feelings revolving around helplessness and powerlessness which are not safe to reveal in the "real world." They talked about sexual experience, or more broadly, bodily experience. And they talked about human longing for connections to others.

We could sort these topics in other ways but I think this is a fair list. These are all aspects of experience that our culture, at least as we know it so far, cannot allow open expression. And society as we know it so far, has been organized by men around only certain aspects of the total human potential. Psychoanalysis turned up things that such a culture cannot encompass in socially approved forms. These are also the parts of life that have been said to be associated with women. They are all labeled "womanly."

I'm suggesting then that these are the parts of life which a male-organized society has not provided well even for men. It cannot do so if it is based on allowing only the members of one sex to become full-fledged people. Such "full-fledged people" become dominant people. If you have to become a dominant person, you cannot allow the existence of all these parts of life. Such a society cannot see gender difference as enlarging of men but must see it as a threat—because it has made the other sex the embodiment of all the parts of life which it has cast out. The cultural explanations such a society constructs and carries through all of its institutions do not derive from what it is to be human; instead, they reflect what it is to be dominating. These explanations become accepted "truth."

In general, our cultural concept of men's psychological development rests on a process of separating psychologically from others as a prerequisite of reuniting as master. This is the cultural prescription and our theories have taken it over completely. I believe it is a distorted view of human need and potential but it follows logically if you have not questioned the notion that one sex has to be superior and dominant. If you do question that assumption, then you might ask, for example, not how does the child develop a sense of separateness, but how does the child become more connected to others as the goal of development. Connection does not mean "dependent," "merged," or any of the other pejorative terms with which it is often confused.

Viewed in this light, I see the specific content of Freud's theories (and others' theories) as a male construction about how to become separated and dominant. The boy is forced to do this if he is to become acceptable to adult men who live by this construction of reality. The notion is not that men should use the parts of their potential which would make them more fully human or more totally developed but that they must overdevelop the parts of their potential which will make them fit the pattern of a dominant sex.

Meanwhile, of course, all of this is chasing an illusion. Men are taken care of personally by women all of other lives. They are much better taken care of than are women. Indeed, the performance of this kind of care was the essential definition of womanhood, a definition which psychoanalytic theories also took over.

It is understandable that a society dominated by one sex could believe that there is a powerful desire for connections with others only if it gave such a powerful desire a base in sexuality. This was a way of not giving full credence to the human wish for connections in its own right. Actually this tendency to sexualize all connections is reflected in our social life in very concrete ways. We still see many men who are able to express their desires for connection only in sexual terms. (Many women understand this; many women also resent this.) Combined with his 19th-century view of science, I think Freud could not fully believe the psychological processes he, himself, astutely observed. He could believe them only if he said that at bottom they all arose from biology. This was in marked contradiction to his great gift which was a psychological gift. He could talk of psychic representations of biological drives, but he could not believe in psychological constructions in their own right as we can today. Thus, he didn't go the next step and fully believe that psychic representations are really determined by interaction with other psychic representations, that is, the effect of other people on the developing child and the adult throughout the relationships between them.

I've tried to say very quickly that I think Freud and the psychoanalysts who followed him have given us a great opening but that the great danger for psychoanalysis lies in the threat of ridigity. I believe there has to be a total change in the content of our theories if they are to encompass new understandings, in particular, those created by modern feminism. I don't believe in the specific concept of psychological development or even the construction of the unconscious as Freud and others have laid it out so far. After all, how could Freud or any other one theorist have the whole truth? I do believe that our great hope of building on the contributions of psychoanalysis is an openness to new thought and an openness especially to what I think is the most stimulating and creative work occuring today—the new formulations arising from the very close description of women's experience and the attempt to describe this experience within new categories, not the categories we have inherited. When we do this new thinking, we find not only new understandings of women's lives, which certainly is an important reason to do it, but we also find hidden factors which illuminate—the lives of everyone—the total human experience.

33

Feminist Scholarship and the Training of Psychoanalytic Psychologists: A Feminist Psychotherapist's Perspective

Lenore E. A. Walker

There is a growing empirical and clinical data base which challenges the psycho-analytic view of human behavior because it has not provided an accurate understanding of the psychology of women. In the past 15 years, much of the empirical information Freud would have needed to answer his plaintive plea about not understanding women, has been gathered. There are always a few historical moments that seem to represent the *Zeitgeist* of any particular move-ment. I have organized by discussion of feminist scholarship's contributions to the psychoanalytic training of psychologists around those "moments."

The first moment occurred around the publication of two unrelated works about 1970. Both Phyllis Chesler's (1972) book, *The Myth of Madness* and Inge Broverman and her colleagues' study of mental health professionals' attitudes toward males and females (Broverman, Broverman, Rosencrantz, & Vogel, 1970) documented the negative experiences of women at the hands of the mental health professionals. This followed several years of women's participation in consciousness-raising (C-R) groups. The C-R groups were conducted according to feminist principles provided by the newest women's liberation movement, and were not based on any therapeutic model (cf. Kravetz, 1980). They were political and not therapy-based group sessions, but nonetheless yielded important infor-mation according to women, some of whom then discussed their experiences with therapists. This has led to an erroneous belief that feminist psychology itself is more political than scientific and that at least one component of feminist philosophy must include an angry denouncement of men if not actually outright man-hating. While individuals may integrate personal, political, and scientific analyses, feminist psychology is based on the same scientific and professional principles as is any other school of psychology.

Chesler draws attention to the maddening features of the mental health system which ignored the impact of the reality of women's lives. It is not that women need psychotherapy to cure their madness, Chesler contends, but rather they are driven mad by being mishandled by a mental health system designed by men to keep women socialized in inferior sex roles for their own benefit. The system is used to justify the male position of power and punishes women for daring to be different. Chesler made her point by presenting dramatic cases which quickly drew attention to women who were wrongly incarcerated on the back-wards of mental hospitals, or were overmedicated, or were encouraged to stay in psychoanalysis for many years without an end in sight to change a personality which was healthy except for the need to challenge the male patriarchy. Her message was that women who used the mental health system to feel better were encouraged to adapt to their oppression rather than overcome it by changing the social conditions since that would be less beneficial for men.

Marcia Guttentag (1983) later empirically replicated Chesler's findings utilizing the National Institute of Mental Health's systematically collected national statistics. Not only were women seen as 70% of the consumers of mental health, their gender was found to be a differentiating characteristic for both diagnosis and treatment (Russo, 1984). This, emphasis of duality by gender, of course, is not so different from our most current controversy over the proposed addition of diagnoses to the DSM–III (APA, 1980) that do not reflect women's psychology and simply exaggerate the mental health risk of being born a woman in our society. (see, e.g., Garfinkel et al., 1986; Walker, 1987).

The Broverman et al. (1970) study is so classic that most graduate students still learn about it. In this research, a variety of mental health professionals were asked to choose from a list of attributes of mentally healthy people, which would best describe the mentally healthy man, the mentally healthy woman, and the mentally healthy person. Their results stunned the mental health community but not the feminists; the mentally healthy man and person shared the same characteristics but the mentally healthy woman did not. Women were rated as being more emotional, less assertive or aggressive, more nurturing, warmer and more skilled at relationships and just "being." The mentally healthy man, however, was rated as more aggressive, more rational, less emotional, more intellectual, less nurturing, and more skilled at "doing." There obviously is a no-win situation here. For a woman to be mentally healthy, she cannot demonstrate the characteristics by which we judge a healthy person. This study provided the impetus for a great deal of social psychology research, including looking at the role of attribution on motivation and attitudes and better definitions of what have been labeled as male or female attributes (c.f. Frieze et al., 1978; O'Leary, Unger, & Wallston, 1985).

Certainly it is reasonable to believe that views reported are now outdated, 15 years after the women's movement and women professionals have forced mental health professionals to deal with their gender biases! Well, there is a new study reported by Rosencrantz, DeLorey, and Broverman (1985) which replicated their original one. Mental health professionals have not changed their attitudes very much. They still believe that the mentally healthy woman cannot be the same as the mentally healthy man, who is the only one of the two considered to be a mentally healthy person!

The dangers of this double standard to the therapy process are so obvious that I shall not belabor the point. It does tell us that our long list of theoretical, empirical, and clinical-based studies on the psychology of women are going unread or unheeded. And, the American Psychiatric Association's proposed DSM–III–R additions underscore their ignorance (Garfinkel et al., 1986)

By the latter 1970s there were a few more significant "moments" rising from the ongoing efforts to define feminist therapy. It was at that time that several books appeared, (Brodsky & Hare–Mustin, 1980; Franks & Burtle, 1977; Rawlings & Carter, 1977), all trying to modify psychotherapy, especially psychoanalytic theory and practice. The American Psychological Association appointed a Task Force on Sex-Role Stereotyping and Sex Bias in Psychotherapeutic Practice, which among other findings resoundingly criticized psychoanalysis for its gender bias (APA, 1975, 1978). Most noted during this period are Carol Gilligan's (1982) book, *In A Different Voice*, on women's moral development and Jean Baker Miller's (1976) *Toward A New Psychology of Women*. As Jean Baker Miller is on this panel I shall not presume to cover her work, except to note that hers is the first serious attempt to deal with the contradictions between psychoanalysis's emphasis on early childhood as the internalized determinate of personality development and the feminist theoretical emphasis on an externalized psychosocial explanation that accounts for the continuous oppression from a antiwoman culture. Miller's concept of women's developments of a relational ego and not the previous standard of an autonomous ego forms the basis for psychoanalysis to redefine mentally healthy relationships in feminist rather than androcentric terms. Her work is an elegant attempt to compromise on the nature/nurture questions. Early childhood is still seen as the major determinant of personality but it is also shaped by cultural as well as interpersonal factors. And, most importantly, the mother–daughter relationship is more clearly articulated, providing a feminist framework for object-relations analysis. I shall talk about the issue of merger and boundaries a little later, as it has important significance for women in therapy.

Also raised by the ongoing Stone Center Work-in-Progress but not yet fully investigated is the issue of whether autonomy was ever really representative of the male ego state. This kind of investigation is critically needed but to date only has not yet been done. Psychoanalytic psychologists, trained in clinical research, have the skills to continue the investigation. I believe that if psychoanalysis is to become truly relevant to men, the issue of their same or different ego development than women's must be explored.

Gilligan's work also raises similar gender issues about women's development having been erroneously subsumed under the moral development of men. Her work carefully documents the differences in women's moral development as coming from a better developed sense of relatedness. Justice tempered with caring is the women's ethic rather than the more androcentric, absolute, universal standard of justice. Choosing which standard is better varies with who makes the interpretation. Certainly, Gilligan's findings challenge the previously held assumptions of Kohlberg (1964) that absolute justice is of a higher order of psychological development than is a more flexible and individualized interpretation of the rules. Flexibility and adaptability have always been considered a hallmark of good mental health.

By the late 1970s and the early 1980s the next "moment" occurs with the work about violence against women and its impact on women's mental health. My own work as well as others had an important influence on women's mental health policy (Walker, 1979, 1984a, 1984b). The revelation that millions of women were being subjected to cruel and abusive treatment by their mates, no matter what constituted their personality, caused many to revise Freud's theories about masochism and sadism (Symonds, 1979). Except for those who will not look at or be swayed by the overwhelming empirical data (Blum, 1982; Shainess, 1979), the sheer numbers of cases of battered women, abused children, and rape victims suggest that situational factors must be accounted for prior to or during any long-term psychoanalysis. It is no longer adequate to analyze the woman's provocative behavior and judge her to have a personality disorder (cf. Walker & Browne, 1985). It is the man's deficits, not hers, that are responsible for his use of violence even if he does believe he needed to discipline her or control her behavior (Sonkin, Martin, & Walker, 1985). Rosenbaum and O'Leary's (1981) research analyzing the interactions between violent couples support the feminist position here.

Crisis intervention techniques, support groups, and short-term cognitive behavioral therapy all provide useful means to promote directly women's healing from men's violence. In fact, psychoanalysis has been severely criticized for its iatrogenic effects; in many cases it did make things worse by both subtly and not-so-subtly blaming the victim for her own predicament (cf. Caplan, 1985). I would have hoped the empirical data would have convinced the American Psychiatric Association's DSM–III–R committee of the dangerousness of adding categories such as Self-Defeating Personality Disorder a/k/a Masochistic Personality Disorder and Sadistic Personality Disorder, without first clearly delineating the Post Traumatic Stress Disorders and Abuse Disorders categories, but those of you reading the professional psychology and popular press know that did not happen. It has been our worst-case scenario come true; inflexible male psychiatrists, some of whom are psychoanalysts, are refusing to hear anything that does not validate their world view. It is that characteristic alone which I believe has the potential to bring on the demise of psychoanalysis; that is the psychoanalyst's inability to deal with theoretical contradictions and incongruity in any other way but *invalidation*, a process sometimes called *denial* when evidenced by clients.

The area in women's mental health where the negative effects of professional denial have been most obvious is the issue of father's sexual abuse of their daughters, also called incest. When the social *Zeitgeist* about battered women changed in the early 1980s it was followed by the moment of clarity about incest. Although Florence Rush (1981), Judith Herman (1981), Hannah Lerman (1986), and other feminist scholars have been documenting Freud's (1896/1959) erroneous switch from first recognizing his patients' actual experiences, to then believing they were fantasized incest stories, it took Jeffrey Masson's (1984) exposure of the ultimate betrayal in the Fliess letters to capture the mental health community's attention. These letters and missing paragraphs from previously translated and published letters revealed that even those in the general psychoanalytic community were denied access to Freud's total writings on the subject by those in power, who believed it would only be confusing to be exposed to all of his thoughts. Once again, omission rather than thoughtful deliberation was the chosen method to deal with contradiction and inconsistency by the orthodox.

Aside from the content revealed by the new data, including exposure of some of the more ludicrous ideas of the times, such as nose surgery to relieve masturbation and menstrual dysphoria, (perhaps analogous to the DSM debates today), what is highly significant is the revelation of a profound lack of integrity within the body of psychoanalytic scholarship. The highest-status psychoanalysts have been caught with their proverbial fingers in the cookie jar. Feminist scholarship, which has placed such a high premium on open debate until consensus is reached, simply cannot tolerate the unwillingness of psychoanalytic scholars to demonstrate openly its ability to repair its own integrity. Defensive when exposed, the official position has been to ostracize Masson and pretend that the Freud/Fliess correspondence was not deliberately edited to protect Freud's reputation or even worse, that the whole sordid coverup doesn't have any relevance to psychoanalytic theory. Of course it does, and if psychoanalysis is ever to become relevant to women, discussions on its relevance must be begun. Hannah Lerman's (1986) new book, *A Mote in Freud's Eye*, begins the needed polemic analysis.

Data of Elaine Hilberman Carmen, Reiker, and Mills (1984) on inpatients at a psychiatric facility reveals just how prevalent an abuse history is for those who are seriously enough disturbed to be hospitalized. Not only are masochistic or self-defeating personality disorder labels inaccurate, they are also far too simplistic to account for the varieties of impact the abuse traumas have on both women's and men's mental health. Diana Russell's (1986) epidemiological survey suggests that 38% of all women have been sexually abused as children, 25% under the age of 14 and most by fathers and stepfathers. While the incest can take place anytime during childhood, one of the most likely periods for it to begin is from age 7 to 10, just the time period psychoanalysts label *latency* and believe the child has less energy invested in sexuality. Maybe psychoanalysts' misunderstanding of the developmental stage of latency has been confounded by the child's early introduction to secrecy, boundary violations, and genital rather than emotional intimacy. And, the numbers of psychologists guilty of violating boundaries and sexually exploiting clients may perpetuate the damage (Bouhoustos, 1984).

The whole area of psychosexual development needs to be re-examined given the data gleaned from feminist scholarship. The overemphasis of the influence of mothering on personality development does not account for variations in parenting styles which existed in Freud's day as well as today. Women-blaming is too rampant in the psychoanalytic view of child development and child abuse. Such attitudes by therapists' do not allow women's mental health needs to be met. Mothers no longer spend enough time with children to have the kind of impact still attributed to them. But when they do, it is rarely acknowledged for its quality. Instead, psychoanalysis seems to criticize mothers for everything they do. Feminist therapy attempts to support women's strengths rather than criticize or deal with deficiencies unless destructive behavior is evidenced (cf. Rosewater & Walker, 1985).

Developmental psychology has broadened our knowledge about the interrelationship among fitness, maturation, environmental, and interpersonal factors on development of affective, cognitive and behavioral domains. New theories about women's development are being constructed (cf. Silverman & Conarton, in press). Research demonstrates the effectiveness of therapies that deal with all three domains; not just the affective area in which psychoanalysis specializes (Johnson & Auerbach, 1984). There are no empirical data to support the claim that changes in the affective domain will generalize to analysands' thinking and behavior. It is too narrow for psychoanalysis to continue to concentrate only on the nuclear family dyad or triad of parent/child relationships and subsequent emotional development.

For example, Alexandra Kaplan (1933), Judith Jordan (1983), and Janet Surrey, (1983), working at the Stone Center have published an excellent discussion of the concept of empathy, redefining it to include both affective and cognitive features and suggesting that women's capacity for affective merger with another is greater because of the cognitive boundaries learned during early development of female infants and their mothers. But, how do we know it is merger and not simply overlap which defines women's relationships with one another? How do we know that it is the mother–daughter relationship and not any other factor or interrelationship of factors occurring at that time period?

Clinical observations tell those of us who work in the area of domestic violence that men who batter women and children who witness abuse do not demonstrate empathy. But we do not know if that is across all situations or only when witnessing abuse. Here is where empirical data from within the discipline of psychoanalysis as well as other disciplines could be helpful. Developmental psychology research has demonstrated that a lack of empathy can be simulated in the laboratory where children are exposed to witnessing verbal as well as physical violence (cf. Cummings, Lannotti, & Zahn–Waxler, 1985). What about exposure to early sexual abuse? Does witnessing violence stimulate too much empathy in girls and too little empathy in boys? Or, is selflessness in women a necessary stage to go through before a more integrated balance is found as in the Silverman and Conarton (in press) feminist developmental model. These are important research questions and psychoanalytic psychologists could make contributions to finding the answers.

What does account for the gender differences in the transmittal of violent behavior? Is aggression genetically gender-linked as the sociobiologists and psychoanalytic determinists would have us believe? If so, then how do we explain the battered women who fight back, some who actually kill their mates or children? Is aggression simply learned behavior? If so, then how do we explain those who were abused but do not use aggression? The longitudinal studies by Stechler (1986) and his colleagues tell us that curiosity to know and not aggression characterize infant's responses.

The observational data collected by Gerry Patterson (1982), John Reed, Taplin, and Lorber (1981) and their colleagues in Oregon and those by Robert Burgess (1985) and his colleagues at the University of Pennsylvania may offer some explanations. Patterson and Reid found a higher rate of cross-gender aggression displayed in abusive families. Thus, sex-role socialization in those abusive families may contribute to shaping male/female violence patterns. Burgess found that children who were abused did not use abusive behavior if they developed social competence. Thus, good social skills with peers may be an important mediating factor and supporting peer relationships may be a good preventive or even early intervention strategy when we learn about family violence. Those of you who remember the monkey studies of Harry Harlow may recall that some monkeys could overcome poor parental attachment by learning to play with other monkeys closer to them in age. Yet, psychoanalysis has not emphasized interpersonal relationships in its quest for self-understanding.

These empirical findings, from other branches in psychology, add much to our quest for promotion of positive mental health. We have learned of the positive healing effects of support groups for battered women and rape victims through the experiences of rape crisis centers and battered women shelters. Can or should these findings be integrated into psychoanalysis? Given the large numbers of the population, across all demographic groups, who have experienced or witnessed abuse in their family, I believe integration is critical to the survival of psychoanalysis for women.

One area which seems natural to me is in the promotion of women's friendships. Glenace Edwall (1986) has recently completed a review of different views of women's friendships and did a particularly good job of comparing the psychoanalytic and sociocultural positions. She concludes that an integration of both may be the most useful for women in order to move out of the position of being "the other" in a patriarchal world. She broadens the view of psychoanalytic learnings of "sameness" in mother/daughter relationships as underlying the development of friendships to include the incorporation of first being viewed as the same as the mother, then as different from men and then, learning to view oneself as "the other." Thus, in Edwall's view, women learn to be flexible and adapt to friendships that contain elements of both sameness and difference. She believes then, that reparation of faulty parenting or changes in personality can be facilitated by healthy same-sex friendships. This fits with my own views that women who have been repeatedly abused in their homes by men who also love them have lost at least some if not all of their capacity for emotional intimacy. Women therapists can provide the reidentification with the idealized mother rather than the idealized father common in orthodox psychoanalysis. We know psychoanalysis has had much to say about emotional intimacy but the assumptions must be integrated with other relevant issues raised by this newer feminist scholarship.

Feminist psychotherapy has much to learn about the client/therapist relationship from the reformulation of the psychoanalytic concepts of transference and countertransference. Again, using the area of violence against women as an example, since it is the one I know best, relationship issues between client and therapist are paramount to the healing process. Resuming the belief in the ability to keep herself safe is the critical factor for abuse victims to become survivors. This calls for *re-empowerment*, to use the feminist political term, in how the woman thinks about herself, how she behaves, as well as understanding her feelings. It is not enough to stay in the affective domain when her thoughts and behavior may be controlled by situational factors. Cognitive restructuring or reframing, to borrow from behavioral or systems theory techniques may be even more important before feelings can be explored. Legitimate anger and rage will flood the client without those cognitive controls in place.

In my own therapy practice I usually spend the first 6 months developing support, trust, and validation in preparation for the flood of feelings which must be uncovered slowly in abuse victims. It is harder to work with those who have not been dealing with their feelings completely. Some label such clients as having a borderline personality disorder. But that label may be given to women struggling with moving from one stage of development to another (cf. Silverman & Conarton, in press) or those women whose behavior makes male-identified therapists anxious (Walker, 1984b, p. 15). I prefer to wait to see if a therapeutic relationship can be established before I give such a label and simply note the incongruence in such client's affective, cognitive, and behavioral domains. I try to avoid power struggles and manipulation by reducing the distance often created in an authoritarian doctor and submissive patient relationship by trying to be more egalitarian. This means each of us bring some expertise to the therapy relationship. I bring my expertise as a psychotherapist and she brings her expertise about her life experiences. Together, we explore their meaning while respecting the inherent power I have as the therapist. The reduction of the distance between doctor and patient in the therapy relationship has been an important contribution of feminist theory.

Women victims of violence have learned to use their sexuality or seductiveness as a way to keep themselves safe. A good therapy experience with a woman therapist who has her own boundaries clearly, identified, can provide a positive model of emotional intimacy as the client works toward re-empowerment. This considerably broadens the whole definition of what is or is not good for transference and countertransference. Traditional issues in psychoanalysis, such as client resistance, really have no place in feminist analysis. Responsibility for the progress or lack of progress in therapy are equally shared.

The development of a feminist therapy theory is the last significant "moment" that I want to discuss here. By the mid-1980s it became clear that simply borrowing techniques from other therapy systems to integrate within feminist philosophy was not good enough. The beginning attempts are articulated in the 1985 publication, *The Handbook of Feminist Therapy* (Rosewater & Walker, 1985). This has caused some dissension within the ranks of women therapists who do not want to reject their primary affiliation but do embrace the feminist philosophy. In two other books, the articulation becomes clearer. My book on *Women and Mental Health Policy* (Walker, 1984b) illustrates the impact of a variety of feminist approaches on policy while a soon to be released book, *Feminist Psychotherapies: Integration of Therapeutic and Feminist Systems*, edited by Mary Ann Douglas and myself outlines the changes in various theories impacted by feminist scholarship (Douglas & Walker, in press).

Psychoanalysis has never been popular with most feminists for numerous reasons, the most obvious having to do with what is perceived as its elitism, high-status needs, exclusionary practices, and lack of empirical validation of its content, especially where relevant to women. It didn't help that Freud finally told his psychoanalytical colleagues that he left the understanding of women to the poets. The controversy stirred up by Masson showed how Freud's male affiliation needs got in the way of science.

Psychoanalysts today are still in danger of making the same mistakes even though there are more women involved in the process. Psychologists are in the best position to use our professional training to make the badly needed changes. First, psychologists are trained as behavioral observers. We can use this scientific training to try to stop psychoanalysts from discarding that which is incongruent with the official party line. Inconsistencies are always expected in human behavior and all mental health professionals including orthodox analysts, can be trained to think about them as challenges to rather than attacks on prevailing theories. Psychology's strong identification with the scientific method can become a model for all psychoanalysts to learn how to respect empirical data while also remaining both positive and skeptical in the face of contravening clinical data. Not that science is free from sexism. I refer you to the excellent article on guidelines for sex-fair research authored by McHugh, Koeske, and Irene Frieze (1986) in the August issue of the *American Psychologist* that came out of an APA, Division 35, Psychology of Women project.

It is the closed-mindedness of the psychoanalytic tradition which has provided both the elegance of its theories but also the stagnation of its ability to integrate new findings such as those provided by feminist scholarship. I personally do not know if feminist psychoanalysis is possible. The language as well as some of the ideas are so riddled with male dislike of and distrust of women that I find it too oppressive to stimulate my own thinking. I couldn't shake off the racism, sexism, and classism I encountered once again when reviewing the masochism literature for my DSM–III–R battle with the psychiatrists (Walker, 1987). And the contempt shown for women's attempts to formulate psychological analyses separately from men is shown by the refusal to change the gender-based language, including the rampant use of the masculine pronoun to denote men and women used at this very conference without regard for the empirical data demonstrating the cognitive limitations for women that such usage reflects (cf. Henley, 1977, and the APA Publication Manual, 1983).

It is interesting that psychoanalytical training with all its emphasis on the therapeutic relationship in is just beginning to deal with the important data from therapeutic outcome studies. The Orlinsky and Howard (1980) studies show clearly that young men just out of their training have the lowest success rate with women clients. Newly trained women are closer to experienced men and experienced women do the best therapeutic work with women. Obviously, we cannot continue to allow newly trained men to practice on their women clients until they gain experience. Psychoanalytic training, like training in other therapy schools, must help design new methods of training and supervising these men. Certainly, insisting on coursework on the psychology of women in the curriculum is one solution. Bibliographies such as the annotated one recently edited by Dilling and Claster (1985) is another. Placing a symposium such as this one in a plenary session at the front of the program gives the strong message to all attendees that this information is an integral part of psychoanalysis and not a specialized option. Implementing strategies to reverse the hostility shown for feminist scholarship by some of the more orthodox psychoanalysts is also a task for the future.

So, I, myself, have abandoned the effort to develop a feminist psychoanalysis theory and prefer to put my energies to try to develop a truly new psychology of women. But, many of you among the conference participants have a long history of commitment to psychoanalysis. If it can be done at all, it will be you, the revisionists, who will chart the new territory. You must resist the temptation to identify with androcentric analysis and learn to live with the contradictions and incongruence. You must stop using the more blatantly woman-blaming aspects of the theory, and replace them with the separate but at least equal data already available. Of course, properly obtained data should be reported even if they cast aspersion on favorite feminist political ideas. So, too, for data which make some orthodox psychoanalytic concepts outdated. Regurgitation of old, pejorative, and largely unprovable assumptions about women need not be reified by psychoanalytically trained women who join together with other women ostensibly to deal with women's issues. Even the questions chosen to be studied reflect one's values and gender politics. And you must be willing to give up the status that comes from agreeing with "the other," those men and women who prefer not to deal with anything but their insular version of truth.

Hopefully, women psychologists can give up the antagonism which frequently exists between women of different persuasions. Unfortunately, many men are more receptive to feminist concerns than are the women psychoanalysts. Feminist theory calls for women to make choices from an array of possible alternatives. I encourage you all to continue in your work on psychoanalysis and women with an open mind about a feminist perspective. We who endeavor to find answers to women's issues from a feminist perspective need your creative scholarship to keep our minds open to a psychoanalytic perspective, as well. I am hopeful, we can form our bond around our common concerns for the positive mental health of women. Perhaps feminists and psychoanalysts can coexist. To do so we will have to choose areas of consensus and use them to build trust so we can also learn to tolerate our disagreements without personal hostility. Only time will tell if we can do this. I am willing to join with you all to try to find the way.

REFERENCES

American Psychiatric Association. (1980) *Diagnostic and statistical Manual of mental disorders* (3rd ed.). Washington, DC: Author.

American Psychological Association. (1983). *Publication Manual.* Washington, DC: Author.

American Psychological Association Task Force on Sex Role Stereotyping and Psychotherapeutic Bias. (1975). Report. *American Psychologist, 20,* 1169–1175.

American Psychological Association Task Force on Sex Role Stereotyping and Psychotherapeutic Bias. (1978). Report. *American Psychologist, 33,* 1122–1123.

Blum, H. P. (1982). Psychoanalytic reflections on the "beaten wife syndrome." In M. Kirkpatrick (Ed.), *Women's sexual experiences: The dark continent.* (pp. 263–267). New York: Plenum.

Bouhoustos, J. C. (1984). Sexual intimacy between psychotherapists and clients: Policy implications for the future. In L. E. A. Walker (Ed.), *Women and mental health policy.* Beverly Hills, CA: Sage.

Brodsky, A., & Hare–Mustin, R. (1980). *Pschotherapy with women: An assessment of research and Practice.* New York: Guilford Press.

Broverman, I. Broverman, D. Rosencrantz, P., & Vogel, S. (1970). Sex role stereotypes and clinical judgments of mental health. *Journal of Consulting and Clinical Psychology, 34,* 1–7.

Burgess, R. C. (1985). Social incompetence as a precipitant to and consequence of child maltreatment. *Victimology: An International Journal, 10*(1–4), 72–86.

Caplan, R. J. (1985). *The myth of women's masochism.* New York: Dutton.

Carmen, E. H., Reiker, P. P., & Mills, T. (1984). Victim of violence and psychiatric illness. *American Journal of Psychiatry, 141*(3), 378–383.

Chesler, P. (1972). *Women and madness.* New York: Avon

Cummings, E. M., Lannotti, R. J., & Zahn–Waxler, C. C. (1985). Influence of conflict between adults on the emotions and aggression of young children. *Developmental Psychology, 21,* 295–307.

Dilling C., & Claster B. L. (Eds.). (1985) *Female Psychology: A partially annotated bibliography.* New York: New York City Coalition for Womens Mental Health, 320 W. 86th St., New York City 10024.

Douglas, M. A., & Walker, L. E. A. (in press). *Feminist psychotherapies: Integration of therapeutic and feminist systems.* New York: Ablex.

Edwall, G. E. (1986). *Women's friendships.* Unpublished doctoral dissertation. University of Denver.

Franks, V., & Burtle, V. (1977). *Psychotherapy and women.* New York: Brunner/Mazel.

Freud, S. (1896/1959). The aetiology of hysteria. In E. Jones (Ed.), *The collected papers of Sigmund Freud (Vol. 1,* pp. 183–219). New York: Basic Books.

Garfinkel, R., Allagna, S., Brown, L., Rosewater, L., Walker, L., & Lerman, H. (1986). *Science or politics.* Presented at the American Psychological Association annual convention, Washington, DC, August.

Gilligan, C. (1982). *In a different voice: Psychological theory and women's development.* Cambridge MA: Harvard University Press.

Guttentag, M. (1983). *Too many women.* Beverly Hills, CA: Sage.

Henley, N. (1977). *Body politics: Power, sex, and non-verbal communication.* Englewood Cliffs, NJ: Prentice–Hall.

Herman, J. (1981). *Father-daughter incest.* Cambridge MA: Harvard University Press.

Johnson, M., & Auerbach, A. H. (1984). Women and psychotherapy research. In L. E. A. Walker (Ed.), *Women and mental health policy.* Beverly Hills, CA: Sage.

Jordan, J. V. (1983). *Empathy in the mother-daughter relationship.* Stone Center Work-in-Progress, No. 82–02, Wellesley MA.

Kaplan, A. G. (1983). *Empathic communication in the psychotherapy relationship.* Stone Center Work-in-Progress, No. 82–02. Wellesley MA.

Kohlberg, L. (1964). Development of moral character and Moral ideology. In M. L. Hoffman & L. W. Hoffman (Eds.), *Review of child development research* (Vol. 1, pp. 383–431). New York: Sage.

Kravetz, D. (1980). Consciousness-raising and self help. In A. Brodsky & R. Hare–Mustin (Eds.), *Women and psychotherapy* (pp 267–283). New York: Guilford Press.

Lerman, H. (1986). *A mote in Freud's eye.* New York:

Masson, J. (1984). *The assault on truth: Freud's suppression of the seduction theory:* New York: Farrar, Straus, & Giroux.

McHugh, M., Koeske, R., & Frieze, I. (1986). Issues to consider in conducting non-sexist research. *American Psychologist, 41,* 879–890.

Miller, J. B. (1976). *Toward a new psychology of women.* Boston: Beacon Press.

O'Leary, V., Unger, R., & Wallston, B. (1985). Women, gender, and social psychology. Hillsdale, NJ: Lawrence Erlbaum Associates.

Orlinsky, D., & Howard K., (1980). Gender and psychotherapeutic outcome. In A. Brodsky & R. Hare–Mustin (Eds.), *Women and psychotherapy* (pp. 3–34A). New York: Guilford Press.

Patterson, G. (1982). *Coercive family processes.* Eugene, OR: Castaglia Press.

Rawling, E., & Carter, D. (1977). *Psychotherapy for women: Treatment toward equality.* Springfield, IL: Charles C. Thomas.

Reid, J., Taplin, P., & Lorber, R. (1981). A social interactional approach to the treatment of abusive families. In R. Stuart (Ed.), *Violent behavior: Social learning approaches to prediction, management, and treatment,* New York: A. Rosenbaum & D. O'Leary.

Rosenbaum, A., & O'Leary, D. (1981). Marital violence: Characteristics of abusive couples. *Journal of Consulting and Clinical Psychology, 49*, 63-71.

Rosencrantz, P. DeLorey, C., & Broverman, I. (1985). *One half a generation later: Sex-role stereotypes revisited.* Presented at American Psychological Association annual meeting, Los Angeles, August.

Rosewater, L. B. & Walker, L. E. A. (1985). *Handbook of feminist therapy: Psychotherapy issues with women.* New York: Springer.

Rush, F. (1981). *The best kept secret: Sexual abuse of children.* New York: McGraw–Hill.

Russell, D. E. H. (1986). *The secret trauma: Incest in the lives of girls and women.* New York: Basic Books.

Russo, N. F. (1984). Women in the mental health delivery system: Implications for research and public policy. In L. E. A. Walker (Ed.), *Women and mental health policy.* Beverly Hills, CA: Sage.

Shainess, N. (1979). Vulnerability to masochism: Masochism as a process. *American Journal of Psychotherapy 33*(2), 174–189.

Silverman, L. K., & Conarton, S. (in press). Feminist development through the life cycle. In M. A. Douglas & L. E. A. Walker (Eds.), *Feminist psychotherapies: Integration of therapeutic and feminist systems.*

Sonkin, D. J., Martin, D., & Walker, L. E. A. (1985). *The male batterer.* New York: Springer.

Stechler, G. (1986). *The integration of family systems and psychodynamic approaches to treatment.* Clark Conference on Psychoanalytic Training for Psychologists, October, Worcester, MA.

Surrey, J. (1983). *The relational self in women: Clinical implications.* Stone Center Work-in-progress, No. 82–02, Wellesley, MA.

Symonds, A. (1979). Violence against women: The myth of masochism. *American Journal of Psychotherapy, 33*(2), 161–173.

Walker, L. E. A. (1987). Inadequacies of the masochistic personality disorder. *Journal of Personality Disorders, 7*(2), 183–189.

Walker, L. E. A. (1984a). *The battered woman syndrome.* New York: Springer.

Walker, L. E. A. (1984b). *Women and mental health policy.* Beverly Hills, CA: Sage.

Walker, L. E. A. (1979). *The battered woman.* New York: Harper & Row.

Walker, L., & Browne, A., (1985). Gender and victimization by intimates. *Journal of Personality, 53*, 179-195.

34

A Model for Integrating New Ideas From the Psychology of Women Into Training Programs

Dale Mendell

This chapter focuses upon some ways in which new information about women can be integrated into psychoanalytic training programs. I will not discuss theory as such but rather suggest methods of disseminating such knowledge. It is my impression that too often this is done infrequently or inconsistently.

Let me present some limited and limiting scenarios frequently found in analytic Institutes, one or more of which will easily be recognized. At an extreme, there are no specific courses in female development, teachers or developmental courses are not particularly interested in or knowledgeable about the topic, and supervisors and teachers of clinical courses do not relate changing theories of female development and the attendant changes in concepts about normal adult women to the specifics of clinical work. A somewhat more palatable situation involves giving a well-intentioned but passing nod to the subject. Examples include a single, elective, course in female psychology or an occasional staff meeting or lecture on the topic. (These meetings or courses are generally attended almost totally by female students, in spite of the fact that more than half of all patients are women. This does seem odd, as male candidates might well be expected to be interested in the dynamics of the majority of their patients.)

Missing from the programs just outlined is a real, living integration of newer analytic thinking about women into most relevant areas of curriculum. This is a lack perceived by many candidates. I have heard numerous students complain bitterly about not having been exposed to teaching which would enable them to understand their female patients sufficiently. However, given the proper interest and atmosphere, I believe it is possible to achieve such a goal. To illustrate, I shall choose one of many available vantage points, that of the gender of the analyst *vis-à-vis* the gender of the patient. (I could easily have chosen many alternate topics, for example, psychophysiological events unique to women; however, the gender of the therapeutic dyad has attracted considerable recent interest; see Alonso & Rutan, 1978; Kaplan, 1984; Person, 1983, etc.).

This is clearly a topic of interest to women. On a practical level, three of the four possible gender dyads include women. Historically, the realization that differences in the gender of the therapeutic dyad results in differences in treatment is relatively recent and is a special example of the importance of the real characteristics of the analyst. Conceptually, changes in theory about female development and the related changes in ideas about what constitutes normality in adult women have profoundly influenced treatment. And dynamically, the particular interactions between each therapeutic dyad are rooted in childhood perceptions and fantasies of the nature of women and of their relationships with men and with other women.

I'll now present a model for disseminating conceptualizations about gender dyads throughout Institute training. For illustrative purposes I'll confine myself to the male analyst/female patient dyad, the most traditional one. Courses in the developmental track would stress normative tendencies in male development such as the disidentification with the omnipotently perceived mother of early years and the subsequent tendency toward defensive exteralization of dependent feelings onto women. The girl's tendency toward using her father to assist in separation from the mother of early years and his falling heir to many of her feelings of attachment to her mother would be discussed in terms of later relations between the sexes. The culturally sanctioned notion that women should behave charmingly, ingratiatingly and nonaggressively toward men would be understood as a partial resultant of these psychodynamics.

In clinical courses, particularly those dealing with transference and countertransference, differences in treatment resulting from the gender of the therapeutic dyad would be an assigned topic, complete with readings from the current literature. The dynamics of interaction between men and women as a consequence of differences in development would be utilized to understand certain frequently occurring therapeutic impasses. For example, it has been pointed out that male analysts, beginning with Freud, tend to have difficulty accepting a preoedipal maternal countertransference, as it requires a degree of regression to identification with the early mother. The potential problem in the treatment situation is that of colluding with the female patient's own fear of forming a transference to the preoedipal mother. In addition, the male analyst tends to be uncomfortable with his female patient's rage, both in its castrating and annihilating aspects; in seeking to deny or neutralize this anger, he may unwittingly accede to the cultural stereotype of the ingratiating, nonaggressive woman. On her part, the female patient frequently utilizes defensive measures, such as dissembling or maintaining a fixed erotic transference as she tends to fear that her male therapist will not be able to tolerate anger or confrontation.

In supervisory sessions, technical implications for the male analyst/female patient dyad which grow out of these dynamics would be held in mind. I will give two examples from my supervisory experience of male candidates' "countertransference deafness" to their female patients which are taken from my paper, "Cross-gender supervision of cross-gender therapy: female supervisor, male candidate, female patient." (Mendell, 1986).

The first candidate was near the end of his training in psychoanalysis when he began supervision with me. The patient was beginning her sixth year of twice-a-week treatment and he was becoming increasingly frustrated with the lack of therapeutic movement. The therapist, a scholarly, responsible man, tended to inhibit his agile and incisive thinking when with patients—consciously out of a compassionate wish to let them proceed at their own pace, but on another level as a defense against his own impatience.

The patient, a professional woman in her early thirties who had lost both parents and was about to be divorced, presented herself as helpless, fragile, and in need of rescue by the therapist. Her anger at men, while at time conscious, was never connected with her feelings of helplessness.

While the therapist empathized with her feelings of helplessness and demonstrated his belief both in her real competence and in the validity of her angry feelings, she became increasingly less able to stand up for herself. It was necessary for me to point out to him that an interpretation ascribing her feelings of helplessness to her rage at being abandoned and the function of helplessness as a furious demand for restitution was in order. Interestingly, although the therapist acknowledged the validity of the interpretation, he found it difficult to utilize, especially transferentially. He mistook his patient's stubborn silence for evidence that the interpretation was "too hard on her." Not until she produced a dream in which she was driving a car that had stopped with smoke coming from the engine did he realize that the therapeutic impasse was ending as the patient accepted the linkage between her helplessness and her rage and, not so incidentally, her therapist's newfound ability to accept this.

The second candidate's analysand was a former call girl whose presenting symptom was her hatred for men. She chose her therapist, a former member of a religious order, with the conscious hope that the best of men might sway her from her perception of men as cruel and sexually exploitative. She was less aware of her sadistic wish to exploit men cruelly in retaliation for her own exploitation and abandonment by father and, ultimately, by the precedipal mother. Her longing to be cherished for herself rather than her sexy facade, was too threatening to surface for years.

The analyst was a technically competent candidate with a good grasp of unconscious processes; however, his need to control both the analytic process and himself led him to use isolation and denial to defend against his patient's more intense feelings, particularly primitive dependency longings.

While the analyst had initially offered the patient four sessions a week, for the first year she insisted on three visits per week. Her attachment grew as the summer break approached and she demanded the four sessions she'd been "promised." The analyst put her off, ostensibly on the grounds that he had no time at that point. He was, indeed, overworked, but as he reported one of the exchanges to me, I was struck by his tone, subtly triumphant and rejecting. He had difficulty acknowledging that the patient's demands had angered and frightened him considerably and that he was, unknowingly, pushing her away by indulging in a form of sadistic teasing.

At another point, when the patient was expressing sexual feelings for the analyst and contrasting this to her past feelings as a call girl, he referred to her as a prostitute and then had difficulty understanding her shock and indignation. It was necessary for me to focus on her exposure of her vulnerability to him in order for him to see that once again he had pushed her away due to his fear of the intensity of his response. Surprisingly, the analyst was able to work this through so that treatment did not founder in an eroticized, sadomasochistic morass. His growing empathy for the patient went hand-in-hand with a recognition of his own long-denied need to be protected and mothered.

In the first vignette, there was unconscious collusion and a resulting lengthy therapeutic stalemate between a woman who concealed her rage behind a helpless demeanor and a man rendered powerless by his fear of examining her anger or his own. In the second vignette, the patient's sexualized wish for closeness, conflicting with her fear of the sadomasochistic elements contained therein, were mirrored in her analyst's fears of the temptations and dangers to be dealt with once he recognized the strength of his sexual and hostile fears and feelings toward her. Both situations illustrate derivatives of central conflicts which men have about women.

At the level of the supervisory program, the likelihood of particular transferential and countertransferential constellations would be emphasized and questions raised as to how best to address and resolve them. One possible solution is that proposed in the article from which I have just quoted, where I suggested that the female supervisor can be particularly helpful for the male candidate treating patients for a number of reasons, including serving as an identificatory model for the candidate.

I hope I have demonstrated the possibility of addressing issues relating to current psychoanalytic issues and conceptualizations about women throughout all aspects of Institute training.

I'd like to conclude with a brief expression of my discomfort with the all-too-frequent partisan use of scholarship, feminist and other. It is all too tempting, faced with the excitement of new theoretical and clinical formulations, to discard older theories because they are no longer serviceable *in toto* and to disparage them to students by presenting only their negative aspects. The phallocentric bias of Freudian theory about female development makes this particularly tempting. I have come to believe, however, that exciting as the presentation of sharply etched differences and adversarial views is both for teacher and student, it is ultimately less useful than a careful weighing of both positive and negative aspects of each position. Our zest for new conceptualizations and new methods of data gathering—for new scholarship—should not lead us to discard earlier psychoanalytic work or to disparage the formulations of revisionists who, for example, still find drive theory useful or have not abandoned retrospective reports from the analytic couch as one source of developmental data. The literature on the gender of the therapeutic dyad derives from a range of theoretical vantage points and thereby gains in breadth and richness. Ours is a field of widely divergent views, in which the search for "truth" is hardly within foreseeable grasp. Even if by dint of forcefully presented views, we win a battle of slogans with our students, I am convinced that we would be doing them and ourselves a disservice.

REFERENCES

Alonso, A., & Rutan, S. (1978). Cross-sex supervision for cross-sex therapy. *American Journal of Psychiatry, 135*(8), 928–931.

Kaplan, A. G. (1984). *Female or male psychotherapists for women: New formulations.* Work-in-progress, No. 83–02, Wellesley, MA.

Mendell, D. (1986). Cross-gender supervision of cross-gender therapy: Female supervisor, male candidate, female patient. *American Journal of Psychoanalysis, 46*(3), 270–275.

Person, E. (1983). Women in therapy. Therapist gender as a variable. *International Review of Psychoanalysis, 10,* 193–204.

35 Workshop Reports

Summarized by Ester R. Shapiro

The Clark Conference workshops, meeting four times during the conference, were designed to provide an opportunity for faculty to lead small-group discussions of the many issues stimulated by the panel presentations. Most of the faculty were listed on the original program as available to lead either discussions to follow the conference presentations, or else discussions with a focused topic, such as child development workshops, or Jungian analysis workshop, which would discuss the conference topics as they were relevant to a particular theoretical orientation or special interest group.

At the time of registration, we had asked participants to rank-order their particular workshop choices, and we planned to assign registrants to one of their top choices of a workshop with a particular faculty member or with a specific focus of interest. In planning the conference, the committee felt that it would be important for participants to experience the continuity of meeting for all four workshop sessions with one particular group. We assigned registrants ahead of time to specified workshops in order to limit group size to allow for small-group discussion, to predict which faculty would have enough enrollment to run a workshops, to distribute the number of participants across workshops more or less evenly, and to anticipate and organize room assignments.

The workshops turned out to be a test case for our commitment to offer flexible, participant-centered learning, and to place educational concerns over administrative or institutional concerns. Right from the beginning, many conference participants made it clear that they preferred to sample different workshops at different times, rather than to be committed to attending just one. On the basis of both prior enrollment, as well as student and faculty interest, we posted the room location of a dozen or so faculty who were available to lead workshops, and encouraged participants as well as faculty to attend the workshops of their choosing. With this arrangement, then, the eight workshops which were held for the four sessions of the conference had a consistent core of faculty and participants who came for all the meetings, and a changing group who attended just one or two of the meetings, so that they could attend several. While this arrangement did not meet our original, preconceived notion in favor of small groups of predictable size and of group continuity, it did provide most of the participants with the workshop arrangement of their choosing.

In addition, we requested that each of the workshops assign a reporter to take notes of the group discussion, so that the insights gained within the different small-group discussions could be brought back to the large group. The following workshop summaries are based on workshop reports presented on Sunday evening, after eight of the workshops had met four times, and on additional materials submitted by faculty prior to the conference and published in the agenda books.

Carol Marshall, Ph.D., reported on a workshop led by Stanley Gochman, Ph.D., who entitled his preconference workshop summary "A Model For Innovative Training In Psychoanalysis." Gochman participated in the development of the Institute for Analytic Psychotherapy in New Jersey in the 1960s, and currently teaches clinical psychology at American University. In his work, he emphasizes the integration of diverse points of view in psychoanalysis, including Adler's theoretical work, with other areas of psychology, such as child development research, systems theory, and cultural and social factors.

In the workshop meetings, Marshall reported that the group began the discussion of training by reflecting what they believed distinguished the psychologist psychoanalyst from other psychoanalysts. They concluded that psychologists as psychoanalysts are more scientifically oriented, concerned with confirming their ideas before proceeding. Psychologists have a broader interest in diverse theories, models, and methodologies, as well as diverse patient populations. Often, psychologists emphasize a wellness orientation rather than an illness orientation emphasized by the medical model. Psychologists appreciate the role of learning, the importance of behavior, and processes of normal personality development.

Having elaborated these unique qualities of the psychologist psychoanalyst, the Gochman workshop participants then discussed what kind of a credentialing process would encourage and enhance these unique qualities, rather than borrowing the criteria for evaluating training for medical analysts. The group referred to Dr. Stephen Appelbaum's presentation, in which he stated that a psychoanalyst should have a coherent theory of individual development, and a theory of how the mind works which would inform and direct the clinical work.

With this model, the candidate, after completing a program of study, would be asked to present a statement of his or her coherent theory of human development and of human psychology, and illustrate how the theory directs his or her clinical work. This would enable the candidate's clinical work to be judged for the coherence of the theoretical approach as it guided the clinical work, rather than on extrinsic technical factors, such as frequency of sessions. The workshop participants felt that this would enhance theoretical diversity rather than forcing a narrow choice of theoretical orientation.

In their concluding points, participants in this workshop felt that graduate students in clinical psychology were not sufficiently informed of the value of a psychoanalytic orientation, and that the division should support the section of local chapters to provide information directed at the graduate students in their communities. An awareness of psychoanalysis as a resource would provide opportunities to learn about and integrate psychoanalytic concepts into their clinical work early in their training. This group felt it was too early in the development of training programs for the Division to create a board that would provide national credentialing by mandating uniform requirements. Finally, the group recommended that the Division support the study of social issues in psychoanalysis, by pursuing a committee for the study of social issues which would give feedback to developing training programs.

Zenia Fliegel, Ph.D., reported on her own workshop, which discussed the general questions of theory, technique, and training brought up by the program presentations. This group oriented their workshop discussions by focusing on the issue of diversity, and asking the question, what can be included, and what has to be excluded, from psychoanalysis? What is extrinsic, and what is intrinsic? The group agreed that systems theory could be integrated into psychoanalysis, as a means of conceptualizing the expectable or unexpectable environment of individual development. In contrast, the group felt that hypnotherapy, unless it was accompanied by rigorous psychoanalytically informed theory, was a parameter that assumed too much as to what was good for the patient, with the therapist as magical helper. On the other hand, workshop participants were impressed with the effectiveness of therapeutic results provided by hypnotherapy, and would feel comfortable referring patients for this kind of treatment.

Fliegel added that her workshop's discussion of theoretical diversity inadvertently provided some confirmation of the male/female split described by Stephen Appelbaum, because the only man attending the workshop was the only group member concerned about the conceptual compatibility of the various models psychoanalysis might employ, while the women in the group accepted that these different models could coexist. In further discussing theoretical diversity, the group argued that often new ideas in psychoanalysis that form new schools, much as the beehive phenomenon brought up by Murray Bilmes, are often restating ideas already in the psychoanalytic literature. In considering this phenomenon, though, the group concluded that this process of reinventing the wheel has some benefits, in that it encourages fresh perspectives on psychoanalytic insights, and interferes with rigidity or ossification of thinking.

Stanton Marlan, Ph.D., reported on the Jungian workshop which he led. He provided several articles and key references for conference participants to use as resources in understanding Jungian psychoanalytic perspectives and views of psychoanalytic training (Hillman, 1975; Marlan, 1986; Samuels, 1985; Singer, 1982; Stein, 1982). He began by stating that the Jungian tradition is not monolithic, but rather is represented by at least three main orientations: the classical, the developmental, and the archetypal. Typically, Jungian Institutes are concerned that analysts be exposed to a rich variety of cultural, literary, and mythic studies as well as clinical training, agreeing with many of the speakers that the absence of such broad cultural and literary training from most traditional Institutes leads to limited perspectives on complex human phenomena.

Marlan reported that in the Jungian tradition, training emphasizes the personal development of the training analyst in the sense of developing depth and personal wholeness, rather than on technique per se. From the Jungian perspective, the distinction between open and closed or lockstep models poses a classical archetypal polarity, and that both sides need to be included and integrated. Similarly, Appelbaum's discussion of the romantic and classical perspectives has been extensively addressed in the Jungian literature, and the Jungian perspective would emphasize the exploration and personal integration of these typological polarities. A lot of Jung's early theorizing about psychological types, in fact, came from Jung's response to the contrast in the personal styles of Freud and Adler, and his attempt to forge a theory that would account for both sides of the continuum. Jungians have always emphasized the study of both the individual typology or psychology of theories, as well as the cultural countertransference that is at the base of any theoretical approach.

The Jungian workshop also discussed the question of the number of sessions per week, emphasizing that the depth of the exploration of the unconscious in terms of its personal and archetypal levels as well as the transference is what determines the depth of the analysis, and not frequency of sessions. Prior to acceptance at most institutes candidates are required an initial personal analysis of 100 hours preliminary to enrolling in training and kept totally separate from the Institute. In addition, the training analysis within the Institute is always nonreporting, so as to preserve the privacy of the personal analysis, which is seen as the heart of the training process.

Marlan described Jungian analysts as following Jung in emphasizing both scientific method or scholarly approach and the artistic, expressive side of psychoanalysis. In reaction to Paul Wachtel's paper, his group agreed with the statement that creative development of psychoanalysis has to achieve better separation from Freud and Freud's methods. He felt that Jung encouraged innovation rather than imitation in his followers, and quoted him as saying, "I'm glad I'm Jung and not a Jungian," encouraging his students to create for themselves as well. Although Jungians work with symbols in a way reminiscent of Dan Brown's hypnotherapy presentation, the Jungian work with symbols would be far slower, more exploratory at greater depth, and would not prematurely exploit the symbol or the unconscious for the purpose of ego development.

Marlan concluded by stating that just as Jungian analysis has been excluded from the history and development of traditional psychoanalysis, so was he disappointed that the Jungian workshop was a group of Jungians talking with one another, rather than with the larger group as a whole. Jungian Institutes have been training psychologists and other nonmedical analysts all over the world, share interests with their Freudian colleagues, and are very interested in new developments in psychoanalytic theory.

Ester Shapiro, Ph.D., reported on the family therapy workshop, led by Gerald Stechler, Ph.D., and Paul Wachtel, Ph.D. The family therapy group began with a paradoxical question: What are we, as a group of family therapists, doing here, at a psychoanalytic conference? Some group participants described their experiences of doing family therapy within a psychoanalytic Institute "in secret," because family theory and technique are not known or accepted. The exclusion of family therapists from Institute faculty, and the exclusion of family theory from the psychoanalytic curriculum, in themselves powerfully restrict the educational process, by limiting the theoretical and technical options candidates are educated to consider and to have available in their repertoire.

The family therapy workshop next discussed the nature of psychic structure, when viewed both from a traditional psychoanalytic and from systemic perspectives. Both Stechler and Wachtel have written extensively about their own integration of psychoanalytic and systemic perspectives, and the shared discussion focused on the need to distinguish between processes for the early development of psychic structure and processes for the current maintenance of psychic structure in the patient's adult life. Stechler referred to George Klein and other writers, who emphasize that psychoanalytic metapsychology needs to be discarded in favor of a clinical theory based on the dynamics of conflict.

He stated that in this form psychoanalytic concepts, such as multideterminism, nonlinear causality, as well as concepts such as conflict and ambivalence, are very compatible with modern systems theory, especially the work of Prygogine on discontinuous, self-regulating biological systems. Rather than choose between an intrapsychic model of psychic structure as slow to develop and slow to change, or an interpersonal or systemic model of psychic structure as generated by transactions in current relationships, it is possible to look at the interplay between internalized psychic structure and its collaborative organization and maintenance in transactional exchanges with important others. With this integrative perspective, it is possible to consider how something as profound as intrapsychic structure can in fact be altered by interpersonally or systemically oriented therapies.

The family therapy workshop concluded its work with a discussion of a sexual abuse case presented by Myron Lazar, Ph.D. The case was discussed from the point of view of Boszormenyi–Nagy's contextual therapy (Boszormeny–Nagy, & Krasner, 1988), which emphasizes family attachments and invisible family loyalties, and the importance of acknowledging the intergenerational nature of normal family processes and family dysfunction.

Etta Sax, Ph.D., reported for the child analysis workshop, which was collaboratively led and included Jan Drucker, Ph.D., Ava Siegler, Ph.D., and Carol Michaels, Ph.D., from the conference faculty. The workshop began with the discussion of the developmental perspective as the orienting approach to lifespan development, and therefore relevant to both child and adult psychoanalytic training. A number of workshop participants were considering child training, and the workshop participants discussed and compared different kinds of programs, their theoretical and treatment goals, and the success of different programs in meeting those goals.

The group discussed the problem that child psychoanalytic training often emphasizes frequent sessions as the best means of getting to the inner life of the child, but after psychoanalytic training most child work takes place with less frequent meetings. Child training should try to achieve a balance so that candidates experience this depth approach to the inner life of the child, but then have a range of technical skills which are more broadly, pragmatically applicable in a child psychotherapy practice.

John Herman, Ph.D., reported on a general discussion workshop with varied faculty and participant membership. The group began with a discussion following the panel on Institute and open training models, and concluded that not enough attention had been paid to the major factors in psychoanalytic Institutes which are psychodynamic or intrapsychic in nature. The workshop participants felt that any Institute can be described as a compromise formation of a variety of fantasies and conflicts. These conflicts have to be respected and discussed rather than eliminated.

In response to the presentations on psychoanalytic supervision, the group asserted that most learning is self-taught, and that it is important to look at supervision as supporting an active approach to personal learning. The emphasis on process applies to the analytic process itself, where what matters is not what the therapist says, but what the therapist says next, so that what is important is the process of responsiveness and not the original intervention. The group suggested that Institutes should have seminars for supervisors, in helping them achieve this kind of teaching. The group also addressed the question of evaluation in Institutes, and agreed that evaluation feedback needs to be part of an educational which maximizes the candidate's learning.

The group recommended the use of videotapes, for example of videotaping clinical interviews with confederates such as actors or actresses, and perhaps then videotaping a feedback session with the supervisor as well, so that these discussions become part of the educational process. In a final discussion of the Wachtel and Silberschatz presentations, the group discussed the nature of research in the clinical situation, and felt that the clinical situation could still offer opportunities for the exploration of hypotheses which could then be more formally tested.

Larry Hedges, Ph.D., reported for Dr. John Gedo's workshop. As Gedo is a physician who has been very involved in psychoanalytic training conferences of the International and the American, the group posed the question to Gedo, how is this conference sponsored by psychologists different? He commented, first, that he had seldom seen so many complex administrative issues discussed in such good form, and that the contributions themselves were at an extremely high level. He found it inspiring to be at the conference, because in this group there is as yet no training tradition, everything is open to question and nothing has yet been decided. In conferences of the American or the International, the enemy is the traditional training program, and the problem is how to identify what is wrong and how to change what has already been established and is resistant to change.

Gedo asserted that although the psychologists tend to see the medical analysts as the enemy, most medical analysts will welcome the insights offered by these new perspectives which expand the psychoanalytic community. He finds that psychologists, with their intellectual and scientific tradition, have functioned for psychoanalysis as "epistemological referees," for example David Rappoport, George Klein, or Roy Schaeffer, who review and critically examine different perspectives in psychoanalysis. Finally, Gedo raised the point that the group of psychologists seemed very concerned with being validated by the fathers of psychoanalysis. Rather, he feels that it is the job of the fathers to address and be accountable to the younger generation, who represent the creative future of psychoanalysis.

Robert Aguado, Ph.D., reported on the Melanie Klein workshop which he conducted. Because the Kleinian perspective is often not taught in traditional training programs, Aguado first presented Kleinian theoretical concepts and their application to child and adult clinical material. He noted that the Kleinian approach begins with a very different definition of the object than is prevalent in Freudian psychoanalysis. Klein emphasises fantasy in the earliest object relationships, the importance of the infant's experience of anxiety and the mechanisms, such as introjection, projective identification, and splitting, which are defenses against this early anxiety. From this perspective, the clinical work addresses the internal fantasy life of the patient, and transference manifestations of these early defenses, and does not intervene in any way in the patient's real life. In case discussions, he reviewed the paranoid/schizoid position and the depressive position, both involving fragmentation of the self and attempts to reconstitute object relationships. In the ensuing discussion, he encouraged the workshop participants to apply these clinical and theoretical concepts from early object relational experience to issues of training.

REFERENCES

Boszormenyi-Nagy, I., & Krasner, B. (1986). *Between give and take: A clinical guide to contextual therapy*. New York: Bruner/Mazel.

Marlan, S. (1986). *Jungian psychoanalysis*. Unpublished manuscript.

Samuels, A. (1985). *Jung and post-Jungians*. London: Routledge & Kegan Paul.

Singer, J. (1982). The education of the analyst. In M. Stein (Ed.), *Jungian analysis*. London: Routledge & Kegan Paul, pp. 367–385.

Stein, M. (1982). The aims and goals of Jungian analysis. In M. Stein (Ed.), *Jungian analysis*. London: Routledge & Kegan Paul, pp. 27–43.

36

The Future of Psychoanalytic Education: Intergenerational Conflict and the Balance of Tradition and Innovation

Ester R. Shapiro

INTRODUCTION

The future of psychoanalysis, and the future of psychoanalytic education, are closely intertwined, as the early psychoanalytic community knew from the very beginning. Who could become a psychoanalyst, what did they have to do to become one, who in the psychoanalytic community would train them, these questions have been intensely debated since the fifth psychoanalytic congress in Budapest in 1918, when Hermann Nunberg suggested that all analysts should be analyzed, and the ninth congress in Bad Homburg in 1925, when Max Eitingon proposed that analysts should be required to have their analytic work supervised (Sandler, 1982).

Between 1920 and 1924, the Berlin Psychoanalytic Institute, headed by Karl Abraham, formalized the requirements of a tripartite model for psychoanalytic education which was endorsed by the International Training Commission appointed by the International Psychoanalytic Association (IPA) in 1925. By the mid-1930s the Berlin Institute's training program had been adopted by most of the psychoanalytic community worldwide (Bernfeld, 1962; Gay, 1988; Jacoby, 1983; Lewin & Ross, 1960). This was true in both Europe and the United States, even though the American Psychoanalytic Association (APsaA) had initiated a "Declaration of Independence" in 1936, formalized in 1938, asserting the independence of its own Institutes in setting their own requirements for who could train as an analyst in the United States. Since the APsaA adopted the same training standards as recommended by the IPA's Training Commission (Schecter, 1979), clearly the only point of difference or independence was the APsaA's right to determine that nonmedical graduates of IPA Institutes could not practice psychoanalysis in the United States as they could in Europe.

The question of lay analysis has been intertwined with the developmental history of psychoanalysis since 1927, when Freud wrote *The Question of Lay Analysis* in response to a lawsuit for quackery brought against Theodore Reik by a disgruntled American analysand. In response to Freud's strong statement in favor of lay analysis, the International Psychoanalytic Association held a congress on the question of lay analysis (Jones et al., 1927). In those papers, the psychoanalytic community overwhelmingly agreed that psychoanalysis was a medical therapy which should be practiced by physicians. At the time of the 1927 Congress, no other licensed mental health practice group existed, psychiatry itself was a suspiciously regarded medical specialty, and medical analysts argued that if psychoanalysis was practiced by just anybody then most physicians would not take psychoanalysis seriously.

The Americans at the 1927 Congress made the strongest statement that psychoanalysis was exclusively a medical specialty, while Jones and others argued that nonmedical analysts could be trained if they agreed to practice under medical supervision. Brill, Jones, and other speakers at the 1927 Congress stated with regret that here was the one and only issue on which they felt forced to disagree with the Master. Oberndorf of the New York Psychoanalytic Association, less apologetic for disagreeing with Freud, compared Freud's publication of *The Question of Lay Analysis* before the IPA's discussion with a physician who prematurely intervenes in a situation which might otherwise naturally heal itself—thinly veiling his accusation that Freud's public support of lay analysis was professionally irresponsible, in itself a kind of "quackery" (Kohon, 1986). In response to the discussion at the 1927 Congress, Freud wrote an even stronger 1928 postscript to his book, in which he argued that if psychoanalysis were allowed to become a medical specialty, it would eventually become nothing but a footnote in a psychiatric textbook on the treatment of neuroses.

Both these developments—the creation of a rigorous, universally applied program of study monitored by the APsaP for the United States, the IPA for the rest of the world; and the resolution that psychoanalysis was a medical specialty—were initiated with the goal of preserving psychoanalysis on behalf of its future. As Anne–Marie Sandler wrote in her 1982 review of the training procedures in Europe, the early psychoanalytic movement concentrated on preserving the unique identity of psychoanalysis, "maintaining and developing that which Freud has created" (Sandler, 1982, quoting Eitingon) and protecting it from fusion with other fields of thought or technical approaches.

Consistent with the goals of preserving the integrity of psychoanalysis, and therefore ensuring its survival, the early participants in the psychoanalytic movement were expected to learn Freudian psychoanalysis, and to confirm clinically or expand theoretically on Freud's psychoanalytic findings. In the early history of psychoanalysis, especially in the banishment or control of those disciples who strayed too far from the core of psychoanalytic concepts, the attempt to maintain the continuity of the past into an uncertain future often conveyed the quality of a struggle to the death between past and future, master and disciple, parent and child. The early history of psychoanalysis is marked by bitter excommunications of once cherished disciples (Alfred Adler, Carl Jung, Otto Rank) and equally acrimonious close calls (Sandor Ferenczi, the Ernest Jones/Melanie Klein alliance).

Of course, there have been new developments in psychoanalytic theory, within the IPA, such as the Kleinian, object-relations, and self-psychology theories and technical revisions, and outside the IPA, such as the culturalists or the interpersonalists (Eagle, 1984; Greenberg & Mitchell, 1983; Wallerstein, 1988). Further, research and theory within child development and psychology of women have begun to be integrated into psychoanalytic thinking (Drucker, Mendell, Miller, Stechler, in this volume). Yet these expanded theoretical perspectives continue to be regarded as separate, distinct schools, still not part of the mainstream psychoanalytic perspective, even less often part of psychoanalytic education as offered in psychoanalytic Institutes, most especially the Institutes of the American Psychoanalytic Association.

Sandler (1982) notes that psychoanalysis succeeded in the important task of self-preservation. Now, she argues, psychoanalysis is contending with the danger of "a tendency to unhealthy conservatism which may result in rigidity, in a kind of ossification and a lack of openness to adaptive change" (Sandler, 1982, p. 386). In the relatively brief century since its inception, how did the cultural, intellectual, and therapeutic revolution of psychoanalysis become a stagnant field, reasoning by authority rather than persuaded by new evidence, within the United States viewed as an instrument of social conformity rather than of social reform?

Social critics, from the early Marxists to contemporary feminists, have been drawn to psychoanalysis as the most radical tool for understanding the interplay between cultural oppression and the internalization of oppression within the individual psyche. At its inception, psychoanalysis was seen as revolutionizing the sexually repressed Victorian culture, and was allied with many socialist political and educational critics (Gay, 1988; Jacoby, 1983). Freud was of two minds about the proper relationship between the instincts and society. Especially in his early writings, he argued that overly strict repression of sexual and aggresive instincts, familial or cultural, resulted in crippling neurosis. By the end of his life, after witnessing the horrors of World War I, the political and economic deterioration of the Austrian nation, and the fascist takeover of Central Europe, Freud felt more pessimistic about the fundamentally destructive nature of the instincts. In his postwar writings, beginning with *Beyond the Pleasure Principle* (1920), Freud came to emphasize more the need for social structures, external and internal, to restrain this human capacity for destruction. However, Freud continued to hope that psychoanalysis could influence social reform, through public education and through critique of social forms, in such a way that individuals would not be as crippled by the fruitless task of maintaining harsh restrictions against the instincts.

The capacity for psychoanalysis to offer social critique seems to depend in part on its relationship to the larger society. In the United States, psychoanalysis became established as an economically successful branch of the powerful medical profession. Increasingly, it became associated as well with an emphasis on adaptation to a conventional society's expectations. Clarence Oberndorf, with Brill, a founder of the New York Psychoanalytic Society and with Jones a founder of the American Psychoanalytic Association, lamented of psychoanalysis in 1953: "Psychoanalysis had finally become legitimate and respectable, perhaps paying the price in becoming sluggish and smug, hence attractive to an increasing number of minds which find security in conformity and propriety" (Oberndorf, 1953, p. 207). What Oberndorf failed to bring together in his thinking, quite possibly because his own actions were so central in restricting lay analysis in the United States, was the role that the medicalization of psychoanalysis played in the creation of a conventionally acceptable psychoanalysis which had become professionally self-protective at the expense of its intellectual independence.

It seems that orthodox psychoanalytic theory and practice in the United States has been uniquely characterized by a combination of emphasis on social conformity and rigid identification with certain narrow aspects of Freudian psychoanalytic theory and technique. Freud generated an enormous body of work in his lifetime, which he frequently expanded and revised as his thinking evolved, as he matured from young man to ailing elder, as he ceased to be an outcast and became a world leader, as he observed the 20th century's political disasters and corresponding human suffering from the center stage of Austria. Freud's writings, the products of a complex mind, are themselves models for his own theories of unconscious conflict, resistance, and ambivalence, and are most productively read as such. The tensions between the scientific method and the literary, between object relations theory and drive theory, between preoedipal and oedipal perspectives, between the roles of external reality and internal fantasy in creating inner structure, between analysis of unconscious affects and drives or analysis of ego defenses, permeate Freud's dense, exploratory, contradictory writings. Freud wished for a Nobel prize for medicine, but he won a Goethe prize for literature.

Although the entire international psychoanalytic community uses Freud's writing as a touchstone, the American Psychoanalytic Association has generated the most uniformly narrow reading of Freud. Three important factors distinguished the development of psychoanalysis in the United States from the development of psychoanalysis in other parts of the world. First, the central control of the American Psychoanalytic Association limited theoretical development by imposing uniform courses of study emphasizing drive theory and ego psychoanalytic perspectives. Second, the medicalization of psychoanalysis limited interdisciplinary participation, narrowed the scientific scope of psychoanalysis to its medical application, and imposed a diagnostically oriented medical model. In addition, the medical model encouraged uncritical acceptance of professional authority, in both training relationships and in the view of the psychoanalytic relationship itself. Because of the success of the American Psychoanalytic Association in making psychoanalysis an accepted part of an economically powerful medical establishment, North American psychoanalysis had more to gain from embracing the cultural status quo than did a more culturally marginal psychoanalytic community, such as in Britain or Latin America.

Finally, more subtly, the absorption of refugees from the Central European psychoanalytic community in the United States also added to the conservative direction of North American psychoanalysis, because of the immigrant's natural tendency to idealize the lost country, as well as the political requirements of refugees from an enemy country adapting to the politically conservative climate in the United States after World War II. The psychological adjustments encouraged in American acculturation, represented by cherished American tradition of the "melting pot," offer greater educational and economic opportunities, as well as greater political freedom, in exchange for a degree of cultural homogenization. The historical and cross-cultural dimensions of psychoanalysis, the discontinuities of immigration and their psychological consequences for the psychoanalytic movement, will be discussed more fully later in this chapter.

The fragmentation of the European psychoanalytic community during World War II, and the economic success and stability of psychoanalysis in the United States, has given the status of psychoanalytic theory and practice in the United States a disproportionate impact on the definition of psychoanalysis worldwide. As one example, the IPA was surely influenced, in accepting the APsaA's "declaration of independence" (1936–1938) by the fact that in 1933 Hitler came to power in Germany, in 1938 in Austria, and that many European analysts fled for their lives to the United States.

Both psychoanalysis as a scientific discipline and psychoanalysis as a treatment technique have suffered from this fragmentation and isolation. The current developments in the American Psychological Association's Division of psychoanalysis, especially the lawsuit challenging the medical monopoly, and the creation of diverse interdisciplinary communities of psychoanalysts in the United States in dialogue with the International, offer a new opportunity for the developmental integration of psychoanalysis within the United States and in the international psychoanalytic community.

The question of the future of psychoanalysis has far greater relevance for the society, and for the field of mental health, than is believed by those who denigrate psychoanalysis as an obsolete treatment model or an esoteric cult studied by obsessional worshipers of Freud. Psychoanalytic psychotherapy, based on psychoanalysis and its dynamic theory of the unconscious, continues to be a highly respected form of postgraduate training for most mental health professionals. As the popularity of psychoanalysis declines in psychiatry, with the remedicalization of psychiatry, interest in psychoanalysis is growing among clinical psychologists and other mental health professionals, for example as reflected in the popularity of psychoanalytically oriented internships, or in the growing membership of Division 39.

The power of the psychoanalytic method, as well as potentially its fundamental limitation, lies in the fact that the analyzing instrument is the self within a human relationship, one experiencing human being knowing another and enhancing the other's self-knowledge through deep involvement and self-awareness. Freud discovered that there was no other avenue for the full understanding of the complex human psyche, as powerful as the psychoanalytically trained observer, required to observe simultaneously self and other.

The relational tension between knowledge of others and self-awareness characterizes the unique psychoanalytic definition of objectivity, a self-reflective attitude toward one's own subjectivity arrived at in the psychoanalytic interchange (Racker, 1968). Because of the analyst's power in the psychoanalytic relationship, however, the psychoanalytic stance can degenerate into a self-protectively authoritarian attitude in which the analyst always knows best, the patient's disagreement is always resistance, where interpretation can take the form of aggressive attacks designed to induce compliance with the analyst's view of the patient's reality. Psychoanalysts in the interpersonal and British object relational traditions (e.g., Balint, 1953/1986; Bollas, 1987; Greenberg & Mitchell, 1983; Hoffman, 1983; Levenson, 1983; Searles, 1979; Will, 1962) have argued that a psychoanalytic interchange which does not acknowledge the mutuality of relationship, where analysts cannot learn about themselves from their patients, can deteriorate into behavior modification or thought control.

As can be seen from this discussion, there is an enormous gap between psychoanalysis at its best and psychoanalysis at it worst. At its best, psychoanalysis offers not only an invaluable, but an indispensable contribution to the field of mental health and to the scientific understanding of individual and social psychology. Even the scientific method itself can be productively studied from a psychoanalytic perspective, as suggested by Keller (1985) a mathematical biophysicist who uses psychoanalytic theory to analyze the gender bias in the scientific method.

> My use of psychoanalytic theory is premised on the belief that, even with its deficiencies, it has the potentiality for self-correction. The mode of analysis it provides is sufficiently penetrating to enable us to examine developmental failures not only in the human psyche but in the theory itself. (1985, p. 73)

In the history of psychoanalysis, this is a good developmental moment for those of us who cherish psychoanalysis and wish to address its problems honestly and constructively. With the opening of the Freud archives, new opportunities for more realistic historical study of psychoanalysis have been made available. The lawsuit against the APsaA and the IPA has re-established an interdisciplinary psychoanalytic community worldwide, making it possible for both theory and treatment to be more fully informed by the contributions of other intellectual and mental health disciplines besides the medical.

Medicine itself is changing, with the proliferation of medical information and technology, so that paradoxically, modern medicine itself is questioning the old apprenticeship and medical authority model in favor of more collaborative, independent study formats, such as Harvard Medical School's New Pathways curriculum. In this new era of complex medical judgment calls, with an increase in malpractice litigation in which patients hold their doctors accountable for promoting the image that the doctor does always know best, physicians are increasingly cooperating with their patients in making treatment decisions. Within and outside of organized medicine, the benefits of a fragmented, technological approach are being questioned in favor of a more holistic and humanistic approach to healing as a process involving body, psyche, soul, and environment.

Because Division 39 developed outside of APsaA and IPA strictures, the Clark Conference papers could offer intellectually diverse reviews and critiques of current psychoanalytic educational practices, representing perspectives from both medical and interdisciplinary Institutes as well as from eminent psychoanalysts trained by independent study. Because Division 39 is open to the entire American Psychological Association membership, participants also included interpersonalists, culturalists, Jungian, and Adlerian analysts who might not ordinarily be heard from in discussions of training offered by the IPA or APsaA. The opportunity provided by the Division for communication among diverse groups who addressed one another's contributions with interest and intellectual respect was in itself a powerful stimulus to collaboration and mutual learning.

Yet in spite of the diversity of presenters' backgrounds, theoretical orientations, and topics, the papers offer remarkably consistent, recurrent themes in identifying problems in psychoanalytic education, and in suggesting new directions. Consistently, the papers in this conference address the question, what is the reality, and especially the relational reality, of our psychoanalytic educational institutions? How do these institutional organizations and relationships impact on the vision of psychoanalysis which is integrated by the candidate? The relational, developmental perspective implicit in the papers offers an alternative definition of authority in educational relationships which emphasizes mutuality, collaboration, and exploration of differences.

However, many of these critiques have been offered before, and have not been successfully integrated in such a way as to generate the recommended organizational changes. For this reason, discussions of the future of psychoanalytic education need to address explicitly the structural and relational barriers to new learning, established over the history of the psychoanalytic movement, which have impeded the implementation of previous critiques. I will propose that the traumatic developmental history of psychoanalysis—including Freud's child and adult developmental history—created barriers to the adaptive integration of new information which parallel the intrapsychic defenses of the individual, and the interpersonal defenses of an enmeshed family.

At the heart of these barriers to learning from experience is the self-protective exploitation of authority due to a fear of difference in interpersonal relationships, motivated by a fear of what will be seen and learned about the self through the recognition of differences in others. In analyzing these interpersonal barriers to learning from experience, I will apply an intergenerational lifespan development theory which examines the process of individual development in the context of the relational capacity to balance closeness and independence, continuity with the past and creative discontinuity, during life-cycle transitions (Shapiro, 1986, 1987, 1988). I will argue that a focus on the definition of authority in intergenerational relationships, and on the capacity of relationships to tolerate collaboration and difference, provides a way of understanding the current impasse in psychoanalysis. I will point to important historical developments in psychoanalysis restricting discussion of differences, as Central European psychoanalysis became first an export and soon after an exile transplanted into varying cultural contexts.

Finally, I will describe the attempts in the Boston and Michigan local chapters to create psychoanalytic training programs informed by these critiques and discussions of the psychoanalytic educational process. The Boston chapter has chosen an Institute or "closed" model training program, while the Michigan chapter has chosen an "open" model or independent study system. With very different organizational structures, both groups have maintained open dialogue among a diverse group of psychoanalytically oriented clinicians. These two groups created different educational programs, but share the common goal of creating a balance between structure and flexibility, requirements and independent study, community and autonomy, in offering a psychoanalytic education.

TRADITION AND INNOVATION: TOWARD
A DEVELOPMENTAL INTEGRATION

The Clark Conference papers, with their diverse presentations from different psychoanalytic backgrounds, offer process as well as content in expanding the critical study of psychoanalytic education. The organization of this conference reflects the realization that the exploration of many points of view, the process of dialogue across differences, will lead to a diversity of educational visions which will enrich the future of psychoanalysis. The subtitle of the Clark Conference, "Tradition and Innovation in Psychoanalytic Training," was chosen to imply the conference goal of a process of exploration and dynamic integration of the wisdom of the past with the creative innovation required for the future of psychoanalytic education. Too often in human development, whether of individuals, families, or institutions, there is a polarization and isolation of tradition and innovation, as reflected by the categories of orthodoxy and heresy, or conformity and revolution.

Most intellectual and scientific disciplines find themselves posing dualities in polar opposition, and psychoanalysis is no exception. These dualities recur throughout these conference papers: "drive theory" versus "relational theory," "open" versus "closed" training models, "feminine" versus "masculine" approaches to theory and technique, "classical" versus "romantic" perspectives, and so on. In his paper for this conference, Stephen Appelbaum suggests that the hallmark of a first-rate mind is the capacity to tolerate paradox, and to extend one's thinking by facing and exploring contradictions. He concludes that a complete psychoanalytic theory needs to explore the tension between opposing polarities and their integration into a more complete psychoanalytic theory addressing human development and gender differences as part of a general psychoanalytic psychology.

The Clark Conference papers implicitly offer a view of psychoanalytic education from a dialogic or dialectical developmental perspective, in which the tensions created by the open-minded exploration of differences or of conflicting points of view are themselves the stimulus for shared intellectual growth. In this spirit, both the papers and the concluding summary chapter offer a perspective on a process of learning, rather than a proposal for a specific educational form or outcome. This process orientation has emerged from the conflict-ridden collaboration of diverse groups of psychoanalysts who formed Division 39, and from the collaborative development of local chapters in diverse communities, which have received the Division's support in acknowledging that different communities will need to evolve their own training programs appropriate to their particular needs.

Most stage theories of human development encourage the polar perspective, by offering a view of development which is discontinuous and linear. In contrast, process-oriented developmental theories, such as Werner's organismic developmental theory (1948) or Riegel's dialectical, lifespan developmental theory (1976), propose that it is the exploration and integration of opposing forces or contradictory perceptions into a coherent unity which moves human development forward throughout the life cycle. From the point of view of these theories, a stage of polarization can be a preliminary step in a developmental process, which first articulates differences and then integrates these differences into a coherent whole.

This developmental process of exploration and integration of contradictory forces or perspectives can best be understood as an intergenerational relational process. Throughout the life cycle, the individual's inner capacity to explore and integrate the complexities of a developing self depends on the capacity of important others to support and tolerate the expression of interpersonal differences. For this reason, the definition of authority in a relationship where one person nurtures the development of another establishes the developmental course for the future, whether the relationships be parent and child in the family, student and teacher in the psychoanalytic Institute, or analysand and analyst in the therapeutic relationship conducted within the psychoanalytic community. Intergenerational relationships, and the institutional forms which follow from them, vary enormously in their capacity to create a cohesive community which supports both the connectedness required for a sense of continuity and stability, and the autonomy of its individuals required for spontaneity and creativity.

If development depends on the exploration and integration of conflict or difference, what interferes with this normal developmental process? Both psychoanalysis and intergenerational family therapy conceptualize psychopathology as the failure to learn from experience because of the defensive, inflexible imposition of unexamined old assumptions—intrapsychic or interpersonal—on current experience. While psychoanalytic theory emphasizes the intrapsychic process of defense, family systems theory emphasizes the interpersonal enlisting of close others in the defensive protection of the self.

The intrapsychic system of the neurotic and the family system of the enmeshed family have a great deal in common. Both mobilize defenses, whether intrapsychic or interpersonal, to avoid conflict or to control overwhelming emotions, especially as a means of coping with the emotions generated in the process of developmental change. These self-protective defenses, which at one time served a useful equilibrating function, do create a manageable view of self and others, but at the expense of learning from new information. If defenses are indiscriminately applied to new situations, they will prevent the acknowledgment of difference between the old and the new which permits change.

A relational developmental perspective assumes that all persons exist in relationships and that a complex sense of the self is interpersonally established, maintained, developmentally modified, and reorganized through transactions in close relationships throughout the life cycle (Shapiro, 1987, 1988). Changes in relationships, whether in a shared response to the environment outside the family or in response to the developmental changes of individual family members, require that relational identity be redefined. This process of mutual identity change is facilitated when it is balanced by a sense of stability or continuity. During life-cycle transitions that are emotionally overwhelming or traumatic, or by their nature radically discontinuous, it is more likely that the process of change will be restricted or controlled, so as to create a tolerable balance or equilibrium of continuity and discontinuity.

While interpersonal defenses are fundamentally collaborative, parents have a disproportionate power due to the dependency of the children, who rely on the parent for physical and emotional care and for guidance in self-understanding and self-regulation. The child's knowledge of the self and experience of the world is arrived at through both self-generated exploration and through interchanges with the parents, and children will often give priority to their parent's definition of their own, inner experience. In addition, from earliest infancy, children consciously and unconsciously respond protectively to their parents' emotional distress and collaborate with their parents' attempts to cope.

Because of this relational asymmetry of power and dependence between parents and children, appropriately constructive parental protection or socialization of the child can become confused with the self-protective exploitation of the parental power to define the child's experience. For example, a distressed or highly defended parent may respond to a child's distress with criticism or negative character attributions, as a means of avoiding one's own empathic emotional response. When sufficiently overwhelmed by their own emotional experience, adults can exploit their parental authority to restrict the emotional expressions or actions of their children which might contradict their defensive assumptions about self-as-parent in relation to the child. These parental defenses, in turn, create the interpersonal environment for the child's development in which emotions are experienced as manageable and integrated or overwhelming and defended against.

The view of the parent/child relationship discussed from this intergenerational developmental perspective offers a model for understanding the nature and definition of authority in any asymmetrical relationship where one person is responsible for nurturing the development of another. As psychoanalysis has found, the internalization of the parent/child relationship provides the subsequent structure not only for intrapsychic organization, but also for the organization of social and cultural institutions. Any group with the power to dominate others is extremely vulnerable to the self-protective exploitations of this power. When a dominant group takes the liberty to define the experience of another so as to avoid insight into the self, as in social class, racial, gender, or national stereotypes, both groups lose their capacity for the greatest human freedom. Psychoanalysis can make a significant contribution to an understanding of these relational process, both in the family and in the social institutions derived from family relationships.

CLARK CONFERENCE PAPERS: CHANGING THE DEFINITION OF EDUCATIONAL AUTHORITY

From the developmental vantage point described here, the Clark Conference papers can be seen to address consistently the relational process of change in psychoanalytic education. The Clark Conference papers explore the qualities of relationships, institutional and interpersonal, that enable the greatest autonomy while retaining the supportive nurturance of an experienced, established educational community. Under what circumstances does the authority of the parental generation become oriented toward dominance or control, restricting new information or new learning in others so as to project against change in self? Under circumstances of overwhelming change, adults are more likely to insist on conserving a view of the world which does not require disequilibriating change in self. An educational attitude that inflexibly imposes the teachings of the past on the next generation reflects a defensive restriction of change in others, so as to defend against new information that might change the self. An attitude of authority which emphasizes control over new information and restriction of independent thinking interferes with the autonomous identity development of the next generation and with a flexible, creative response to present and future.

Although the content and background reading for each of the panels and papers was summarized in the introduction, it seems worth reviewing these briefly here, as seen from the relational developmental framework. Beginning with Murray Meisels's introductory chapter, on the background of the conference in the light of the Division's development, Meisels notes the importance of the Division as a home for psychologist psychoanalysts which has supported new developments, such as the lawsuit, the development of training programs, without homogenizing differences as does the APsaA. In his discussion he describes two fantasies which have stood in the way of change, the fantasy of a higher justice which will rectify an unjust situation, and the fantasy of the perfectly analyzed analyst whom one must strive to become. Meisels notes that both are childhood fantasies which appeal to the higher authority of a perfect, all-knowing idealized parent, and both are barriers to change through action in the real world.

Helen Block Lewis's theoretical contributions on the superego emotions of shame and guilt focus explicitly on the nature of relationships with inequality of status, and the intrapsychic consequences of interpersonal dominance or exploitation of authority. Lewis also addressed the major problem of the silencing of difference of opinion or diversity in any relationship as resulting in intellectual and emotional stagnation. Anne–Marie Sandler's keynote address discusses the costs and benefits of a requirement-oriented system, which creates a supportive community offering a sense of certainty, in which the faculty takes educational responsibility and the students are more compliant, with an independent-study system which allows more autonomy and creativity but more uncertainty and revolt.

The papers on open and closed systems follow with the question, what is the proper balance between creating a supportive, experienced community while preserving the autonomy and creativity of its participants, especially of its students? Charles Spezzano's paper notes that because psychologists in the United States have been excluded from training in medical Institutes, we have overemphasized the quest for legitimacy as defined by the external authority of the American, echoing Meisels's statements that the quest for authority and definition outside the self interferes with the development of self-definition, and with the action required for change.

The papers on the components of psychoanalytic training, personal analysis and supervision, argued that when the training analysis is an institutional requirement defined as the most important dimension of the psychoanalytic educational process, candidates become extremely vulnerable to conscious and unconscious coercion to become analysts in the image of their training analyst or institution. In the panel addressing the candidate's theoretical learning, "Becoming a psychoanalyst of one persuasion or another," the panelists emphasized that psychoanalytic learning at its best involves a relational process of communication of diversity and systematic exploration of differences toward unique personal integration. Such an exploration and integration of differences in a supportive relational climate not only enhances the capacity for relatedness which candidates bring to their psychoanalytic treatment, it also offers the best chance of advancing the growth of psychoanalytic theory.

The papers on the relationship of psychoanalysis to other forms of therapy and to research on psychoanalytic technique suggest that psychoanalysis has failed to develop, both technically and theoretically, through its isolation from other disciplines and from scholarly and experimental challenge of its established assumptions. The dialogue with different perspectives will enhance the development of psychoanalysis. The discussion of the relationship between the Division and local chapters emphasized the importance of active self-determination, for example, in initiating the lawsuit against the APsaA or in creating our own educational programs, in promoting the autonomous self-definition of psychologists as psychoanalysts.

Finally, the concluding papers on the contribution of family theory and research—psychology of women, child development, infant research, and family systems theory—argued that the direct study of child development within family relationships, especially the study of relational attachments, adds a perspective that an exclusively individual, adult male-oriented perspective fails to add to psychoanalytic thinking. The cultural realities of male dominance, including the devaluation of emotional expressiveness in relationships, and the familial realities of parent/child relationships, have been found to be important determinants in the construction of the self for both men and women, adults and children.

These papers convey the hopefulness that psychoanalysis can recapture some of the innovative spirit which characterized the appeal of psychoanalysis in its early years. It is no coincidence that these critiques were generated by Division 39, a psychoanalytic group outside the established psychoanalytic groups of the IPA and APsaA. Rather, the Division has been somewhat freer to operate outside the rules of family loyalty and family obligation that are part of being a member of a close-knit community with a shared history. However, as a number of the speakers noted, it won't do to congratulate ourselves for our greater freedom and independence as outsiders to an established organizational or family system. We outsiders are family members too, and we need to turn our attention to the psychoanalytic family history and relationships which are ours as well.

THE FAMILY DEVELOPMENTAL HISTORY
OF PSYCHOANALYSIS: FAMILY TRAUMA
AND FAMILY LOYALTY

Psychoanalysis has taught us that in understanding current problems and creating new solutions for the future, the greatest personal freedom is achieved through a thorough understanding of one's own past. In this spirit, I will now turn to a brief discussion of our psychoanalytic history, which highlights important intergenerational factors and crucial cultural transitions in the development of psychoanalysis and its institutional forms.

In the following discussion, I will argue that the powerful defenses against theoretical and technical development which have characterized psychoanalysis exist because of the powerful confluence of internal and external realities in the history of the psychoanalytic movement and in the development of its educational forms in response to that history. The family developmental history of psychoanalysis, especially during the period when the vision for psychoanalytic education was consolidated, took place in an overwhelming emotional context, the bloody political struggles in Europe marked by the two World Wars. The traumatic upheavals and losses of this historical period in Central Europe, and the dispersal of the psychoanalytic community, propelled the struggle to preserve psychoanalysis toward a far more conservative direction.

In addition, Freud's personal developmental and relational history, his early individual history and the ways his individual life course, both in its career and family aspects, intersected with these world events, powerfully shaped the course of the psychoanalytic movement and its intergenerational attitudes as reflected in its educational institutions. Freud studies have tended to either idealize or repudiate Freud, and the new possibilities for study with the opening of the archives creates the opportunity for a more balanced view of Freud's personal life and its impact on psychoanalysis. A family life-cycle orientation, taking into account the formation of Freud's personality through his early family relationships and the expression of that personality in his family of procreation and in his adoptive family, the psychoanalytic movement, can illuminate the relational developmental history of the psychoanalytic movement.

The exploration of the past requires the rediscovery of what has been known but repressed because of unbearable conflicts or affects. There are fewer family secrets in psychoanalytic history than there used to be, with expanding access to Freud's correspondance and other historical documents which had previously been withheld from study or published in edited form. However, as in any system, intrapsychic, familial, or organizational, a great deal can be out in the open and still hidden from view, through the power of isolation, disassociation, and repression. Paradoxically, what is isolated or repressed, in both intrapsychic reality and in family relationships, has a disproportionately powerful impact on the developmental course, because isolation interrupts the ongoing process of change stimulated by learning from new experiences. Further, the unconscious conflicts of the adults are passed on to the next generation through the medium of the parent–child relationships.

As Siegfried Bernfeld discusses in his paper "On Psychoanalytic Training," the formation of the Berlin Psychoanalytic Institute in the early 1920s, in which psychoanalytic education was formalized very much as it is practiced today throughout most of the psychoanalytic communities, took place at an extraordinary moment in political, cultural, and historical time in Europe between the two World Wars. After World War I, and with the success of the Russian revolution, European socialists, especially in Central Europe, expanded their radical political activities, confident that the socialist movement would sweep through Europe. Siegfried Bernfeld, Otto Fenichel, Wilhelm and Annie Reich, Edith Jacobson, Kate Friedlander, and many others of the second-generation psychoanalytic circle were socialists for whom psychoanalysis and political reform were intimately intertwined. After World War I, Berlin was the center of a political, cultural, and artistic avant-garde which was very sympathetic to the radical theories of psychoanalysis.

Unfortunately, the Central European community experienced a brutal fascist backlash to the socialist political activity. Hitler's defeat of the German Democratic government in 1933 was preceded by a brief socialist takeover in Budapest in 1919, followed by a fascist overthrow with such violent antisocialist as well as antisemitic policies that many Hungarians, including Melanie Klein and the Balints, emigrated to Berlin. Jacoby, in *The Repression of Psychoanalysis*, argues that the rise of fascism in Europe, the Americanization of psychoanalysis into a branch of conventional psychiatry, the American hostility toward socialism, and the status of Central European analysts as refugees to countries at war with their own, led to the suppression of the socialist political commitments which were an integral part of the Berlin psychoanalytic community.

Jacoby describes a secret correspondence, a *Rundbriefe*, in which a circle of these immigrant psychoanalysts continued to discuss their political aspirations and ideals. However, their realistic fear of anticommunist reprisal led these analysts to discuss their ongoing political commitments only in this secret form. Fenichel, the leader of this correspondence, stated that psychoanalysis could no longer afford to dedicate itself to political aims, and his public statements and writings were devoted to the development or psychoanalytic theory, so that psychoanalysis would be ready when a more receptive, reformist political climate returned.

In addition to these catastrophic political events, important events in Freud's personal life at that time had an enormous impact on the emotional climate as well as the practical decisions which were made in the psychoanalytic community at that time. Bernfeld notes that the initial diagnosis of Freud's cancer in 1923 created conscious concern within the psychoanalytic community about safeguarding the future of the psychoanalytic movement, as well as unconscious rebellion and guilty self-suppression at the welcome death of the oppressive father. Freud's lifelong preoccupation with death, stimulated by his experience of the death of his first sibling, a brother born when Freud was 11 months old, who died when Freud was 18 months old, was deepened by his reaction to the horrible carnage of World War I. All three of Freud's sons fought in the war, and in his correspondence at that time he describes himself as preparing for the worst, that he would lose at least one.

Ironically, Freud's sons survived, but it was his favorite daughter, Sofie, who was the family casualty of World War I. She died of influenza in 1920, during her third pregnancy, in an epidemic which Gay (1988) describes as raging throughout postwar Austria, so completely decimated by the war both economically and politically. The death of Sofie's second son and Freud's favorite grandson in 1923, the same year Freud's cancer was diagnosed, devastated Freud. His state of mind at the time was sufficiently morose that his physician, Felix Deutsch, and the circle of analysts closest to Freud, decided to withhold from Freud and his family that Freud had a malignancy, for fear that he might become suicidally depressed.

Although Freud lived until 1939, surviving with cancer for 16 years, his illness became a major part of his exchanges with the psychoanalytic movement from that time forward. Freud had a lifelong tendency to experience relationships with men as rivalries to the death. Both before and after his illness, he interpreted not only hostility but disagreements and even gifts of compliments as hidden wishes to see him dead. The developmental background to this relational experience has been alluded to in the major Freud biographies (Gay, 1988; Jones, 1957; Roazen, 1971), and is a subject which deserves further study for what it illuminates of the relational realities within the psychoanalytic movement.

The transmission of knowledge in psychoanalysis is made deeper and more complex by the interweaving of educational, collegial, and therapeutic relationships. Freud analyzed many of the analysts in the early psychoanalytic movement, including his daughter Anna, and profoundly influenced the development of psychoanalytic ideas through those relationships as well through his intellectual power. Freud's equation of disagreement with a death wish against him added to the practical prohibitions, such as his disapproval, or the threat of excommunication from the psychoanalytic community, which limited discussions of difference and restricted the expansion of psychoanalytic theory.

Further, the informal standards for psychoanalytic training practiced in Vienna, which required minimal supervision or personal analysis, along with the complicated interweaving of personal, educational, and professional worlds, led to interrelationships which erupted in a number of public scandals. The dramatic suicides of Victor Tausk, Otto Gross, and Herbert Silberer, the murder of child analyst Hug–Hellmuth by her nephew, whom she had brought up and analyzed, the psychotic breakdown of Horace Frink, whom Freud analyzed and encouraged to divorce his wife and marry a patient, were among the most notorious examples. In addition to the factors described by Bernfeld and Jacoby, the history of the early psychoanalytic movement suggests that the pressure to create a more conservative climate for psychoanalytic education emerged from the wish to contain the intensely creative but also erratic group within the psychoanalytic community itself. These early psychoanalysts were themselves responding to both internal and social tensions as they underwent extreme personal and cultural changes.

The Berlin society, with Karl Abraham at its head, was a great deal more conservative in its selection criteria for admissions to psychoanalytic training, in the structure of its requirements, and more subtly in its emotional and relational attitudes. The Berlin Institute may have offered needed controls for the quality and uniformity of psychoanalytic education, but seems to have done so along with more problematic controls of personal differences. Karl Abraham is consistently described as "certainly the most normal of the group" around Freud (Jones, 1957), reliable, confident, emotionally controlled, "Prussian," vigilant to emergence of theoretical dissent. Abraham is generally viewed as providing a much needed balance of self-control and common sense in an emotionally volatile movement during a culturally volatile time (Gay, 1988).

The fascist overthrow of the German democratic government with Hitler's victory in Berlin in 1933 and entry into Austria in 1938 marked the dispersal of the psychoanalytic community into exile throughout the world. The emigrations from Central Europe to England and the United States created a radical discontinuity in the psychoanalytic movement, in both the professional and personal lives of the psychoanalysts. The grief reactions of these refugee analysts led them to an idealization of the Viennese and German psychoanalytic communities, and denigration of both the British and American societies (Greenacre, 1961; Grosskurth, 1986; Federn, 1988). Freud had been violently anti-American, associating American psychiatry with a shallow pragmatism and materialism, and his attitude colored European/American tensions from the beginning of the psychoanalytic movement. The immigrant psychoanalysts, lay analysts and physicians alike, were lay analysts in the eyes of American medicine, and fought the reduction of their status as well as the crushing loss of country and culture by retaliating with an idealization of the Central European world view as better suited than the American to the depth psychology view of psychoanalysis.

Jacoby's (1983) discussion of Fenichel's immigration experience is emblematic of the personal impact of the interplay between cultural politics, immigration, and psychoanalytic politics. Fenichel, a physician, stated that in order to preserve classical psychoanalysis in the United States, he would have to qualify for his American medical credentials, because he wanted to fight for Freud's vision of psychoanalysis, including the support of lay analysis, with unassailable medical credentials. His citizenship, a requisite for completing requirements for U. S. medical training, was delayed for some years because of suspicion of his political affiliations. In 1945, at the age of 47, Fenichel died of a ruptured cerebral aneurysm, 6 months into his medical internship at the Los Angeles Cedars of Lebanon Hospital.

Similarly Ernst Federn (1988), Paul Federn's son, complained bitterly of his father's ordeals in attempting to establish his medical credentials after immigrating to New York. He argues that the German language, its scientific and philosophical traditions, as well as its culture, which provided the essential foundation for psychoanalysis, were lost to the immigrant analysts, along with their social and professional status. He comments on the current American psychoanalytic scene:

> We know that Freud was opposed all his life to two developments: the creation of
> an orthodoxy, a church, and the subordination of psychoanalysis to the medical
> profession. Both became true of psychoanalysis in the USA. Therefore in my eyes
> Freudian psychoanalysis has ceased to exist there. (p. 159)

From the American standpoint, the influx of refugee analysts into American Institutes, with their highly valued Central European psychoanalytic training, direct contact with Freud and his culture, and denigration of the American culture, created enormous institutional problems as well. Greenacre (1961), in a review of the literature on selection of candidates for psychoanalytic training, punctuates her discussion with careful commentaries on the enormous impact of the Central European emigration on the dynamics within American Psychoanalytic Institutes. "One hears occasional but most empathic statements regarding the improbability or even impossibility that the American culture can furnish worthwhile analysts" (p. 673). Although she was concerned that the postwar problems might have been at that time too current to be researched, Greenacre concluded that the "mutually ambivalent attitudes" between American and European analysts needed to be discussed as soon as historically possible, because of their enormous impact on psychoanalytic training programs, including the assumptions underlying candidate selection and the definition of desirable qualities in the analyst.

As an example of how the complex, unconscious tensions, miscommunications, and conflicting loyalties between the Americans and the Central Europeans led to the creation of institutional forms which express and contain these unconscious processes, it is interesting to examine the use of the words "candidate" and "control" to designate the psychoanalytic student and the student's first analytic cases. Lewin and Ross (1960), in a summary of historical factors in psychoanalytic education, describe the following:

An interesting vestige of the German influence on American psychoanalytic institutes is the word "candidate" used in many of them as the official designation of the student. In Germany and Austria, a *Kandidat* is a certain grade of university student (e.g. *Kandidat der Medizin*) and aspirant for the degree, and the cognate English word, hardly ever used in English-speaking countries in this academic context, was taken over to designate the students in the London and American institutes. *Kontrolle* is another such word. In German it means supervision or inspection, and one of the arguments about a provision in the Treaty of Versailles was about this word. The Germans thought that their armament was to be *kontrolliert* by the victorious Allies, that is, supervised. The English version read "controlled" (i.e. ruled), and this led to the debate. (p. 31)

For Lewin and Ross, the association to the problems in the Treaty of Versailles was simply an interesting illustrative aside, a problem of translation, added to the main point that connection to the German language and culture of the early psychoanalytic movement was highly valued and incorporated into American psychoanalytic training.

In the context of this discussion, though, it is a relevant and meaningful example of the multiple though unconscious implications of these cross-cultural tensions and loyalty decisions which have formed the psychoanalytic movement and its educational institutions. The political and economic retaliation against the German and Austrian people contained in the 1919 Versailles Treaty planted the seeds for the buried resentment which grew into the monstrous counterretaliations of World War II. The conditions of physical deprivation and economic hardship were far worse in the aftermath of the war than during the war, and it was in this context that infant mortality, tubercolosis, and influenza epidemics decimated the population, including Freud's daughter Sofie and grandson Heinz.

Freud was, understandably, extraordinarily preoccupied with these personal and national consequences of the Versailles Treaty, and he saw Woodrow Wilson as the culprit in the decimation of his country's political and economic life, so much so that he coauthored a biography on Woodrow Wilson which stands as an extraordinary exercise in psychoanalysis as retaliatory character assassination (Gay, 1988). The fact that at the foundation of the tripartite training model the Americans mistranslate the word "control" with the same implicit misunderstanding in the description of student analyses and in the Versailles Treaty is not a simple coincidence. The background and consequences of the mistranslation reflects the depth of admiration, mutual, ambivalently regarded need, and animosity which tied together the Americans and the Central Europeans in world politics and in the politics of psychoanalysis.

Both European critics, and critics within the American Psychoanalytic Association, have corroborated that at the time of the European immigrations, members of the New York Psychoanalytic and the American Psychoanalytic Association competed for theoretical dominance of the Institutes, especially the right to become a training analyst, closely related to economic motives (Jacoby, Federn, Schechter). Because theoretical and technical disagreement was equated with disloyalty, the history of the American Psychoanalytic Association has been punctuated with splits, such as the formation of the William Alanson White Institute and the Karen Horney Institute in the early 1940s, and the establishment of the American Academy of Psychoanalysis in 1956. These dissenting groups felt that the rigid requirements for the theoretical beliefs and technical orthodoxy of training analysts interfered with educational and scientific goals in psychoanalysis.

In contrast to the evolution of a psychoanalytic community in the United States, the British psychoanalytic community developed very differently (Grosskurth, 1986; Kohon, 1986; Steiner, 1985), in its tolerance of dissent, its encouragement of lay analysis, and in its marginal role within the British culture. Kohon (1986) suggests that the important developments of object relations theory in Britain took place because the British Psychoanalytic Institute was able to house the conflicts between Freudian and Kleinian analysis under one roof. Following the "controversial discussions" of 1942–1944, a clinical and theoretical battle over the right to train, a truce or "ladies' agreement" was established forming three groups, Freudian, Kleinian, and the "middle school," each with their own trainees. In the middle ground between Anna Freud's and Melanie Klein's followers the "independent tradition" developed a unique object relations approach, which offers one of the most innovative schools of thought in modern psychoanalysis.

French psychoanalysis, too, has evolved with greater intellectual discourse between psychoanalysis and other disciplines, especially literature and cultural anthropology (Turkel, 1978). While Jacques Lacan and his followers are no longer members in good standing of the International Psychoanalytic Association, primarily for their technical departures, Lacan's work on the symbolic function of language in the expressive and defensive construction of the self has made a vital contribution to the understanding of human development within the constraints of a particular culture's construction of inner reality.

It is clear from this exploratory sketch that the development of psychoanalysis has been fragmented by the realities of its political and historical place in time. The restriction of lay analysis in the United States, and the development of a homogeneous and conservative American psychoanalytic Association, can be interpreted as symptomatic of developmental difficulties in the history of psychoanalysis as it struggled first for acceptance and then for survival, first in Central Europe and then in exile around the world.

A study of the development of psychoanalysis in different cultures suggests important directions for expanding our understanding of the relationship between culture and psyche as reflected in the psychoanalytic relationship itself. As Jean Baker Miller notes in her paper for this conference, psychoanalysis brings to light within the individual elements of the emotional life which are unacceptable to culture and family and therefore repressed. In England, known for the distance between parents and children, especially as it is encouraged in the upper classes, psychoanalysis has devoted itself to an exquisite understanding of the mother's role in the child's development through its exploration in the analytic relationship (Kohon, 1983). In France, where the intellectual life is revered, psychoanalysis devotes itself to understanding the way words and symbols contribute to the alienation of self (Cardinale, 1983).

What does North American culture repress, that psychoanalysis can help us find? The United States welcomes its refugees, but encourages assimilation into an ahistorical "melting pot" culture in which cultural differences are lost to the conscious mind though retained in unconscious, invisible loyalties. In a nation with democratic ideals where the refugee can become a "self-made man," and where material success as the measure of social worth is equally available to all newcomers, most immigrants are grateful for the opportunity to establish themselves on their own merits. The refugee who was rescued from religious persecution, or from economic or political disaster, by entry into the United States is not encouraged to enter as a social critic but rather to become a loyal member of a pluralistic new society.

However, we know that the American melting pot falls significantly short of its democratic ideals, and that the worship of money is no replacement for more substantial social and cultural values. The emphasis on material wealth as a measure of status, the growth of a consumer-oriented mass media which emphasizes the value of instant material gratification, along with the growing isolation of self from the relational contexts of family and community, have generated a growing isolation of self from the embeddedness in the contexts that give human life its meaning. The symptomatic expressions of these social processes, evidenced in the fragmentation of families and communities, accompanied by increases in psychological disturbances such as depression, narcissistic or character disorders, and addictions, can be usefully addressed by a psychoanalytic method which offers a critical, historical, and cultural perspective on the individual's psychic suffering (Levin, 1987).

The values of a technologically advanced, materially oriented society which rewards hard work for economic gain at the expense of emotional relatedness are difficult to question through psychoanalysis when the pathway to a psychoanalytic education involves commitment to these values. The potential for learning from cultural differences, acknowledging the problems and integrating the strengths offered by different cultural solutions to life's problems, will be expanded as psychoanalytic practitioners from more diverse cultural backgrounds enter the field. The introduction of an interdisciplinary psychoanalysis with its dialogue of diversity creates new opportunities for the theoretical and clinical development of a humanistic psychoanalysis capable of offering constructive critique of the cultural processes and values which contribute to the suffering of our own people.

RECOMMENDATIONS FOR THE FUTURE: LOCAL CHAPTER DEVELOPMENTS OF ALTERNATIVE EDUCATIONAL MODELS

In his paper on psychoanalytic education, Siegfried Bernfeld criticized the highly organized, much imitated Berlin Institute as the expression of unconscious psychological and political forces, including the battles between socialism and fascism, and a Prussian attitude of authoritarian educational control in the face of radical cultural change. Bernfeld offered as a contrast the Vienna Society, which essentially remained independent-study oriented, centered on Sigmund Freud as an analyst and teacher. Bernfeld reported that Freud referred to the Berlin Society as "the authorities," and felt that the Vienna group around Freud was too independence-minded themselves to accept the control of a centralized authority. Anna Freud, echoing her father's attitude toward "the authorities," never chose to have the Hampstead Clinic apply for official training recognition from the International Psychoanalytic Association, because her clinic would then have to give up its educational independence.

In fact, the Vienna Society had its own rules and requirements, even if they were informal or implicit, which emphasized personal relationships and loyalty to Freud. Anne–Marie Sandler's presentation for this conference, contrasting the current differences between the British Society and the French Society's training programs, similarly notes that the paternalism of a requirements-oriented British Society has a tendency to encourage conformity and mediocrity in students, while the independent study-oriented French Society encourages revolt, and can overlook serious personal problems in the candidate.

The psychoanalytic community's response of strict, authoritarian control of its students as a means of surviving a period of cultural transition has established traditions which constrain the further development of psychoanalysis. James Strachey, at the celebration of the 50th anniversary of the British Society, observed that while "the gradual development of systematic machinery for training candidates" was needed, it was also possible for psychoanalysis to become overinstitutionalized. Strachey commented that he and other "mavericks" in the early psychoanalytic movement would never be accepted for training at a modern institute (Strachey, in Kohon, 1986).

Yet it is clear that neither the open nor closed institutional forms in and of themselves provide the ideal solution to the problems of psychoanalytic education. The creation of thoughtful educational forms which provide the structure of a supportive community and its wisdom while preserving autonomy and vitality seem to require attention to institutional structure and relational dynamics. The

Clark Conference papers suggest that the future of psychoanalytic education will best be served by the exploration of varieties of educational alternatives, rather than rigid reliance on one particular training format. In spite of very different institutional forms, each psychoanalytic educational community has to struggle to arrive at its own balance between structured requirements and the flexibility of independent study, between adherence to existing traditions and creation of new approaches.

In the above discussion, I have argued that the definition of authority and the encouragement of diversity in educational relationships is a more vital determinant of educational freedom than adherence to a particular institutional structure. Although institutes in the APsaA are required to be uniformly structured, a number of institutes in the International, as well as interdisciplinary psychoanalytic institutes in New York, have created programs on a continuum from completely requirement-oriented to completely independent-study oriented. Within that continuum of "open" and "closed" programs, institutes such as the British Psychoanalytic or New York University's Postdoctoral Program offer candidates the choice of different tracks with different technical and theoretical orientations as a means of providing educational structure while allowing individual decisions about their program of study.

The local chapters of Division 39 began to explore the varieties of psychoanalytic educational programs through the series of meetings on training which Murray Meisels described in his Introduction. Beginning in 1984, local chapter groups from around the country met with each other, with members of the Division's Education and Training Committee, with faculty and graduates of established interdisciplinary Institutes, such as the William Alanson White, the New York University and Adelphi programs, the Postgraduate Center for Mental Health, and the Los Angeles Institute. We discussed the widest range of issues involved in creating a psychoanalytic educational program, from practical and administrative realities to broad philosophical issues. We brought back the information from these meetings to our own local chapter groups, and discussed them at length with the goal of arriving at an institutional plan which would address the broad issues of training in a way that was relevant to our community.

While this process of discussion within the Division and its local chapters has generated a number of different programs, in this final section I will briefly highlight the educational programs in Massachusetts and Michigan as offering two contrasting attempts at creating a balance between structure and flexibility in psychoanalytic training. The Michigan Society for Psychoanalytic Psychology (MSPP) organized a local chapter in 1980, and formed its Center for Psychoanalytic Studies in 1983 as part of MSPP. The Michigan Center is an "open model" training program which does not admit students nor issue a graduation certificate, but rather offers a program of recommended courses and advises students on their independent course of study. In the course, no distinction is made between "candidates" and other students, although admission to specific courses may be influenced by the student's background of training with the Center.

With this program, practitioners interested in psychoanalysis can explore the decision to become psychoanalysts in small steps, and are free to tailor their own studies, which can range from taking a course or two to completing a comprehensive, recommended curriculum, a personal analysis, and supervision of psychoanalytic control cases. The emphasis on independent study and on the diversity of pathways toward becoming a psychoanalyst is meant to maximize the personal responsibility of candidates for pursuing their own education. The Michigan Society is currently debating whether to issue formal certificates of graduation, or to retain the independent study format in which the candidate in consultation with faculty determines at what point in a lifelong educational process he or she feels like a psychoanalyst.

In contrast, the Massachusetts Association for Psychoanalytic Psychology (MAPP) which formed in 1984 had developed an independent training program, the Massachusetts Institute for Psychoanalysis (MIP), started in 1988 with admissions, program requirements, and a graduation certificate. While MIP was formed by members of MAPP and has close ties to the local chapter, because it is a formal training program the American Psychological Association guidelines require that such programs be independent of the APA's Divisions.

The MAPP membership participated actively in the decision to form a formal Institute training program, rather than proceed with the development of an open training model such as that organized by the Michigan Chapter. In an initial questionnaire fielded to the membership in 1985, respondents were intrigued by the open model as an alternative, but expressed concern that such a program would not be rigorous enough and would suffer in comparison with the existing medical Institutes. On the other hands, respondents who supported the closed or Institute model expressed their discontent with the rigidity of existing Institutes, and hoped that a program sponsored by MAPP would offer greater flexibility and educational freedom.

In 1986, a committee with MAPP members from diverse backgrounds and orientations was formed to develop an overall training plan, and generated a report which served as the conceptual framework for the formation of the program (Harder & Cohen, 1987). As part of the decision-making process, Charles Spezzano, from Denver, and Marvin Hyman, from the Michigan Center, came to present and discuss their training approaches to our membership. The committee's report was discussed with the MAPP membership at several open meetings, and working committees were constituted to develop specific program recommendations for curriculum (Slavin & Cohen, 1988), admissions philosophy and policies (Shapiro, 1987) an advanced candidates training program (Barron, 1987), and a psychotherapy program (North, 1987). Again, these working committees were selected to represent diverse points of view offered by individuals from different disciplines, theoretical orientations, and psychoanalytic training backgrounds.

Members of all the committees uniformly engaged one another in dialogue of extraordinary depth, and each of the committee reports, although authored by the chairs who were members of the organizing committee, emerged from a collaborative group consensus which addressed the concerns of every group member. To highlight briefly the committee report recommendations, the psychotherapy program committee concluded that the creation of two separate programs training psychoanalysts and psychoanalytic psychotherapists created arbitrary distinctions between psychoanalysis and psychotherapy. The committee recommended that the educational philosophy of the Institute should be broadly conceived as training in the theoretical underpinnings and the continuum of technical approaches that encompass the analytic process in the broadest sense. In this way, the entire psychoanalytic training program should be designed to provide an opportunity to explore systematically these different expressions of the psychoanalytic process.

The admissions committee report proposed that the prevailing approach to admissions in the literature, which emphasized the prospective candidate's diagnosis and psychopathology, had encouraged a selection process which emphasized conservative decisions and minimized selection of diverse groups of creative clinicians and theoreticians. The admissions policy of our program will instead emphasize that the decision to seek psychoanalytic training is a key developmental juncture in the personal and professional life of the applicant. The admissions interviews will be viewed as the first step in a mutual exploration and decision-making process, rather than a judgmental or adversarial one.

The curriculum committee proposed that modern psychoanalysis is a living, evolving field of study, within which active controversy exists at all levels, from basic assumptions about human nature to clinical theory and technique. The curriculum will take a comparative psychoanalytic approach which views psychoanalysis in a broad intellectual context and recognizes the existence of different analytic stances, modes of listening, or attitudes, and different theoretical assumptions underlying them. This broadly inclusive approach and spirit of inquiry is best encouraged with administrative structure and teaching methods which maximize open, critical discussion, and the student's participation in their own education. The curriculum for this reason emphasizes flexible response to the backgrounds and individual needs of each student. Candidates will be free to select their personal analysts and supervisors in consultation with their own advisory committee. The Institute will provide guidelines for recommended level of experience but will have no required list of training analysts or supervisors. An advanced candidates program was developed to provide credit and an individualized program for those experienced clinicians who had acquired a significant amount of psychoanalytic training through independent study or through participation in other programs.

When MAPP started its educational programs, including the plans for developing a psychoanalytic training program, Boston's mental health community included many psychoanalytically oriented psychologists and social workers but no existing interdisciplinary psychoanalytic training program. Jonathan Slavin (1988) described the 5-year process of forming MIP as one in which the working groups struggled to create unique educational solutions. This process required that each of our working groups address the internal barriers which impeded us in accepting our own authority to define a training program that met our own internal standards and was not in reaction, whether blind acceptance or blind rejection, of existing educational models.

Because of the power of the medical community in Boston, with the presence of three major medical schools and their teaching hospitals, as well as two established medical psychoanalytic Institutes, the view of the medical Institutes as the highest standard had to be confronted again and again. Because most of us involved in MAPP and in the development of MIP were self-educated in psychoanalysis and not graduates of formal institutes, we had to confront our own and our community's questioning of our competence to address problems and questions in psychoanalytic education. For example, after our working committees had generated their reports and presented them to the MAPP membership in January of 1988, we then invited the community of formally trained psychoanalysts who were our potential faculty to hear these reports and to become acquainted with the structure and educational philosophy of our program.

Our own planning committee, an interdisciplinary group, made the recommendation that the reports be summarized by a trained psychoanalyst on our organizing commitee rather than by the committee chairs, most of whom were not formally trained analysts, because the group of medical analysts would not be as receptive to recommendations on psychoanalytic training coming from nonanalysts. After quite a heated discussion, our organizing committee proceeded to make the same reports with the same format as in the presentations to our MAPP membership. In fact, it seemed to me that those of us presenters who had no educational ties to the medical Institutes felt more freedom to speak. Our reports were responded to with challenging but sympathetic questions, as the largely medical group struggled with the radically different conceptions of training, especially the nondiagnostic admissions process and the intellectually critical, comparative, and independent-study orientation.

The relationship between MAPP and MIP, especially the collaboration between practitioners from diverse backgrounds, some with and most without formal psychoanalytic Institute training, provided the essential collaboration that generated our own community's solutions to the problems of psychoanalytic training addressed within Division 39. A dialogue which emphasizes mutuality and collaboration rather than which imposes the authority of Institute status or clinical experience ensures that every point of view will be considered and valued. After participating in this creative, dialogic collaboration among our MAPP membership, I hope that our Institute will continue to evolve with MAPP as its society, so that a group of formally trained psychoanalysts will not become isolated from a wider community of psychoanalytically informed clinicians.

In conclusion, I have offered a discussion of two of the emerging educational programs among the local chapters of Division 39 as illustrations of institutional alternatives which strive for an integration of tradition and innovation in psychoanalytic education. I have argued that in the traumatic developmental history of psychoanalysis, its educational forms have evolved toward conservative self-protection which has impeded healthy self-criticism toward continuing adaptive change. I have offered a developmental model for understanding the relational processes by which the parent generation inadvertently interferes with the development of adaptive change by imposing the past on the future in self-protective ways. I have argued that in the family developmental history of the psychoanalytic movement, the medicalization of psychoanalysis in the United States has been a core symptom of a self-protective parental attitude which, like any symptom, represents a defensive process which prevents new learning. Hopefully, the changes in the American Psychoanalytic Association and the International Psychoanalytic Association due to the September, 1988, settlement of the lawsuit and to the integration of diverse, interdisciplinary educational institutions in Division 39 will provide new opportunities for dialogue which will further the developmental integration of the psychoanalytic community.

REFERENCES

Balint, M. (1953/1986). *Primary love and psychoanalytic technique*. New York: DeCapo Press.

Barron, J. (1988). *Report on the advanced candidacy program*. Massachusetts Institute for Psychoanalysis.

Bernfeld, S. (1962). On psychoanalytic training. *Psychoanalytic Quarterly, 23*, 453–482.

Bollas, C. (1987). *The shadow of the object*. New York: Columbia University Press.

Cardinale, M. (1983). *The words to say it*. Cambridge, MA: VanVactor and Goodheart.

Eagle, M. (1984). *Recent developments in psychoanalysis: A critical evaluation*. New York.

Federn, E. (1988). Psychoanalysis–The fate of a science in exile. In E. Timms, & N. Segal, (Eds.), *Freud in exile*. New Haven, CT: Yale University Press.

Freud, S. (1920). *Beyond the pleasure principle. The standard edition of the complete psychological works of Sigmund Freud* (Vol. 18, pp. 3–64). London: Hogarth Press.

Freud, S. (1928). *The question of lay analysis. The standard edition of the complete psychological works of Sigmund Freud* (Vol. 21). London: Hogarth Press.

Gay, P. (1988). *Freud: A life for our time*. New York: Norton.

Greenacre, P. (1961). A critical digest of the literature on selection of candidates for psychoanalytic training. In *Emotional Growth*. New York: International Universities Press, pp. 670–694.

Greenberg, J., & Mitchell S. (1983). *Object relations in psychoanalytic theory*. Cambridge, MA: Harvard University Press.

Grosskurth, P. (1986). *Melanie Klein: Her world and her work*. New York: Knopf.

Harder, D., & Cohen, M. (1987). *Report from the committee on psychoanalytic training*. Massachusetts Association for Psychoanalytic Psychology. Unpublished manuscript.

Hoffman, I. (1983). The patient as interpreter of the analyst's experience. *Contemporary Psychoanalysis, 19*, 389–422.

Jacoby, R. (1983). *The repression of psychoanalysis*. Chicago: University of Chicago Press.

Jones, E., Sachs, H., Oberndorf, C., Rickman, J., Glover, E., Brill, A., Alexander, F., Muller–

Braunschweig, C., Benedek, T., Reik, T., Roheim, G., Hitchmann, E., Schilder, P., Deutsch, F., Horney, K., Reich, W., Simmel, E., Sadger, J., Harnik, J., Walder, R., Jokul, R., & Ophuijsen, V. Hungarian Psychoanalytic Society, New York Psychoanalytic Society. (1929) Congress proceedings on the question of lay analysis. *Journal of the International Psychoanalytic Association, 8*, 174–283.

Jones, E. (1957). *The life and work of Sigmund Freud.* New York: Basic Books.

Keller, E. (1985). *Reflections on gender and science.* New Haven, CT: Yale University Press.

Kohon, G. (1986). Notes on the history of the psychoanalytic movement in Great Britain. In G. Kohon, (Ed.), *The British School of psychoanalysis: The independent tradition.* New Haven, CT: Yale University Press.

Levin, D. (1987). (Ed.). *Pathologies of the modern self: Postmodern studies on narcissism. Schizophrenia and depression.* New York: New York University Press.

Levenson, E. (1983). *The ambiguity of change.* New York: Basic Books.

Lewin, B., & Ross, H. (1960). *Psychoanalytic education in the United States.* New York: Norton.

North, B. (1987). *Report from the psychotherapy committee.* Massachusetts Institute for Psychoanalysis. Unpublished manuscript.

Oberndorf, C. (1953). *History of psychoanalysis in America,* New York: Harper & Row, p. 207.

Racker, H. (1968). *Transference and countertransference.* New York: International Universities Press.

Riegel, K. (1976). The dialectics of human development. *American Psychologist, 31*, 689–700.

Roazen, P. (1971). *Freud and his followers.* New York: New York University Press.

Sandler, A. (1982). The selection and function of the training analyst in Europe. *International Review of Psychoanalysis, 9*(38), 386–398.

Schechter, D. (1979). Problems of training analysis: A critical review of current concepts. *Journal of the American Academy of Psychoanalysis, 7*(3), 359–373.

Searles, H. (1979). *Countertransference and related subjects: Selected papers.* New York: International Universities Press.

Shapiro, E. (1988). Individual change and family development. In C. Falicov, (Ed.), *Family transitions.* New York: Guilford Press.

Shapiro, E. (1987). Report from the committee on admissions, Massachusetts Institute for Psychoanalysis, Unpublished manuscript.

Shapiro, E. (1986). *Identity development at transition to parenthood.* Paper presented at the Massachusetts Association for Psychoanalytic Psychology, Boston.

Slavin, J. (1988). *On the development of a psychoanalytic training program in Massachusetts.* Paper presented at the Midwinter meeting, Division of Psychoanalysis, San Francisco, February.

Slavin, M., & Cohen, M. (1988). *Report from the curriculum committee.* Massachusetts Institute for Psychoanalysis. Unpublished manuscript.

Steiner, R. (1985). Some thoughts about tradition and change arising from an examination of the British Psychoanalytical Society's Controversial Discussions (1943–1944). *International Review of Psychoanalysis, 12*, 27–71.

Turkel, S. (1978). *Psychoanalytic politics: Freud's French Revolution.* New York: Basic Books.

Wallerstein, R. (1988). One psychoanalysis or many? *International Journal of Psychoanalysis, 69*, 5–21.

Werner, H. (1948). *Comparative psychology of mental development.* Chicago: Wilcox & Follett.

Will, O. (1962). Processes in psychoanalytic education. In J. Masserman, (Ed.), *Psychoanalytic education.* New York: Grune & Stratton, pp. 84–102.

Clark Conference Faculty

Nathan Adler, Ph.D.   Center for Integrative Psychoanalytic Studies, California School of Professional Psychology.

Robert Aguado, Ph.D.*   Private practice, Beverly Hills. Workshop on Kleinian training.

Anna Antonovsky, Ph.D.*   William Alanson White Institute, New York.

Stephen Appelbaum, Ph.D.*   University of Missouri, Kansas City School of Medicine, Kansas City.

Sabert Basescu, Ph.D.   New York University Postdoctoral Program in Psychoanalysis and Psychotherapy, New York.

Murray Bilmes, Ph.D.   Center for Integrative Psychoanalytic Studies, California School of Professional Psychology.

Daniel Brown, Ph.D.*   Cambridge Hospital, Cambridge, Massachusetts.

Aphrodite Clamar, Ph.D.*   Lenox Hill Hospital (New York) Psychoanalytic Psychotherapy Training Porgram. Workshop on feminist scholarship and training.

Jan Drucker, Ph.D.*   Sarah Lawrence College, Bronxville, New York. Workshop on child development and training.

Zenia Fliegel, Ph.D.*   Private practice; Institute for Psychoanalytic Training and Research, New York. Workshop on training models.

John Gedo, M.D.*   Chicago Psychoanalytic Society and Institute, Chicago.

Stanley Gochman, Ph.D.*   American University, Washington, DC. Workshop on innovative training models.

George Goldman, Ph.D.   Adelphi University Postdoctoral Program in Psychotherapy, Institute for Advanced Psychological Studies, New York.

Susannah Gourevitch, Ph.D.   Association for Psychoanalytic Study, Washington, DC.

Milton Horowitz, Ph.D.   Los Angeles Institute for Psychoanalytic Studies, Los Angeles.

Marvin Hyman, Ph.D.*   Michigan Society for Psychoanalytic Psychology, Southfield.

Rochelle Kainer, Ph.D.*   Association for Psychoanalytic Study, Washington, DC.

Bernard Kalinkowitz, Ph.D.*   New York University Postdoctoral Program in Psychoanalysis and Psychotherapy, New York.

Bertram Karon, Ph.D.*   Michigan Society for Psychoanalytic Psychology, East Lansing.

Helen Block Lewis, Ph.D.   Past-President, Division 39; Professor Emeritus, Yale University, New Haven.

Stanton Marlon, Ph.D.*   Interregional Society of Jungian Analysts, Pittsburgh. Workshop on Jungian training.

Murray Meisels, Ph.D.   President-Elect, Division 39; Michigan Society for Psychoanalytic Psychology, Ann Arbor.

Esther Menaker, Ph.D.*   New York University Postdoctoral Program in Psychoanalysis and Psychotherapy, New York.

Dale Mendell, Ph.D.*   Psychoanalytic Institute, Postgraduate Center for Mental Health, New York. Workshop on child and adolescent training.

Jean Baker Miller, M.D.   The Stone Center, Wellesley College, Wellesley, Massachusetts.

Stanley Moldawsky, Ph.D.*   Rutgers University, New Brunswick, New Jersey. Workshop for Sunday registrants.

Norman Oberman, Ph.D.*   Los Angeles Institute for Psychoanalytic Studies, Los Angeles.

Fred Pine, Ph.D.   President, Division 39; Albert Einstein College of Medicine, Yeshiva University, New York.

Anne Marie Sandler, M.S.   President, European Psycho-Analytical Federation.

Herbert Schlesinger, Ph.D.*   New School for Social Research, New York.

Ava Siegler, Ph.D.*   Postgraduate Center for Mental Health, New York. Workshop on Child and Adolescent Training.

George Silberschatz, Ph.D.*   Mount Zion Hospital and Medical Center, San Francisco.

Ester Shapiro, Ph.D.   Cambridge Hospital, Cambridge; Psychology Department, University of Massachusetts, Boston.

Jonathan Slavin, Ph.D.   Tufts University, Medford, Massachusetts.

Charles Spezzano, Ph.D.*   Colorado Society for Psychology and Psychoanalysis, Denver.

Gerald Stechler, Ph.D.*   Charles River Hospital, Boston University Medical School. Workshop on psychoanalysis and family systems theory.

Paul Wachtel, Ph.D.*   City University of New York, New York.

Lenore Walker, Ph.D.*   Walker and Associates; Professional School of Psychology, University of Denver, Denver.

---

*Faculty who ran workshops.

Clark Conference Planning Committee

Helen Block Lewis, Ph.D., Chair
Murray Meisels, Ph.D., Co-Chair

Anna Antonovsky, Ph.D.
Aphrodite Clamar, Ph.D.
Rachelle Dattner, Ph.D.
Milton Horowitz, Ph.D.
Bernard Kalinkowitz, Ph.D.
Bertram Karon, Ph.D.
Carol Michaels, Ph.D.
Fred Pine, Ph.D.
Ester Shapiro, Ph.D.
Norma Simon, Ph.D.
Jonathan Slavin, Ph.D.
Charles Spezzano, Ph.D.
Nathan Stockhammer, Ph.D.

AUTHOR INDEX

Numbers in italics denote pages with complete bibliographic information.

SUBJECT INDEX